ATLAS OF TOWN PLANS
SOUTHERN ENGLAND

Published by the Automobile Association
Fanum House, Basingstoke, Hants RG21 2EA

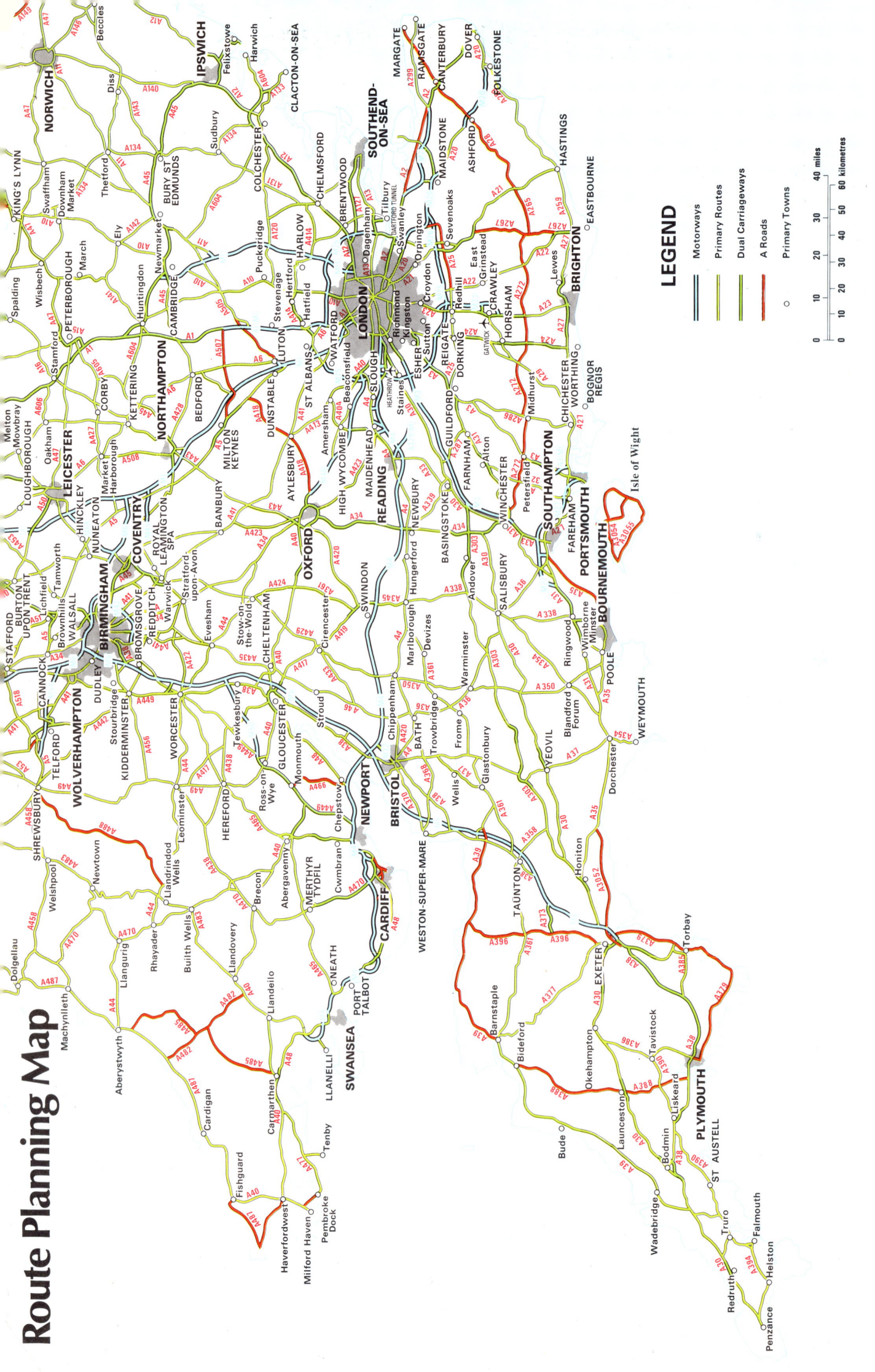

Route Planning Map

London's Orbital Routes

When the M25 is complete it will form a circular motorway route round London, apart from the section between junctions 2 and 31, linked by the Dartford Tunnel. This map shows the latest available information on the progress of the orbital route. The map also shows the North and South Circular roads and the Inner Ring Road.

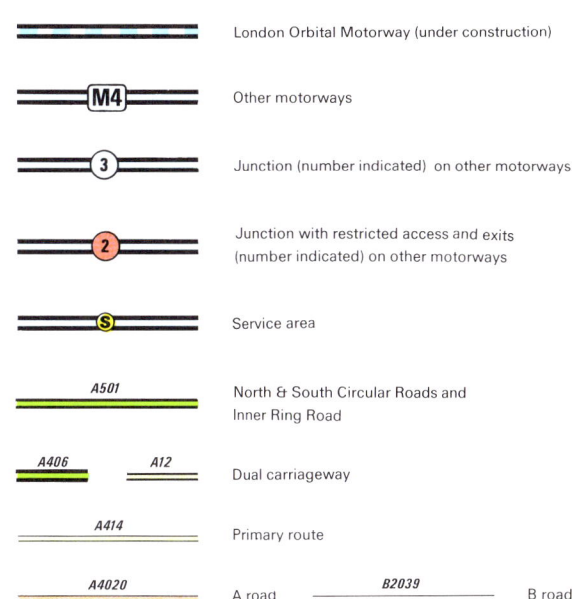

London Orbital Motorway (under construction)

Other motorways

Junction (number indicated) on other motorways

Junction with restricted access and exits (number indicated) on other motorways

Service area

North & South Circular Roads and Inner Ring Road

Dual carriageway

Primary route

A road   B road

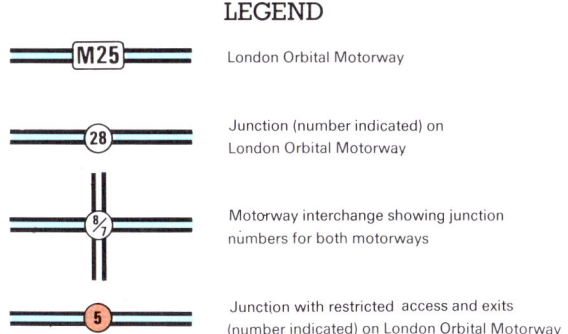

LEGEND

London Orbital Motorway

Junction (number indicated) on London Orbital Motorway

Motorway interchange showing junction numbers for both motorways

Junction with restricted access and exits (number indicated) on London Orbital Motorway

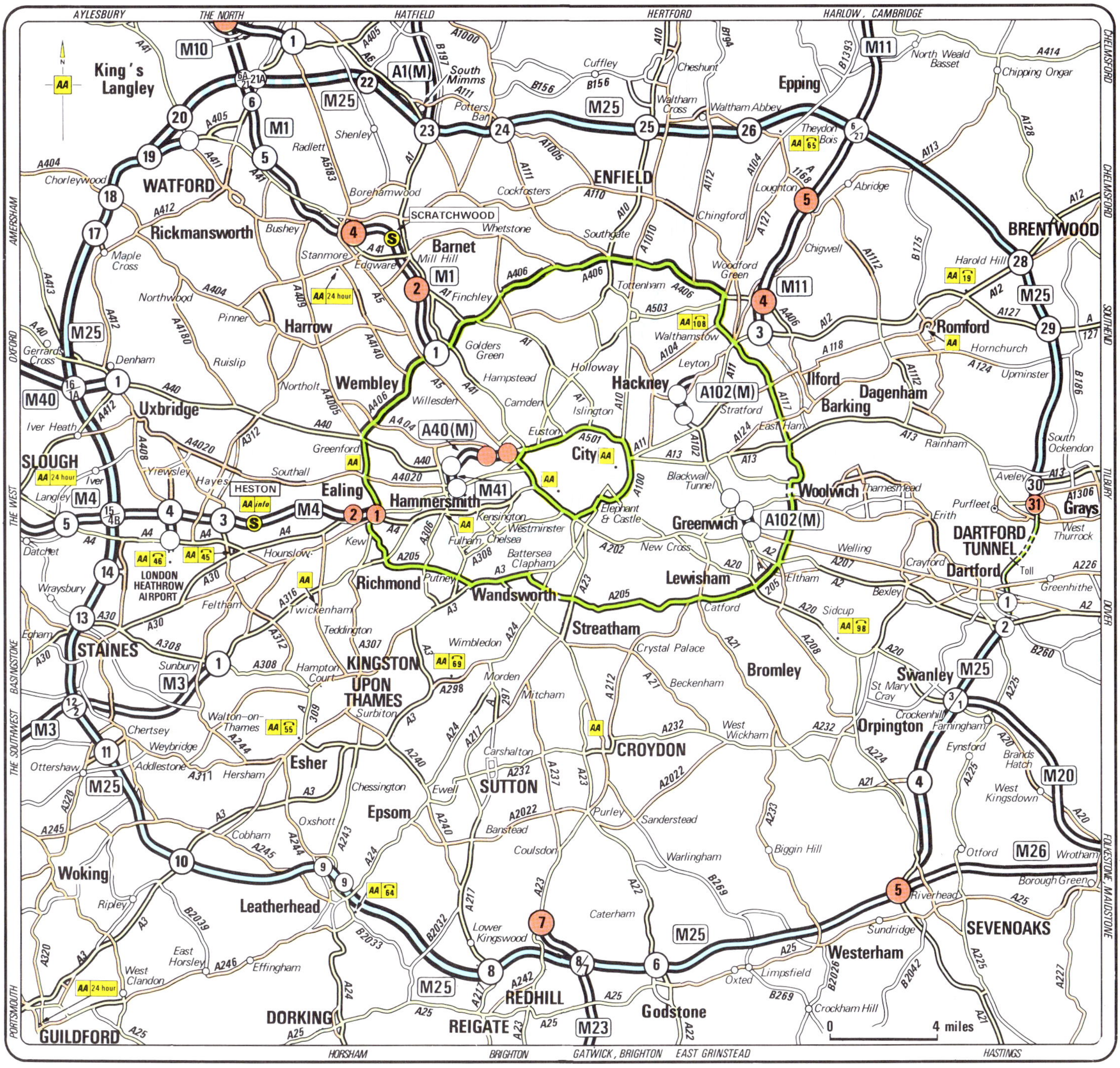

Soft landscapes and the seaside are essential components of the southern scene. The western peninsula is the destination for holidaymakers and the retired and retiring. Towns here have kept much of the quality they had before the vulgar 1960s and beyond, although 'kiss me quick' hats and repellent architecture are sometimes to be seen. The large ports of the south coast were bomber targets during World War II – so many have new centres. But a surprising amount of old townscape can be discovered in all these places, and new efforts are being made to preserve the best of the past. Many towns close to London are under the shadow of the capital, and in these the influence of contemporary culture and commerce is likely to be felt – often unpleasantly. Fortunately, there are scores of towns which retain their provincial character, and these will always be the ones closest to the hearts of tourist and local alike.

This book contains plans of 105 towns and cities in Southern England – from Dover to St Ives, and from Henley to Shanklin. Area plans and descriptions of the towns are included. Street indexes make the plans practical and easy to use.

Produced by the Cartographic Department
Publishing Division of the Automobile Association

The contents of this book are believed correct at the time of printing. Nevertheless, the publisher can accept no responsibility for errors or omissions, or for changes in the details given.

© The Automobile Association 1986

All rights reserved. No part of this publication may be reproduced, stored in a retrieval system, or transmitted in any form or by any means – electronic, mechanical, photocopying, recording or otherwise, unless the written permission of the publisher has been given beforehand.

Published by the Automobile Association, Fanum House, Basingstoke, Hampshire RG21 2EA

Printed and bound in Spain by Graficromo SA, Spain

ISBN 0 86145 366 2

AA Ref 57697

Southern England

AREA MAPS ARE INDICATED IN BOLD.

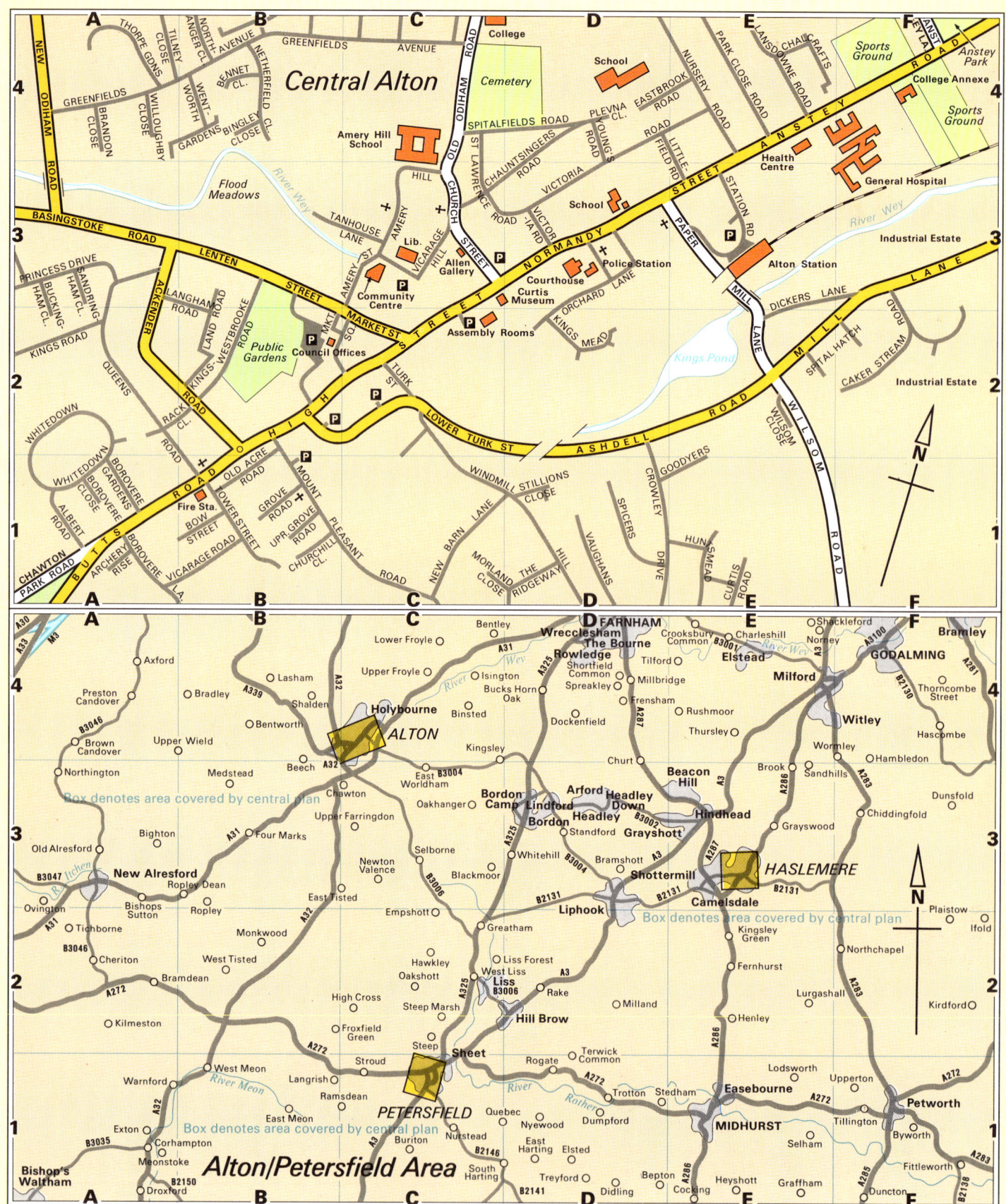

Alton

Locally grown hops and water from the Wey Spring were once the mainstay of the brewers of Alton, a town whose origins stretch back to Roman times. Modern Alton has two attractive parks and a fine modern sports centre which is in great demand from both the locals and those in the surrounding area. The Curtis Museum, founded in 1855, contains local records and natural history.

Petersfield's focal point is The Square, a centuries-old market place, and the town also boasts a number of late 16th-century buildings, dating from before its days as a coaching route staging post. This attractive market town's amenities include the Festival Hall, for opera, concerts and plays, a modern sports centre, and the Heath, which lies to the south and is good for boating, fishing and rambling.

Haslemere in summer re-echoes to the sounds of medieval and Elizabethan music — the speciality of the annual Haslemere Festival, which is one of the oldest in the country. Once dependent on its iron, cloth and leather industries, this is now a popular residential area, and a number of well-preserved old buildings survive, particularly around the High Street. For local organisations, the town's best feature is possibly its Educational Museum, which they use extensively for its archaeology, geology, zoology, and art.

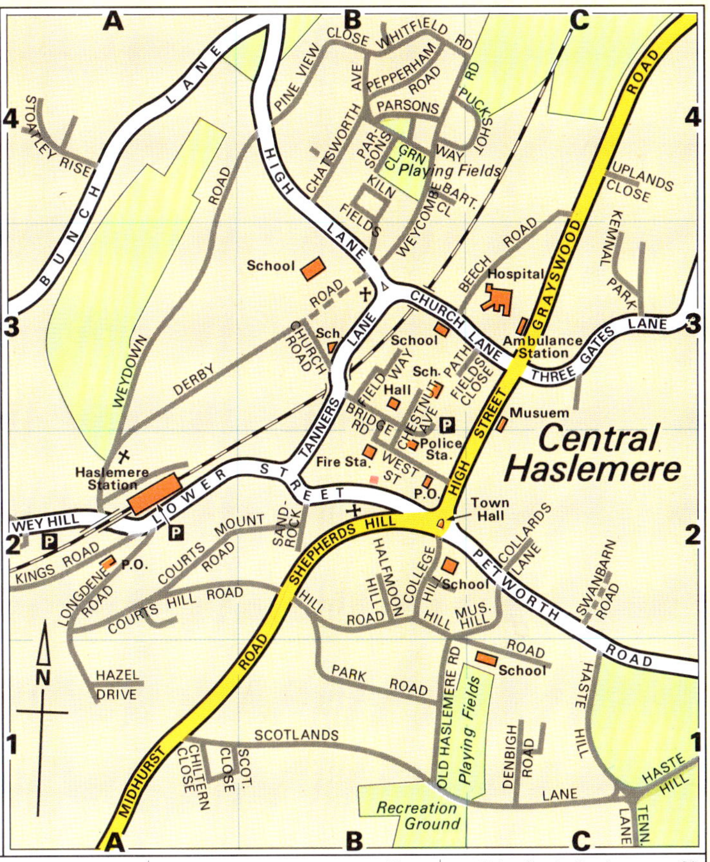

Central Petersfield

(map of Central Petersfield with grid references A–C, 1–4, showing streets including Monks Orchard, Tilmore Gardens, Stafford Road, Cemetery, Kingsfernsden Lane, Churcher's College, Bell Hill Ridge, Woodbury, Highfield Road, North Road, Madeline Road, Health Centre, Recreation Ground, Winchester Road, Princes Road, Queen's Road, Noreuil Road, Gloucester Road, Bedford Road, Hospital, The Borough, Borough Road, Grange Road, Grove Road, Cranford, Playing Fields, School, Petersfield Station, Fire Sta., Cinema, Library, Swan St, The High St, P.O., SQ., Hall, Police Sta., Hylton Road, Dragon St, Sussex Gdns, Sussex Road, The Avenue, County Court, Heath Road, West Road, Heath Pond, Swimming Pool, Town Hall, Causeway)

Central Haslemere

(map of Central Haslemere with grid references A–C, 1–4, showing streets including Whitfield Rd, Pepperham, Parsons, Puckshot Way, Uplands Close, High Lane, Weycombe Rd, School, Hospital, Beech Road, Church Lane, Ambulance Station, Three Gates, Kemnal Park, Weydown, Derby Road, Haslemere Station, Lower Street, Wey Hill, Kings Road, Longdene, P.O., Courts, Mount, Sandrock, Fire Sta., West St, Police Sta., Town Hall, Shepherds Hill, Courts Hill Road, Halfmoon Hill, College Hill, Museum Hill, Petworth Road, Collards Lane, Swanbarn Road, School, Park Road, Denbigh Road, Scotlands, Hazel Drive, Midhurst, Chiltern Close, Scot. Close, Old Haslemere Rd, Playing Fields, Recreation Ground, Haste Hill, Tennysons Lane)

LEGEND

Town Plan

AA recommended route	*(yellow line)*
Restricted roads	--- ---
Other roads	=== ===
Buildings of interest	Court *(orange)*
Car parks	P
Parks and open spaces	*(green)*

Area Plan

A roads	
B roads	
Locations	Froxford ○
Urban area	

Street Index with Grid Reference

Alton

Ackender Road	A3-A2-B2
Albert Road	A1
Amery Hill	C3
Amery Street	C3
Anstey Lane	F4
Anstey Road	E3-E4-F4
Archery Rise	A1
Ashdell Road	D2-E2
Basingstoke Road	A3
Bennet Close	B4
Bingley Road	B4
Borovere Close	A1
Borovere Gardens	A1
Borovere Lane	A1-B1
Bow Street	B1
Brandon Close	A4
Buckingham Close	A3-A2
Butts Road	A1-B1-B2
Caker Stream Road	F2-F3
Chalcrafts	E4
Chauntsingers Road	C3-D3-D4
Chawton Park Road	A1
Church Street	C3
Churchill Close	B1
Crowley Drive	D2-D1
Curtis Road	E1
Dickers Lane	E2-E3-F3
Eastbrook Road	D4-E4
Goodyers	D1-E1-E2
Greenfields Avenue	A4-B4-C4
Grove Road	D2
High Street	B2-C2-C3
Huntsmead	E1
Kings Road	A2
Kingsland Road	B2-B3
Kings Mead	E4
Lansdowne Road	D2
Langham Road	A3-B3-B2
Lenten Street	B3-B2-C3
Littlefield Road	D4-E4-E3
Lower Turk Street	C2-D2
Market Square	B2-C2
Market Street	C3-C2
Mill Lane	E2-F2-F3
Morland Close	C1-D1
Mount Pleasant Road	B2-B1-C1
Netherfield Close	B4
New Barn Lane	C1-D1
New Odiham Road	A4-A3
Normandy Street	C3-D3-E3-E4
Northanger Close	B4
Nursery Road	D4-E4
Old Acre Road	B1-B2
Old Odiham Road	C3-C4
Orchard Lane	D2-D3
Paper Mill Lane	D3-E3-E2
Park Close Road	D4
Plevna Close	D4
Princess Drive	A3
Queens Road	A2-B2-B1
Rack Close	A2-B2
St Lawrence Road	C4-C3-D3
Sandringham Close	A3
Spicers	D1
Spitalfields Road	C4-D4
Spital Hatch	E2-F2
Station Road	E3
Stillions Close	D1
Tanhouse Lane	B3-C3
The Ridgeway	D1
Thorpe Gardens	A4
Tilney Close	A4
Tower Street	B1
Turk Street	C2
Upper Grove Road	B1
Vaughans	D1
Vicarage Hill	C3
Vicarage Road	A1-B1
Victoria Road	D3-D4-E4
Wentworth Gardens	B4-A4
Westbrooke Road	B2-B3
Whitedown	A2-A1
Willoughby Close	A4
Wilsom Close	E2
Wilsom Road	E2-E1-F1
Windmill Hill	C2-C1-D1
Young's Road	D4

Petersfield

Barham Road	B2-C2
Bedford Road	A2
Bell Hill	A4-A3
Bell Hill Ridge	A4
Borough Grove	B1
Borough Road	A1-B1-B2
Buckingham Road	A2
Bucksmore Avenue	A3
Causeway	B1-C1
Chapel Street	B2
Charles Street	B2
College Street	C3-C2
Cranford Road	B1
Dragon Street	C2
Frenchmans Road	A3-A2-B2
Gloucester Road	A2
Grange Road	B1
Heath Road	C2
Heath Road West	C1-C2
Highfield Road	B3
High Street	B2-C2
Hylton Road	B2-C2-C1
Kimbers	B3
King George Avenue	B3-C3-B2-C2
Kingsfernsden Lane	C4
Lavant Street	B2
Love Lane	C3
Lynton Road	A3
Madeline Road	C3
Moggs Mead	C2
Monks Orchard	B4
Noreuil Road	A2
North Road	B3

Haslemere

Oaklands Road	A3
Osborne Road	B3
Penns Road	B3
Princes Road	A2
Queen's Road	A2
Ramshill	C3-C4
Readon Close	C3
Rushes Road	A3-A2
Sandringham Road	B3
Selbourne Close	B4-C4
Stafford Road	B4
Stanton Road	A3
Station Road	B2-B3-C3
Sussex Gardens	C2-C1
Sussex Road	C2-C1
Swan Street	B2
The Avenue	C2
The Borough	B2
The Square	B2
Tilmore Gardens	B4-C4
Tilmore Road	B4-B3
Tor Way	C3-C2
Weston Road	C2
Winchester Road	A2-A3
Winton Road	B3-B2
Woodbury Avenue	A3

Haslemere

Bartholomew Close	B4
Beech Road	B3-C3-C4
Bridge Road	B3
Bunch Lane	A3-A4-B4
Chatsworth Avenue	B4
Chestnut Avenue	B2-B3
Church Lane	B3-C3
Church Road	B3
Chiltern Close	A1
Collards Lane	C2
College Hill	B2
Courts Hill Road	A2-B2
Courts Mount Road	A2-B2
Denbigh Road	C1
Derby Road	A2-A3-B3
Field Way	B3
Grayswood Road	C3-C4
Great Gates Lane	C3
Halfmoon Hill	B2
Haste Hill	C1
Hazel Drive	A1
High Lane	B4-B3
High Street	B2-C2-C3
Higher Combe Road	C3
Hill Road	B2-B1-C1
Kemnal Park	C3
Kiln Fields	B4-B3
Kings Road	A2
Longdene Road	A1-A2
Lower Street	A2-B2
Midhurst Road	A1-B1-B2
Museum Hill	B2-C2
Old Haslemere Road	B1
Park Road	B2-B1
Parsons Close	B4
Parsons Green	B4
Path Fields Close	B3-C3
Pepperham Road	B4
Petworth Road	B2-C2-C1
Pine View Close	B4
Puckshot Way	B4-C4
Sandrock Street	B2
Scotland Close	A1
Scotlands Lane	A1-B1-C1
Shawbarn Road	C2
Shepherds Hill	B2
Stoatley Rise	A4
Tanners Lane	B2-B3
Tennysons Lane	C1
Uplands Close	C4
West Road	B2
Wey Hill	A2
Weycombe Road	B3-B4-C4
Weydown Road	A2-A3-A4-B4
Whitfield Road	B4

PETERSFIELD
Butser Ancient Farm, reconstructed to a prehistoric design, is one of the attractions of Queen Elizabeth Country Park — a serene area of countryside covering over 1,000 acres, which lies just three miles south of Petersfield on the A3.

Ashford

One of Britain's more unusual museums is that of the Intelligence Corps at Ashford's Templar Barracks — but those who only wish to investigate the secrets of this thriving market town might prefer to visit the Local History Museum or the Ashford Heritage Centre, which traces its bygones through to Roman times. Now an important industrial and commercial centre with good shops,

Ashford also enjoys the facilities of the Stour Sports Centre and the greenery of Victoria Park.

Folkestone is a town of contrasts — between the gleaming modern ferries carrying holidaymakers to France and Belgium, and the narrow cobbled streets and old buildings which lie around its harbour. Flanked by 15th-century Martello towers on the clifftop is the Leas promenade, site of the Leas Cliff Hall (a major entertainment centre), and the New Metropolitan Arts Centre, which stages regular

exhibitions. Visitors to the Leas can go by road or by lift — an unusual water-driven model has been in operation here since the 19th century.

Hythe Main terminus for the Romney, Hythe and Dymchurch Light Railway, which runs along the coast from here to Dungeness, Hythe is a peaceful, unspoiled resort. One of the Cinque Ports, its places of interest include the 17th-century Old Manor House and a parish church which has several 13th-century features.

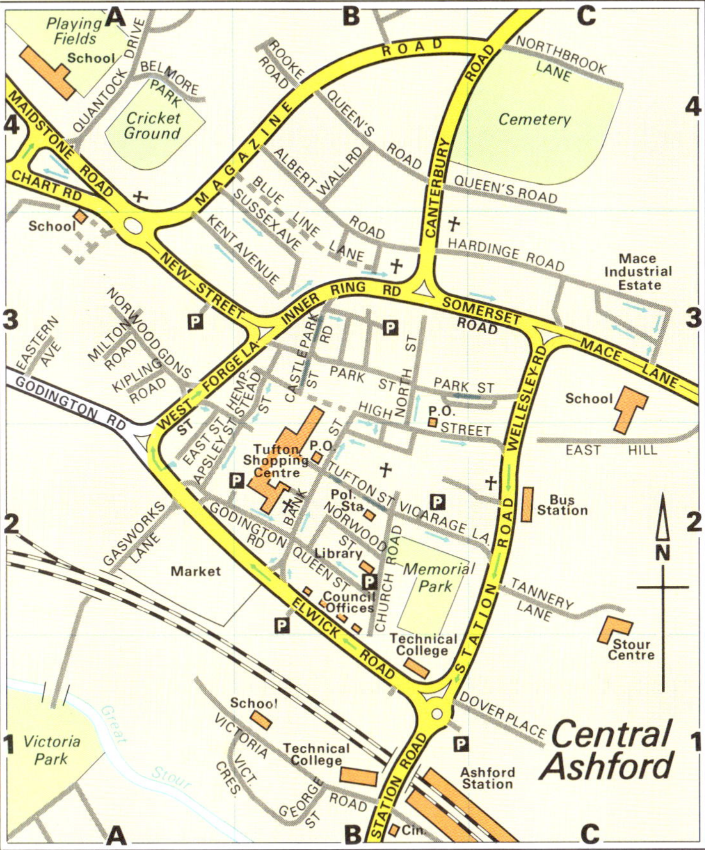

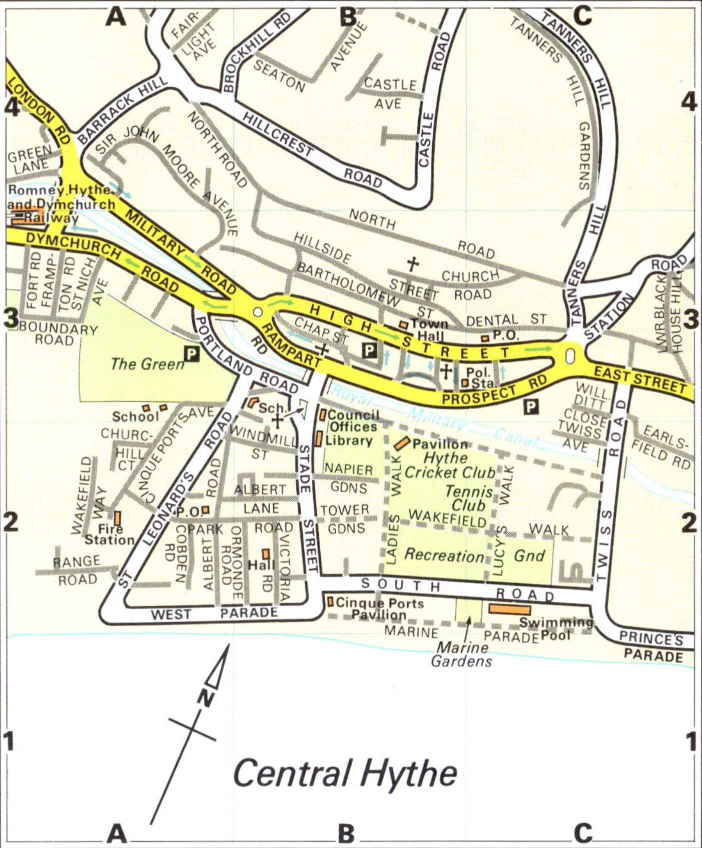

Central Ashford

(map — Ashford town plan)

Central Hythe

(map — Hythe town plan)

LEGEND

Town Plan

AA Recommended roads	*(yellow)*
Other roads	*(white)*
Restricted roads	*(dashed)*
Buildings of interest	Library *(orange)*
Car parks	P
Parks and open spaces	*(yellow)*
One way streets	→

Area Plan

A roads	
B roads	
Locations	Lyminge ●
Urban area	

Street Index with Grid Reference

Folkstone

Alexandra Gardens	D2
Alexandra Street	F4
Archer Road	E4
Bayle Street	E2
Black Bull Road	D4-E4
Bolton Road	E4
Boscombe Road	D4
Bournemouth Road	C4-D4
Bouverie Place	D2
Bouverie Road West	A2-B2-C2
Bouverie Square	C2-D2
Bradstone Avenue	D3-D4
Bradstone Road	D3-E3
Bridge Street	F4
Broadfield Road	A4
Broadmead Road	C4-D4
Brockman Road	C3
Cambridge Gardens	D3
Canterbury Road	E4-F4
Castle Hill Avenue	B1-B2-B3-C3
Charlotte Street	E3
Cheriton Gardens	C2-C3
Cheriton Place	C2
Cheriton Road	A4-B4-C4-C3-D3-D2
Christ Church Road	C2-C3
Church Street	D2-E2
Claremont Road	C3
Clarence Street	E3
Clifton Crescent	A1-B1
Clifton Road	B1
Connaught Road	D3
Coolinge Road	C3-D3
Cornwallis Avenue	B4
Dawson Road	E4
Denmark Street	F4
Dover Road	E2-E3-F3-F4
Dudley Road	F3
Dyke Road	F2
Earls Avenue	A1-A2-A3
East Cliff	F2-F3
Eastfields	E4
Fern Bank Crescent	E4
Folly Road	F3
Foord Road	D3-D4
Foresters Way	D2-D3
Garden Road	D4
Gloucester Place	D2
Godwyn Road	A2-A3
Grace Hill	D3-D2-E2-E3
Grimston Avenue	A2-A3
Grimston Gardens	A2-A3
Grove Road	E3-F3
Guildhall Street	D2-D3
Harbour Approach Road	E1
Harbour Way	E2-E3
Harvey Street	E2-E3
Ingles Road	B2-C2
Jointon Road	A3-B3
Julian Road	B4
Kingsworth Gardens	B3-C3
Langhorne Gardens	B1
Linden Crescent	E4
London Street	E3-E4
Lower Sandgate Road	A1-B1-C1-D1-E1-E2
Manor Road	C2-C3
Marine Parade	D1-E1
Marine Terrace	E1
Martello Road	F3
Marten Road	A3-A4
Metropole Road East	A1-A2
Middleburg Square	C2-D2
Millfield	C2-D2
Morrison Road	F3-F4
North Street	E2-F2
Old High Street	E2
Oxford Terrace	D2
Pavilion Road	D4
Playdell Gardens	C1
Princess Street	F4
Queen Street	E3
Radnor Bridge Road	E3-F3-F2
Radnor Park Avenue	C4
Radnor Park Crescent	C4-D4
Radnor Park Road	C4-D4
Radnor Park West	B4-C4
Raventa Road	A4
Rendezvous Street	D2-E2
Road of Remembrance	D1-E1
Rossendale Road	F3
Ryland Place	F3
St John's Church Road	D4
St Johns Street	E3
St Michael's Street	E2-E3
Sandgate Road	A2-B2-B1-C1-C2-D2-D1-D2
Shakespeare Terrace	C1
Shellons Street	D2-D3
Shepway Close	D4-E4
Ship Street	D4
Shorncliffe Road	A4-A3-B3-C3
The Bayle	E2
The Durlocks	F2
The Leas	B1-C1-D1
The Parade	E2
The Tram Road	E2-F2-F3
Tontine Street	E2-E3
Trinity Crescent	A1-A2
Trinity Gardens	B2
Trinity Road	A2-B2-B3
Victoria Grove	D2-D3
Victoria Road	C4-D4
Walton Road	D4-E4
Wear Bay Road	F2
Westbourne Gardens	A2
West Terrace	D1-D2
Wiltie Gardens	C4
Wilton Road	B4

Ashford

Albert Road	B3-B4
Apsley Street	A2-B2
Bank Street	B2-B3
Belmore Park	A4
Blue Line Lane	B3-B4
Canterbury Road	B3-B4-C4
Castle Street	B2
Chart Road	A4
Church Road	B2
Dover Place	B1-C1
Eastern Avenue	A3
East Hill	A2
East Street	A2-A3
Elwick Road	B1-B2
Forge Lane	A3-B3
Gasworks Lane	A2
George Street	B1
Godington Road	A3-A2-B2
Hardinge Road	B3-C3
Hempstead Street	B3
High Street	B3-B2-C2
Inner Ring Road	B3
Kent Avenue	A3-B3
Kipling Road	A3
Mace Lane	C3
Magazine Road	A3-A4-B4-C4
Maidstone Road	A4
Milton Road	A3
New Street	A3-B3
Northbrook Lane	C1
North Street	B2-B3
Norwood Gardens	A3
Norwood Street	B2
Park Road	B3
Park Street	B3-C3
Quantock Drive	A4
Queen's Road	B4-C4
Queen Street	B2
Rooke Road	B4
Somerset Road	B3-C3
Station Road	B1-C1-C2
Sussex Avenue	A4-B4-B3
Tannery Lane	C2
Tufton Street	B2
Vicarage Lane	B2-C2
Victoria Crescent	A1-B1
Victoria Road	A1-B1
Wall Road	B4
Wellesley Road	C2-C3
West Street	A2-A3

Hythe

Albert Lane	A2-B2
Albert Road	A2
Barrack Hill	A4
Bartholomew Street	B3
Boundary Road	A3
Brockhill Road	A4-B4
Castle Avenue	B4
Castle Road	B4
Chapel Street	B3
Churchill Court	A4
Church Road	B3-C3
Cinque Ports Avenue	A2-A3
Cobden Road	A2
Dental Street	B3-C3
Dymchurch Road	A3
Earlsfield Road	C2-C3
East Street	C3
Fairlight Avenue	A4
Fort Road	A3
Frampton Road	A3
Green Lane	A4
High Street	B3-C3
Hillcrest Road	B4
Hillside Street	B3
Ladies Walk (footpath)	B2
London Road	A4
Lower Black House Hill	C3
Lucy's Walk (footpath)	C2
Marine Parade	B2-C2
Military Road	A4-A3
Napier Gardens	B2
North Road	A4-B4-B3-B2
Ormonde Road	B2
Park Road	A2-B2
Portland Road	A3-B3
Prospect Road	B3-C3
Prince's Parade	C1-C2
Rampart Road	B3
Range Road	A2
St Leonard's Road	A2-A3-B3
St Nicholas Avenue	A3
Seaton Avenue	B4
Sir John Moore Avenue	A2-A4
South Road	B2-C2
Stade Street	B2-B3
Station Road	C3
Tanners Hill	C3-C4
Tanners Hill Gardens	C4
Tower Gardens	B2
Twiss Avenue	C3
Twiss Road	C2-C3
Victoria Road	B2
Wakefield Walk (footpath)	B2-C2
Wakefield Way	A2
West Parade	A2-B2
William Ditt Close	C3
Windmill Street	A2-B2

HYTHE
Running from Hythe to Dungeness Lighthouse, the 15-inch-gauge Romney, Hythe and Dymchurch Railway, with its 11 diminutive steam locomotives and one diesel, proudly claims the title of The Smallest Public Railway in the World.

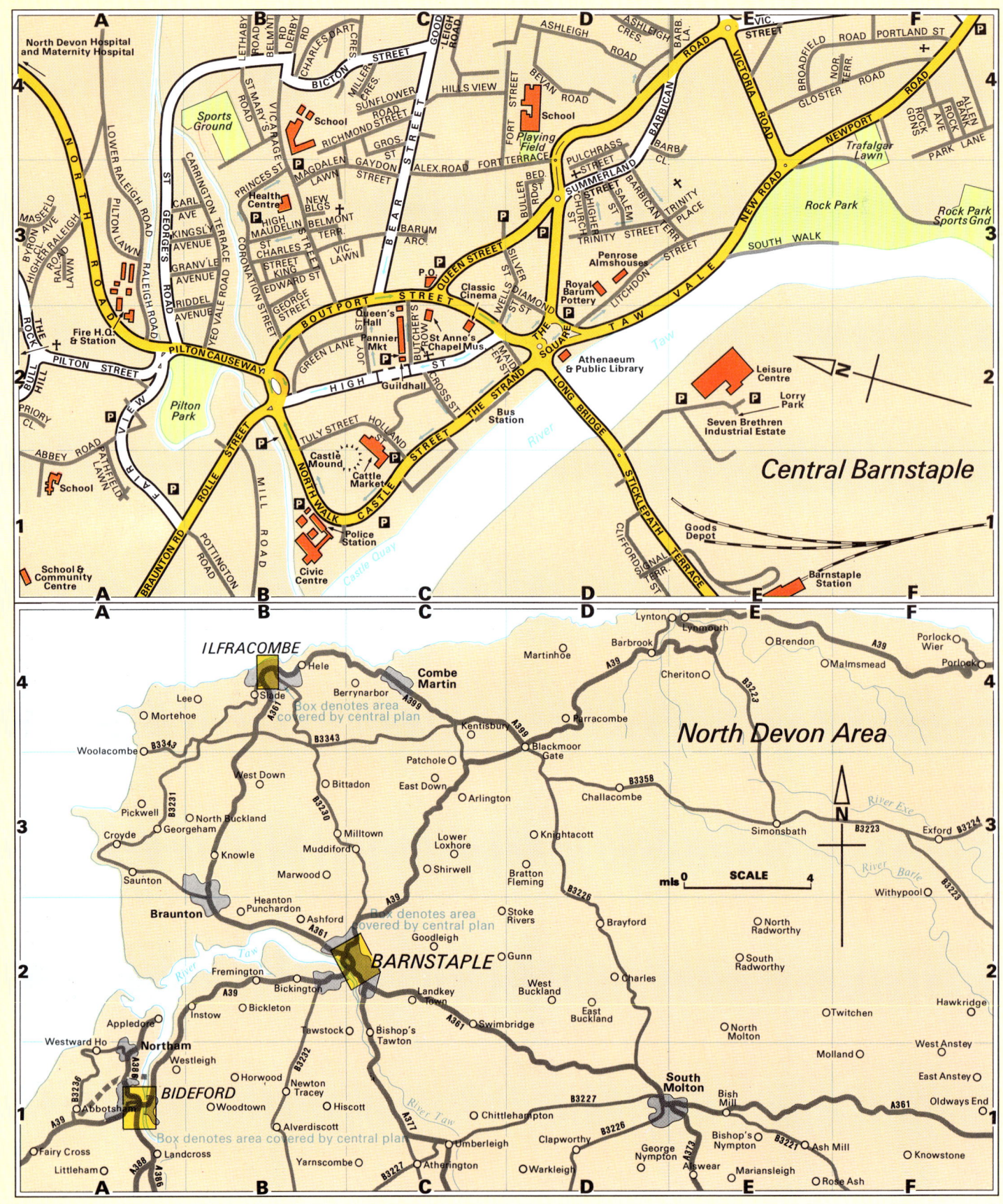

Barnstaple

During the 18th century the wool trade created a prosperity in Barnstaple to which the town's elegant Georgian buildings testify. Queen Anne's Walk, a colonnade where merchants conducted business, is both a fine example of this period and a reminder that Barnstaple has always been a trading centre. This tradition continues as today it is one of the area's busiest market towns. Of the many picturesque shopping streets Butchers Row is particularly attractive.

Ilfracombe This is North Devon's well-established "Queen of the Coast". Originally a fishing harbour, Ilfracombe evolved in the 19th century – when enterprise was all – into one of the typical seaside resorts that mushroomed all over England. Here, terraces of large Victorian hotels and houses follow the contours of the hills down to the harbour and a welter of little coves. The town is also the main departure point for Lundy Island.

Bideford South-west of Barnstaple and Ilfracombe, Bideford too has always made its living by trading and the sea. Sir Richard Grenville, a Bideford man famous for his fight against the Spaniards in the Azores, gained a charter for the town from Elizabeth I and it prospered as a port and shipbuilding centre until the 18th century. A nautical air still pervades Bideford and the long, tree-lined quay is popular.

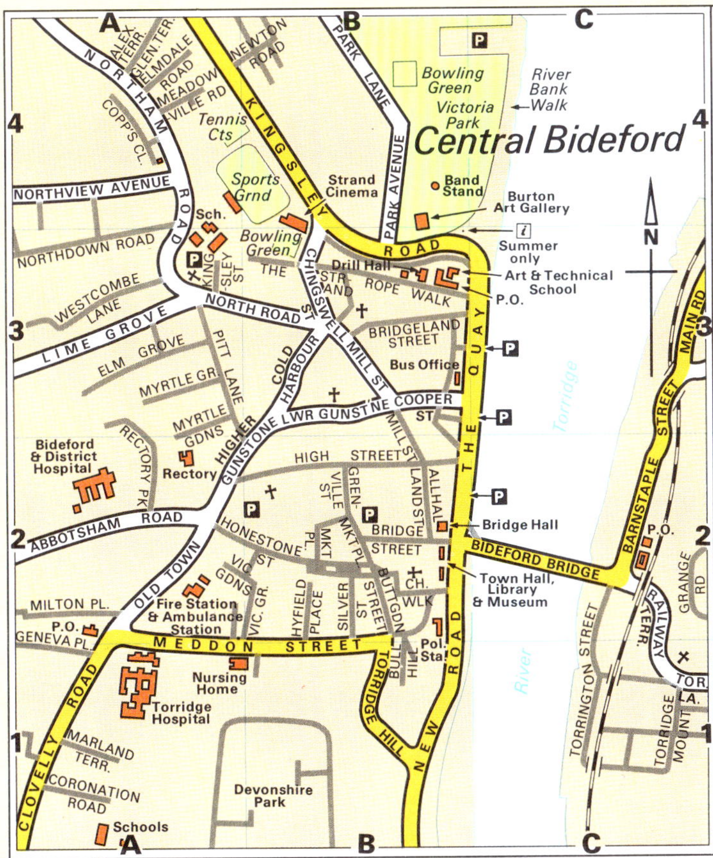
Central Bideford
Bowling Green
Victoria Park
River Bank Walk
Band Stand
Burton Art Gallery
Summer only
Art & Technical School
P.O.
Strand Cinema
Drill Hall
Bus Office
Bridge Hall
Town Hall, Library & Museum
Bideford & District Hospital
Rectory
Fire Station & Ambulance Station
Nursing Home
Torridge Hospital
Devonshire Park
Schools
Tennis Cts
Sports Grnd
Bowling Green
Pol. Sta.
River Torridge
KINGSLEY ROAD
NORTHAM ROAD
NORTHVIEW AVENUE
NORTHDOWN ROAD
WESTCOMBE LANE
LIME GROVE
ELM GROVE
MYRTLE GR
NORTH ROAD
PARK LANE
PARK AVENUE
THE QUAY
BRIDGELAND STREET
HIGH STREET
ABBOTSHAM ROAD
MEDDON STREET
BIDEFORD BRIDGE
BARNSTAPLE STREET
TORRINGTON STREET
MAIN RD
NEW ROAD
TORRIDGE HILL
CLOVELLY ROAD
MARLAND TERR.
CORONATION ROAD
OLD TOWN
HONESTONE ST
MILTON PL.
GENEVA PL.

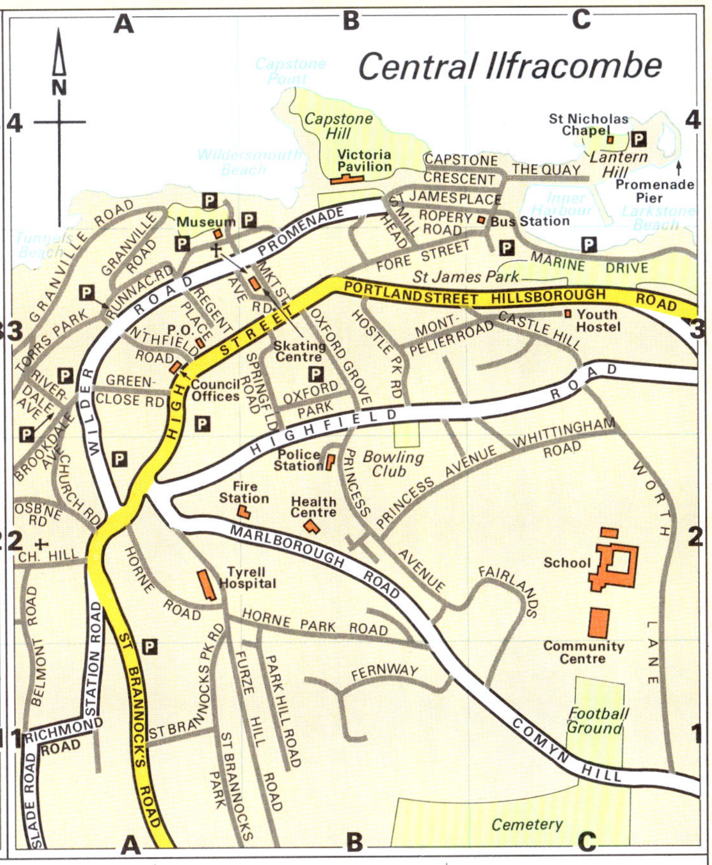
Central Ilfracombe
Capstone Point
Capstone Hill
Wildersmouth Beach
Victoria Pavilion
St Nicholas Chapel
Lantern Hill
Promenade Pier
Inner Harbour
Larkstone Beach
Tunnels Beach
Museum
Bus Station
St James Park
Youth Hostel
Skating Centre
Council Offices
Police Station
Bowling Club
Fire Station
Health Centre
Tyrell Hospital
School
Community Centre
Football Ground
Cemetery
CAPSTONE CRESCENT
THE QUAY
MARINE DRIVE
PROMENADE
FORE STREET
PORTLAND STREET
HILLSBOROUGH ROAD
HIGH STREET
HIGHFIELD ROAD
WHITTINGHAM ROAD
PRINCESS AVENUE
MARLBOROUGH ROAD
HORNE PARK ROAD
HORNE ROAD
FERNWAY
COMYN HILL
WORTH LANE
FAIRLANDS
ST BRANNOCK'S ROAD
STATION ROAD
RICHMOND ROAD
SLADE ROAD
BELMONT ROAD
WILDER ROAD
GRANVILLE ROAD
TORRS PARK
OXFORD GROVE
OXFORD PARK
CASTLE HILL

LEGEND

Town Plan
- AA recommended route
- Restricted roads
- Other roads
- Buildings of interest — Station
- Car parks — P
- Parks and open spaces
- One way streets

Area Plan
- A roads
- B roads
- Locations — Patchole ○
- Urban area

Street Index with Grid Reference

Barnstaple

Abbey Road	A1-A2
Alexandra Road	C3
Allen Bank	F4
Ashleigh Crescent	D4-E4
Ashleigh Road	D4
Barbican Close	D4-E4
Barbican Lane	E4
Barbican Road	D4-E4
Barbican Terrace	D3-E3
Barum Arcade	C3
Bear Street	C3-C4
Bedford Street	D3
Belmont Road	B4
Belmont Terrace	B3-C3
Bevan Road	D4
Bicton Street	B4-C4
Boutport Street	B2-B3-C3-C2
Braunton Road	A1
Broadfield Road	E4-F4
Buller Road	D3
Bull Hill	A2
Butcher's Row	C2-C3
Byron Close	A3
Carlyle Avenue	A3-B3
Carrington Terrace	B3-B4
Castle Street	C1-C2
Charles Dart Crescent	B4-C4
Charles Street	B3
Clifford Street	D1
Coronation Street	B2-B3
Cross Street	C2
Derby Road	B4
Diamond Street	D2-D3
Fair View	A1-A2
Fort Street	C3-C4-D4
Fort Terrace	C3-D3
Gaydon Street	C3
George Street	B2-B3
Gloster Road	E4-F4
Goodleigh Road	C4
Granville Avenue	A3-B3
Green Lane	B2-C2
Grosvenor Street	C4
Higher Church Street	D3
Higher Raleigh Road	A3
High Maudelin Street	B3
High Street	B2-C2
Hills View	C4
Holland Street	C1-C2
Joy Street	C2
King Edward Street	B3
Lethaby Road	B4
Litchdon Street	D2-D3-E3
Long Bridge	D2
Lower Raleigh Road	A3-A4
Magdalen Lawn	B3
Maiden Street	D2
Masefield Avenue	A3
Miller Crescent	C4
Mill Road	B1-B2
New Buildings	B3
Newport Road	E3-E4-F4
New Road	E3
Norfolk Terrace	F4
North Road	A2-A3-A4
North Walk	B1-B2
Park Lane	F4
Pathfield Lawn	A1-A2
Pilton Causeway	A2-B2
Pilton Lawn	A3
Pilton Street	A2
Portland Street	F4
Pottington Road	B1
Princes Street	B3
Priory Close	A2
Pulchrass Street	D3-D4
Queen Street	C3-D3
Raleigh Lawn	A3
Raleigh Road	A2-A3
Richmond Street	B4-C4
Riddel Avenue	A2-B2-B3
Rock Avenue	F4
Rock Gardens	F4
Rolle Street	B1-B2
St George's Road	A2-A3-A4
St Mary's Road	B4
Salem Street	D3
Signal Terrace	D1-E1
Silver Street	D3
South Walk	E3-F3
Sticklepath Terrace	D1-E1
Summerland Street	D3-D4
Sunflower Road	C4
Taw Vale	D2-D3-E3
The Rock	A2
The Square	D2
The Strand	C2-D2
Trinity Place	E3
Trinity Street	D3
Tuly Street	B2-C2
Vicarage Lawn	B3-C3
Vicarage Street	B3-B4
Victoria Road	E4
Victoria Street	E4
Wells Street	C2-D2-D3
Yeo Vale Road	B2-B3

Bideford

Abbotsham Road	A2
Alexandra Terrace	A4
Allhalland Street	B2
Barnstaple Street	C2-C3
Bideford Bridge	B2-C2
Bridgeland Street	B3
Bridge Street	B2
Bull Hill	B1-B2
Buttgarden Street	B2
Chingswell Street	B3
Church Walk	B2
Clovelly Road	A1
Cold Harbour	B3
Cooper Street	B3
Copp's Close	A4
Coronation Road	A1
Elmdale Road	A4
Elm Grove	A3
Geneva Place	A1-A2
Glendale Terrace	A4
Grange Road	C2
Grenville Street	B2
Higher Gunstone	A2-B2-B3
High Street	A2-B2
Honestone Street	A2-B2
Hyfield Place	B2
Kingsley Road	A4-B4-B3
Kingsley Street	A3
Lime Grove	A3
Lower Gunstone	B3
Main Road	C3
Market Place	B2
Marland Terrace	A1
Meadowville Road	A4
Meddon Street	A1-A2-B2-B1
Mill Street	B2-B3
Milton Place	A2
Myrtle Gardens	A2-A3
Myrtle Grove	A3
New Road	B1-B2
Newton Road	A4-B4
Northam Road	A3-A4
Northdown Road	A3-A4
North Road	A3-B3
Northview Avenue	A4
Old Town	A2
Park Avenue	B3-B4
Park Lane	B4
Pitt Lane	A2-A3
Railway Terrace	C1-C2
Rectory Park	A2-A3
Rope Walk	B3
Silver Street	B2
The Quay	B2-B3-C3-C2
The Strand	B3
Torridge Hill	B1
Torridge Mount	C1
Torrington Lane	C1
Torrington Street	C1-C2
Victoria Gardens	A2-B2
Victoria Grove	A2-B2
Westcombe Lane	A3

Ilfracombe

Avenue Road	A3-B3
Belmont Road	A1-A2
Brookdale Avenue	A2-A3
Capstone Crescent	B4-C4
Castle Hill	C3
Church Hill	A2
Church Road	A2-A3
Comyn Hill	B1-C1
Fairlands	B2-C2-C1
Fernway	B1
Fore Street	B3-C3
Furze Hill Road	A2-A1-B1
Granville Road	A3-A4
Green Close Road	A3
Highfield Road	A2-B2-B3-C3
High Street	A2-A3-B3
Hillsborough Road	C3
Horne Park Road	A2-B2-B1
Horne Road	A2
Hostle Park Road	B3
Marine Drive	C3-C4
Market Street	B3
Marlborough Road	A2-B2
Mill Head	B3-B4
Montpellier Road	B3-C3
Northfield Road	A3
Osborne Road	A2
Oxford Grove	B3
Oxford Park	B3
Park Hill Road	B1-B2
Portland Street	B3-C3
Princess Avenue	B3-B2-C2
Promenade	B3-B4
Regent Place	A3
Richmond Road	A1
Riverdale Avenue	A3
Ropery Road	B4-C4
Runnacleave Road	A3
St Brannocks Park	A1
St Brannocks Park Road	A1-A2
St Brannocks Road	A1-A2
St James Place	B4-C4
Slade Road	A1
Springfield Road	B3
Station Road	A1-A2
The Quay	C4
Torrs Park	A3
Whittingham Road	C2-C3
Wilder Road	A2-A3
Worth Lane	C1-C2-C3

BARNSTAPLE
This ancient town stands on the Taw estuary and until the 19th century was an important port. The bridge across the river was originally built in the 1400s but has since been widened and extensively altered.

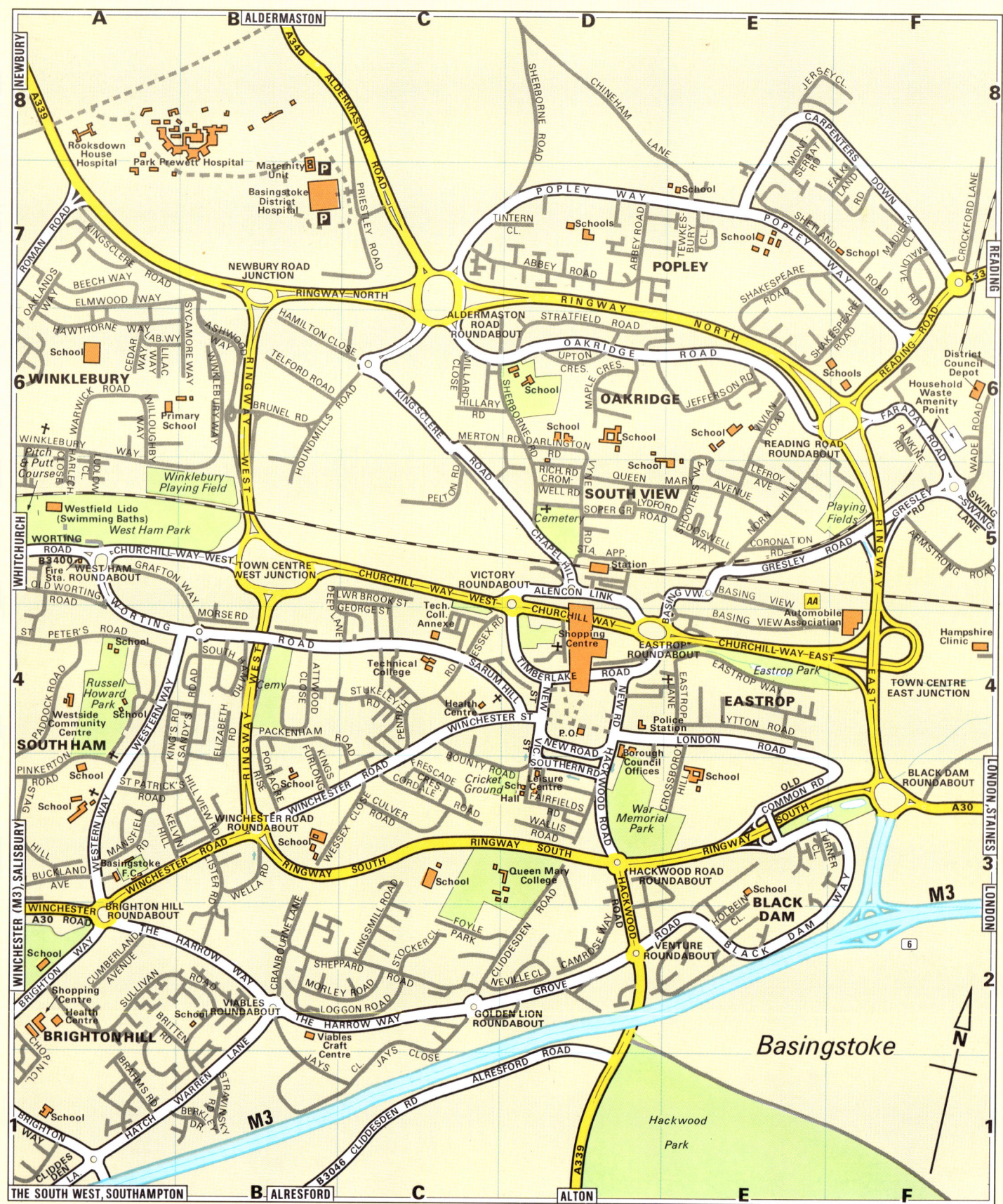

Basingstoke

Ever-expanding Basingstoke has seen a remarkable transformation in the last half-century, from quiet market town to major commercial and industrial centre, with a population of about 90,000. Rehousing for thousands of Londoners in the 1960s began the process, and easy access by road and rail to Heathrow Airport, Southampton Docks and London has made moving here an attractive proposition for large companies.

At the heart of the town is a large pedestrian shopping centre with good parking, a Sports Centre and a thriving theatre. Several specially created sports parks are in easy reach, and Mays Bounty, the local cricket ground, is regularly used by Hampshire for part of its County programme.

Basingstoke still boasts a number of older buildings, notably the 13th-century ruins of the Holy Ghost Chapel, which lie to the north of the railway station on the site of an ancient burial ground. St Michael's Parish Church dates mainly from the 16th century and has traces of Norman influence, although Second World War bombing destroyed most of the stained glass. The church also suffered damage in the Civil War from Cromwell's forces; two miles to the east of Basingstoke lie the ruins of Basing House, destroyed in 1645 by Parliamentary forces after a three-year resistance.

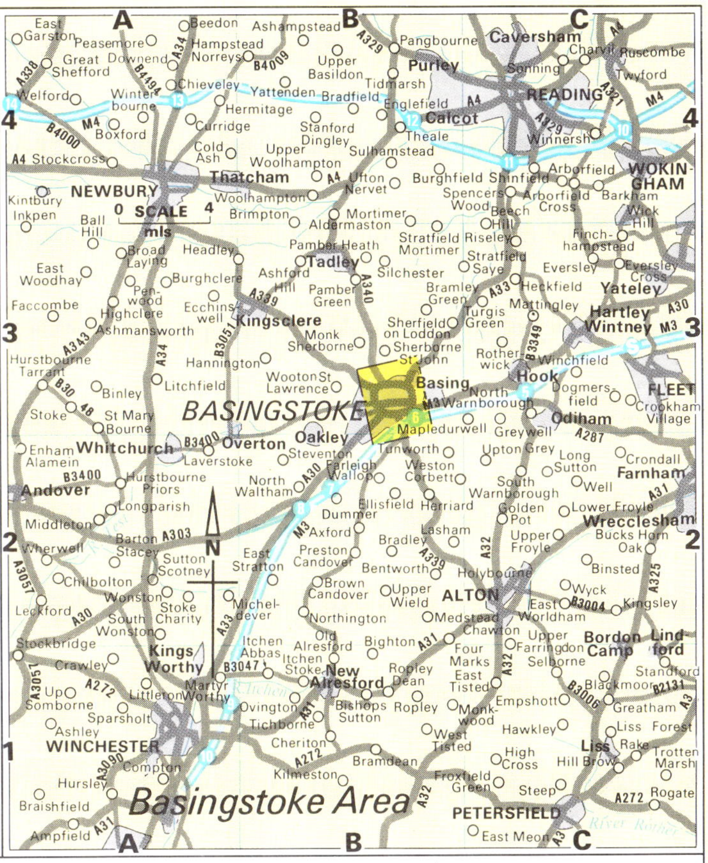

Central Basingstoke

Basingstoke Area

LEGEND

Town Plan

AA recommended route
Restricted roads
Other roads
Buildings of interest — Station
Car parks — P
Parks and open spaces
One way streets

Area Plan

A roads
B roads
Locations — Faccombe ○
Urban area

Street Index with Grid Reference

Basingstoke

Abbey Road	C7-D7
Aldermaston Road	B8-C8-C7
Alencon Link	D4-D5
Alresford Road	C1-D1-D2
Armstrong Road	F5
Ashwood Way	B6
Attwood Close	B4
Basing View	D4-E4-E5-E4
Beech Way	A7
Berkley Drive	A1-B1
Blackdam Way	E2-F2-F3-E3
Bounty Road	C4-C3-D3
Brahms Road	A1
Brighton Way	A1
Brighton Way	A2
Britten Road	A2-B2
Brunel Road	B6
Buckland Avenue	A3
Camrose Way	D2-D3
Carpenters Down	E7-E8-F8-F7
Cedar Way	A6
Chapel Hill	D5
Chineham Lane	D8-E8-E7
Chopin Close	A1-A2
Chuchill Way	D5-D4
Churchill Way East	E4-F4
Churchill Way West	A5-B5-C5-C4
Cliddesden Lane	A1
Cliddesden Road	B1-C1-C2-D2-D3
Cordale Road	C3
Coronation Road	E5
Cranbourne Lane	B2-B3
Crockford Lane	F7-F8
Cromwell Road	D5
Crossborough Hill	E3-E4
Culver Road	C3
Cumberland Avenue	A2
Darlington Road	D6
Deep Lane	B5-B4-C4
Doswell Way	E5
Eastrop Way	E4
Elizabeth Road	B3-B4
Elmwood Way	A6-A7-B7
Essex Road	C4
Fairfields Road	D3
Falkland Road	E7-F7
Faraday Road	F5-F6
Foyle Park	C3-C2-D2
Frescade Crescent	C3
Grafton Way	A5-B5-B4
Gresley Road	F5
Grove Road	C2-D2-E2
Hackwood Road	D4-D3-D2
Hamilton Close	B6-C6
Harlech Close	A5-A6
Hatch Warren Lane	A1-B1-B2
Hawthorne Way	A6
Hillary Road	C6-D6
Hill View Road	B3
Holbein Close	E2-E3
Houndmills Road	B5-B6-C6
Jays Close	B2-B1-C1-C2
Jefferson Road	E6
Jersey Close	E8-F8
Kelvin Hill	A3
Kingsclere Road	C6-C5-D5
Kingsclere Road	A7-B7
Kings Furlong	B3-B4

Kingsmill Road	C2-C3
King's Road	A3-A4
Laburnum Way	A6
Lefroy Avenue	E5
Lilac Way	A6
Lister Road	B2-B3
Loggon Road	B2-C2
London Road	D4-E4-E3-F3
Lower Brook Street	B5-C5
Ludlow Close	A5-A6
Lydford Road	D5-E5
Lytton Road	E4
Madeira Close	F7
Maldive Road	F7
Mansfield Road	A3
Maple Crescent	D6
Merton Road	C6-D6
Millard Close	C6
Montserrat Road	E7-E8
Morley Road	B2-C2
Morse Road	B4
Neville Close	C2-D2
New Road	D4-D3
New Street	D4
Norn Hill	E5-E6
Oaklands Way	A6-A7
Oakridge Road	C6-D6-E6
Old Common Road	E3-F3
Old Worting Road	A5
Packenham Road	B4-C4-C3
Paddock Road	A3-A4
Pelton Road	C5
Penrith Road	C4
Pinkerton Road	A3
Popley Way	C7-D7-E7-F7-F6
Portacre Rise	B3-B4
Priestley Road	C7-C8
Queen Mary Avenue	D5-E5
Rankine Road	F6
Reading Road	F6-F7
Richmond Road	D5
Ringway East	F6-F5-F4-F3
Ringway North	B7-C7-D7-D6-E6
Ringway South	B3-C3-D3-E3-F3
Ringway West	B3-B4-B5-B6
Roman Road	A7
St Patrick's Road	A3-B3
St Peter's Road	A4
Sandy's Road	B3-B4
Sarum Hill	C4-D4
Shakespeare Road	E7-E6-F6-F7
Sheppard Road	B2-C2
Sherborne Road	D7-D8
Shetland Road	E7-F7
Sherborne Road	C6-D6-D5

Shooters Way	E5-E6
Soper Grove	D5
Southern Road	D3
South Ham Road	B4
Stag Hill	A3
Station Approach	D5
Stocker Close	C2
Stratfield Road	D6-E6
Stravinsky Road	B1
Stukeley Road	B4-C4
Sullivan Road	A2-B2-B1
Swing Swang Lane	F5
Sycamore Way	B6-B7
Telford Road	B6
Tewkesbury Close	E7
The Harrow Way	A2-B2-C2
Timberlake Road	D4
Tintern Close	C7-D7
Upton Crescent	D6
Victoria Street	D2-D3
Vivian Road	E6
Vyne Road	D5-D6
Wade Road	F5-F6
Wallis Road	D3
Warwick Road	A6
Wella Road	B3
Wessex Close	B3-C3
Western Way	A3-A4-B4
Willoughby Way	A5-A6
Winchester Road	A2-A3-B3-C3-C4-D4
Winchester Street	C4-E4
Winklebury Way	A6-A5-B5-B6
Worting Road	A5-A4-B4-C4

Basingstoke Central

Alencon Link	A3-B3-B4-C4-C3
Basing View	C3-C4
Beaconsfield Road	B1
Bounty Road	A2-A1-B1
Bramblys Drive	A2
Burgess Road	A4-B4
Castle Road	B1
Chapel Hill	A4-B4
Chequers Road	C2-C3
Churchill Way	A3-B3-C3
Churchill Way East	C3
Churchill Way West	A3
Church Square	B3
Church Street	B2-B3
Cliddesden Road	B1
Cordale Road	A1
Council Road	B1
Crossborough Hill	C1-C2
Doswell Way	C4
Eastfield Avenue	C2-C3
Eastrop Lane	C2-C3
Eastrop Way	C3
Essex Road	A3
Fairfields Road	B1
Flaxfield Road	A3-A2-B2
Frances Road	A2
Frescade Crescent	A1
Goat Lane	C3
Hackwood Road	C1-C2
Hardy Lane	A1-A2
Jubilee Road	B1-B2
Kingsclere Road	A4
London Road	C2
London Street	B2
Lower Brook Street	A3
Lytton Road	C2
Mortimer Lane	A3
New Road	B2-C2-C3
New Street	B2
Norn Hill	C4
Old Reading Road	C4
Penrith Road	A1-A2
Rayleigh Road	A3
Ringway South	C1
Rochford Road	A3
Sarum Hill	A3-A2-B2
Soper Grove	B4
Southend Road	A3
Southern Road	B2
Timberlake Road	A3-B3-C3
Victoria Street	B2
Vyne Road	B4
Wallis Road	B1
White Hart Lane	C2
Winchcombe Road	A2
Winchester Road	A1-A2-B2
Winchester Street	B2
Worting Road	A3
Wote Street	B2

BASINGSTOKE
Fanum House, headquarters of the AA, rises out of the Eastrop business area of town, which overlooks tranquil Eastrop Park.

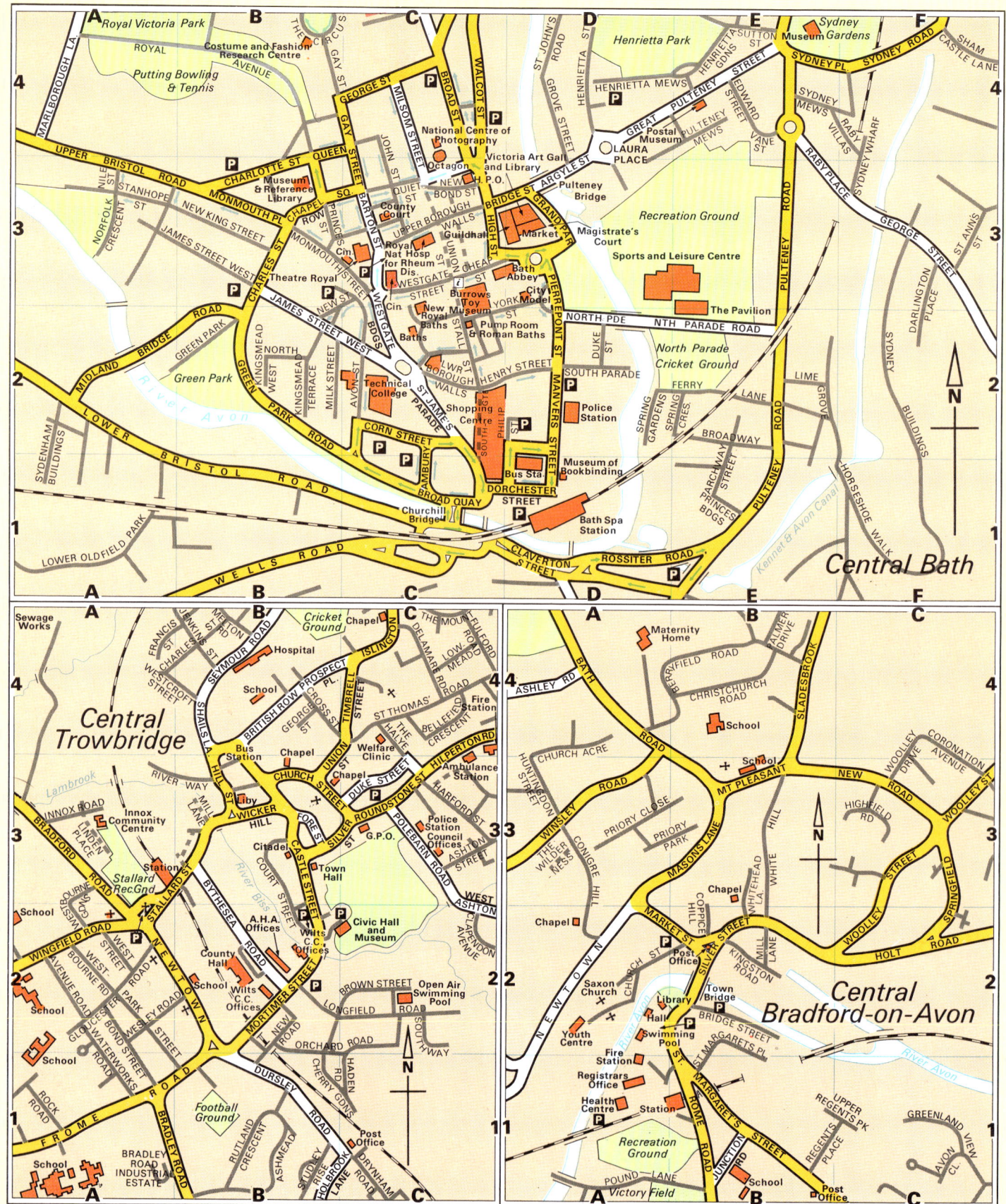

Bath

This unique city combines Britain's most impressive collection of Roman relics with the country's finest Georgian townscape. Its attraction to Romans and fashionable 18th-century society alike was its mineral springs, which are still seen by thousands of tourists who visit the Roman Baths every year. They are now the centre-piece of a Roman museum, where exhibits give a vivid impression of life 2000 years ago. The adjacent Pump Room to which the waters were piped for drinking was a focal point of social life in 18th- and 19th-century Bath.

The Georgian age of elegence also saw the building of Bath's perfectly proportioned streets, terraces and crescents. The finest examples are Queen Square, the Circus, and Royal Crescent, all built of golden local stone. Overlooking the Avon from the west is the great tower of Bath Abbey – sometimes called the "Lantern of the West"

because of its large and numerous windows.

Bath has much to delight the museum-lover. Near the abbey, in York Street, is the Burrows Toy Museum – a treasure-trove of playthings spanning two centuries. The Assembly Rooms in Bennett Street, very much a part of the social scene in Georgian Bath, are now the home of the Museum of Costume, and nearby, in Circus Mews, is the Carriage Museum, which vividly recalls coaching days.

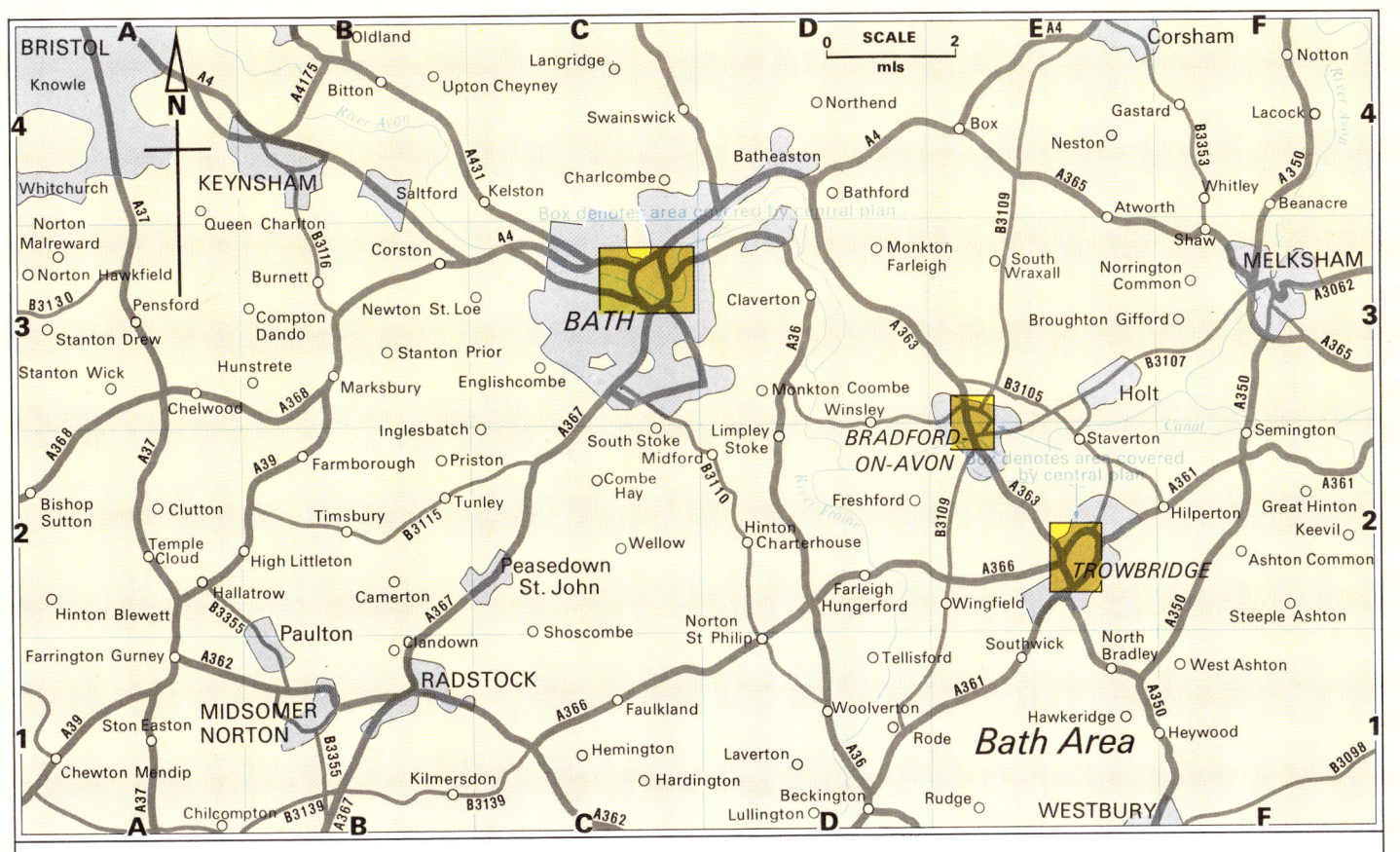

Key to Town Plan and Area Plan

Town Plan

A A Recommended roads
Other roads
Restricted roads
Buildings of interest — Library
Car Parks — P
Parks and open spaces
Churches — †
One Way Streets

Area Plan

A roads
B roads
Locations — Box ○
Urban Area

Street Index with Grid Reference

Central Bath

Ambury	C1-C2
Archway Street	E1-E2
Argyle Street	D3-D4
Avon Street	C2
Barton Street	C3
Bridge Street	C3-D3
Broadway	E2
Broad Street	C3-C4
Broad Quay	C1
Chapel Row	B3
Charles Street	B2-B3
Charlotte Street	B3-B4
Cheap Street	C3
Claverton Street	C2
Corn Street	C1-D1
Darlington Place	F2-F3
Dorchester Street	C1-D1
Duke Street	D2
Edward Street	E4
Ferry Lane	D2-E2
Gay Street	B4-C4-C3
George Street	B4-C4
George Street	F2-F3
Grand Parade	D3
Great Pulteney Street	D4-E4
Green Park	A2-B2
Green Park Road	B1-B2-C2-C1
Grove Street	D3-D4
Henrietta Gardens	E4
Henrietta Mews	D4-E4
Henrietta Street	D4
Henry Street	C2-D2
High Street	C3
Horseshoe Walk	F1
James Street West	A3-B3-B2-C2
John Street	C3-C4
Kingsmead North	B2
Kingsmead Terrace	B2
Kingsmead West	B2
Laura Place	D3-D4
Lime Grove	E2-F2-F1
Lower Bristol Road	A2-A1-B1-C1
Lower Borough Walls	C2
Lower Oldfield Park	A1
Manvers Street	D1-D2
Marlborough Lane	A4
Midland Bridge Road	A2-B2-B3
Milk Street	B2
Milsom Street	C3-C4
Monmouth Place	B3
Monmouth Street	B3-C3
New Street	B2-B3-C3
New Bond Street	C3
New King Street	A3-B3
Nile Street	A3
Norfolk Crescent	A3
North Parade	D2
North Parade Road	D2-E2
Philip Street	C1-C2
Pierrepont Street	D2-D3
Princes Buildings	E1
Princes Street	B3
Pulteney Mews	E4
Pulteney Road	E1-E2-E3-E4
Queen Square	B3-B4-C4-C3
Quiet Street	C3
Raby Place	E4-E3-E3
Raby Villas	E4-F4
Rossiter Road	D1-E1
Royal Avenue	A4-B4
St Ann's Street	F3
St Jame's Parade	C2
St John's Road	D4
Sham Castle Lane	F4
Southgate	C1-C2
South Parade	D2
Spring Crescent	E2
Spring Gardens	D2
Stall Street	C2-C3
Stanhope Street	A3
Sutton Street	E4
Sydenham Buildings	A1-A2
Sydney Buildings	F1-F2-F3
Sydney Mews	E4-F4
Sydney Place	E4-F4
Sydney Road	F4
Sydney Wharf	F3-F4
The Circus	B4
Union Street	C3
Upper Borough Walls	C3
Upper Bristol Road	A4-A3-B3
Vane Street	E4
Walcot Street	C3-C4
Wells Road	A1-B1-C1
Westgate Buildings	C2-C3
Westgate Street	C3
York Street	C2-D2-D3

Trowbridge

Ashmead	B1
Ashton Street	C3
Avenue Road	A2
Bellefield Crescent	C4
Bond Street	A1-A2
Bradford Road	A2-A3
Bradley Road	A1-B1
British Row	B4
Brown Street	B2-C2
Bythesea Road	B2-B3
Castle Street	B2-B3
Charles Street	A4-B4
Cherry Gardens	B1-C1
Church Street	B3-C3
Clapendon Avenue	C2
Court Street	B2-B3
Cross Street	B4-C4
Delamare Road	C4
Drynham Road	C1
Duke Street	C3-C4
Dursley Road	B1-C1
Fore Street	B3
Francis Street	A4-B4
Frome Road	A1-B1
Fulford Road	C4
George Street	B4
Gloucester Road	A2
Haden Road	C1
Harford Street	C3
Hill Street	B3
Hilperton Road	C3-C4
Holbrook Lane	B1-C1
Innox Road	A3
Islington	C4
Jenkins Street	A4-B4
Linden Place	A3
Longfield Road	B2-C2
Lowmead	C4
Melton Road	B4
Mill Lane	B3
Mortimer Street	B2
New Road	B1-B2
Newtown	A2-B2
Orchard Road	B1-B2-C2-C1
Park Street	A2-A1-B1
Polebarn Road	C3
Prospect Place	B4-C4
River Way	A3-B3
Rock Road	A1
Roundstone Street	C3
Rutland Crescent	B1
St Thomas' Road	C4
Seymour Road	B4
Shails Lane	B3-B4
Silver Street	B3-C3
Southway	C2
Stallard Street	A2-A3-B3
Studley Rise	B1
The Hayle	C4
The Mount	C4
Timbrell Street	C3
Union Street	B3-B4-C4-C3
Waterwoks Road	A1-A2
Wesley Road	A2-B2
West Street	A2
West Ashton	C2-C3
Westbourne Gardens	A2-A3
Westbourne Road	A2
Westcroft Street	A4-B4
Wicker Hill	B3
Wingfield Road	A2

Bradford-on-Avon

Ashley Road	A4
Avon Close	C1
Bath Road	A3-A4-B4-B3
Berryfield Road	A4-B4
Bridge Street	B2
Christchurch Road	B4
Church Acre	A4
Church Street	A2-B2
Conigre Hill	A2-A3
Coppice Hill	B2-B3
Coronation Avenue	C3-C4
Greenland View	C1
Highfield Road	C3
Holt Road	B2-C2
Huntingdon Street	A3
Kingston Road	B2
Junction Road	B1
Market Street	A2-B2
Masons Lane	A3-B3
Mill Lane	B2
Mount Pleasant	B3
Newtown	A1-A2-A3
New Road	B3-C3
Palmer Drive	B4
Pound Lane	A1-B1
Priory Close	A3-B3
Priory Park	A3-B3
Regents Place	B1-C1
Rome Road	B1
St Margaret's Place	B1-B2
St Margaret's Street	B2-B1-C1
Silver Street	B2
Sladesbrook	B3-B4
Springfield	C2-C3
The Wilderness	A3
Upper Regents Park	B1-C1
White Hill	B2-B3
Whitehead Lane	B2-B3
Winsley Road	A3-A4
Woolley Drive	C3-C4
Woolley Street	C2-C3

11

Central Dartford

Bexley/Dartford Area

SCALE 0 — 3

Bexley/Dartford

The rural sights and sounds of Stone Lodge Farm Park and Farm Museum — just east of town off the A226 — make an unexpected contrast with the old River Darent market town of Dartford. Its main concerns for many years have been engineering and papermaking, and Dartford enjoys some excellent modern facilities such as the Arndale Centre and the Orchard theatre complex. A number of old buildings

survive in the centre, the oldest being the Norman-towered parish church of Holy Trinity. There is also a local museum.

Bexleyheath was once known simply as Bexley New Town. This is the administrative centre for the Borough of Bexley. Modern development has brought the Broadway Shopping Centre and the swimming pool and solarium of the Crook Log Sports Centre. Out of doors, Danson Park, scene of the July Danson Show, was first designed by Capability Brown.

Gravesend Making a vital link with Essex through the Tilbury ferry service, Gravesend's prime position on the Thames Estuary has always been a major factor in its growth, and the recent restoration of the 1842 Royal Terrace Pier celebrates a long maritime tradition. Much of the town was destroyed by fire in the 18th century, but several older buildings still survive in the Promenade area, including 14th-century Milton Chantry, a former chapel.

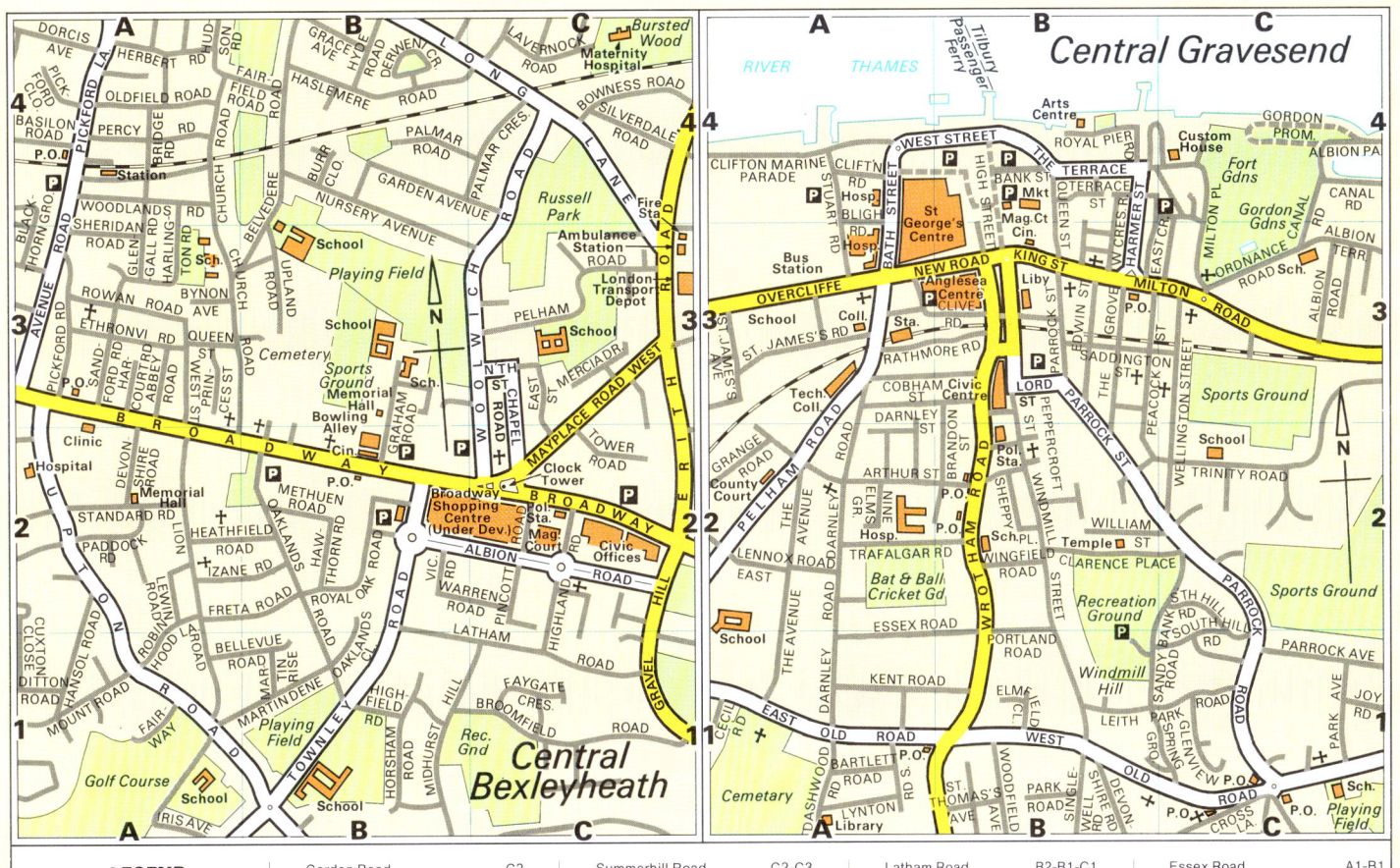

LEGEND

Town Plan

- AA recommended route
- Restricted roads
- Other roads
- Buildings of interest
- Car parks
- Parks and open spaces

Area Plan

- A roads — A210
- B roads — B258
- Locations — Bean○
- Urban area

Street Index with Grid Reference

Dartford

Anne of Cleaves Road	C3-C4
Ash Road	C1
Attlee Drive	F4
Bath Road	A2-A3
Bayly Road	F3
Beech Road	C1
Bedford Road	F2
Berkeley Crescent	E1
Blenheim Road	B3
Bow Arrow Lane	F3
Brent Lane	E2-E1-F1
Broomhill Road	A3
Burnham Road	C4
Carlisle Road	F3
Carrington Road	E3-F3
Cedar Road	C1
Central Road	D4-D3
Christchurch Road	B3
Colney Road	E3-F3
Coniston Close	A1
Cranford Road	D1
Cross Road	A3-B3
Darenth Road	D2-E2-E1
Dartford Road	A4-A3-B3
Dene Road	E2
Derwent Close	A1
Devonshire Avenue	A3
Dorchester Close	E1
Downs Avenue	F1-F2
East Hill	E2-F2
Elm Road	C1
Essex Road	C3
Firmin Road	B4
Francis Road	C4
Fulwich Road	D3-E3-F3
Gainsboro Avenue	B4
Gloucester Road	A2
Gordon Road	C2
Great Queen Street	E2-E3
Green Street	F1
Hallford Way	B4-C4
Havelock Road	A2-A3
Heathclose Avenue	A1-A2
Heathclose Road	A1
Heathlands Road	A1
Heath Lane (Lower)	B1-B2-C1-C2
Heath Lane (Upper)	A1
Heath Street	C2
Heathview Crescent	A1
Highfield Road	C2-C3
Highfield Road South	C1-C2
High Street	C3-D3
Home Gardens	D3
Howard Road	F2-F3
Hythe Street	D3-D4
Ingram Road	D1
Instone Road	C2-D2
Kent Road	C3
King Edward Avenue	C3-C4
Kingsley Avenue	F4
Laburnum Avenue	B1-C1
Lansbury Crescent	F4
Larch Road	C1
Lavina Road	E3
Lawrence Hill Road	D4
Littlebrook Manor Way	E4-F4
Little Queen Street	E2
Linden Avenue	B1
Lower Hythe Street	D4
Lowfield Street	C1-C2-D2
Manor Place	C1
Maple Road	B1-C1
Marcet Road	B4
Market Street	D2
Mead Road	C1
Mill Pond Road	D3-D4
Miskin Road	B2-C2
Moreland Avenue	A4
Morris Gardens	F4
Mount Pleasant Road	D3
Olive Road	C1
Orchard Street	C3-D3
Overy Liberty	D3-D2
Overy Street	D3
Park Road	F1-F2
Penney Close	B2-C2
Phoenix Place	C1-C2
Pilgrims Way	F1-F2
Princes Road	A2-A1-B1-C1-D1-E1-F1
Princes Road North	A2
Princes View	E1-F1
Priory Close	B4-C4
Priory Hill	C3-C4
Priory Road	C3-C4
Raeburn Avenue	A4
Riverside Way	D4
Roseberry Gardens	B2
Rowan Crescent	B1
St Albans Road	E2-E3
St Martins Road	E3
St Vincent's Avenue	E4-F4-F3
St Vincent's Road	F3-F2
Savoy Road	B4-C4
Shenley Road	F2-F3
Shepherds Lane	A2-B2-B3
Somerset Road	A2-A3
Spital Street	C3
Stanham Road	A4-B4-B3

Summerhill Road	C2-C3
Sussex Road	E2-F2
Swaisland Road	A4
Sycamore Road	B1-C1
The Brent	F2
Temple Hill	D3-E3-E4
Temple Hill Square	E4
Tower Road	B3
Tunnel Approach Road	F3-F4
Vale Road	A1
Victoria Road	C4-D4
Waid Close	E3
Wakeley Road	A4
Waldeck Road	E2
Watling Street	F2
Westgate Road	C3-D3
West Hill	B3-C3
West Hill Drive	B3-B4
West View	E3
Willow Road	B1-C1
Wilmot Road	A4-B4
Wyvern Close	B2
York Road	E2

Bexleyheath

Abbey Road	A3
Albion Road	B2-C2
Avenue Road	A3-A4
Basilon Road	A4
Bellevue Road	A1-B1
Belvedere Road	A3-B3-B4
Blackthorne Grove	A3-A4
Bowness Road	C4
Bridge Road	A4
Broadway	A3-A2-B2-C2
Broomfield Road	B1-C1
Burr Close	B4
Bynon Avenue	A3
Chapel Road	C2-C3
Church Road	A4-A3-B3
Cuxton Close	A1-A2
Derwent Crescent	B4
Devonshire Road	A2
Ditton Road	A1
Dorcis Avenue	A4
East Street	C2-C3
Erith Road	C2-C3-C4
Ethronvi Road	A1
Fairfield Road	A4-B4
Fairway	A1
Faygate Crescent	C1
Freta Road	A2-B2
Garden Avenue	B4-C4
Glengall Road	A3-A4
Grace Avenue	B4
Graham Road	B2-B3
Gravel Hill	C1-C2
Hansol Road	A1-A2
Harcourt Road	A3
Harlington Road	A3-A4
Haslemere Road	B4
Hawthorn Road	B2
Heathfield Road	A2-B2
Herbert Road	A4
Highfield Road	B1
Highland Road	C1-C2
Horsham Road	B1
Hudson Road	A4
Hyde Road	B4
Iris Avenue	A1
Izane Road	A2-B2

Latham Road	B2-B1-C1
Lavernock Road	C4
Lewin Road	A2
Lion Road	A2-A1
Long Lane	B4-C4-C3
Martin Dene	A1-B1
Martin Rise	B1
Mayplace Road West	C2-C3
Mercia Drive	C3
Methuen Road	B2
Midhurst Hill	B1-C1
Mount Road	A1
North Street	C3
Nursery Avenue	B4-B3-C3
Oaklands Close	B1-B2
Oaklands Road	B1-B2
Oldfield Road	A4
Paddock Road	A2
Palmar Crescent	C4
Palmar Road	B4-C4
Pelham Road	C3
Percy Road	A4
Pickford Close	A4
Pickford Lane	A4
Pickford Road	A4
Pincott Road	C2
Princes Street	A3
Queen Street	A3
Robin Hood Lane	A1-A2
Rowan Road	A3
Royal Oak Road	B2
Sandford Road	A3
Sheridan Road	A3
Silverdale Road	C4
Standard Road	A2
Tower Road	C2
Townley Road	B1-B2
Upland Road	B3
Upton	A3-A2-A1-B1
Victoria Road	B2
Warren Road	B2-C2
West Street	A3
Woodlands Road	A3
Woolwich Road	C2-C3-C4

Gravesend

Albion Parade	C4
Albion Road	C3
Albion Terrace	C3
Arthur Street	A2-B2
Bank Street	B4
Bartlett Road	A1
Bath Street	A3-A4
Bligh Road	A4-A3
Brandon Street	B2-B3
Canal Road	C3-C4
Cecil Road	A1
Clarence Place	B2-C2
Clifton Marine Parade	A4
Clifton Road	A4
Clive Road	A3-B3
Cobham Street	A3-B3
Cross Lane	C1
Darnley Road	A1-A2-A3
Darnley Street	A3-B3
Dashwood Road	A1
Devonshire Road	B1
East Crescent	B3-B4-C4
East Old Road	A1-B1
Edwin Street	B3
Elmfield Close	B1

Essex Road	A1-B1
Glenview	C1
Gordon Promenade	C4
Grange Road	A2
Harmer Street	B3-B4
High Street	B4-B3
Joy Road	C1
Kent Road	A1-B1
King Street	B3
Leith Park Road	B1-C1
Lennox Road East	A2
Lord Street	B3
Lynton Road South	A1
Milton Place	C3-C4
Milton Road	B3-C3
New Road	A3-B3
Nine Elms Grove	A2
Ordnance Road	C3
Overcliffe	A3
Park Avenue	C1
Park Road	B1
Parrock Avenue	C1
Parrock Road	C1-C2
Parrock Street	B2-B3
Peacock Street	B2-B3
Pelham Road	A2-A3
Peppercroft Street	B3-B2
Portland Road	B1-B2
Queen Street	B4-B3
Rathmore Road	A3-B3
Royal Pier Road	B4
St James's Avenue	A3
St James's Road	A3
St Thomas's Avenue	B1
Saddington Street	B3-C3
Sandy Bank Road	B1-B2-C2
Sheppy Place	B2
Singlewell Road	B1
South Hill Road	C1-C2
Spring Grove	B1-C1
Stuart Road	A4-A3
The Avenue	A1-A2
The Grove	B2-B3
The Terrace	B4
Terrace Street	B4
Trafalgar Road	A2-B2
Trinity Road	C2
Wellington Street	C2-C3
West Crescent Road	B3-B4
West Old Road	B1-C1
West Street	A4-B4
William Street	B2-C2
Windmill Street	B2-B1
Wingfield Road	B2
Woodfield Avenue	B1
Wrotham Road	A1-B1-B2-B3

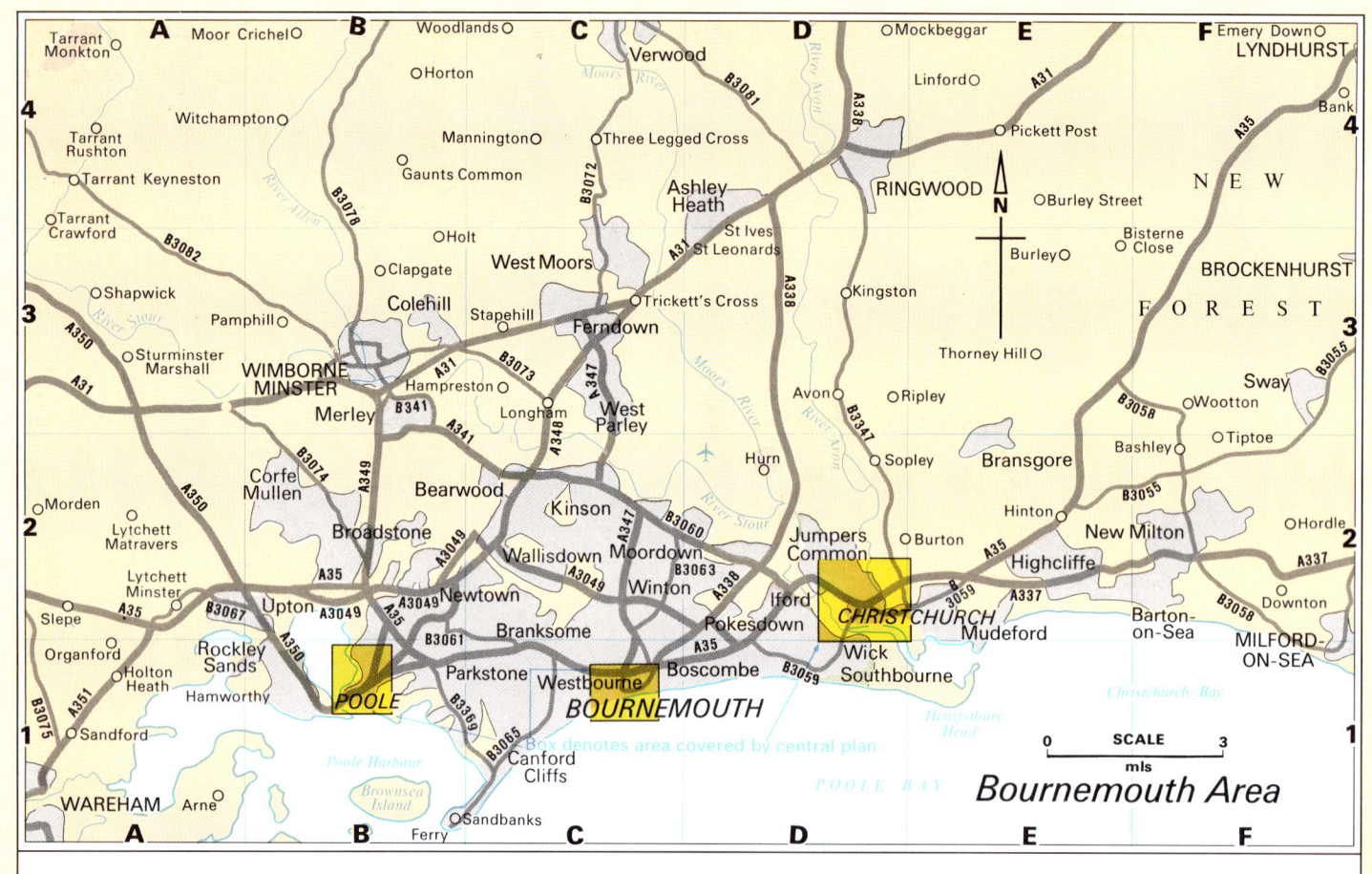

Bournemouth Area

Box denotes area covered by central plan

SCALE 0 — 3 mls

Street Index with Grid Reference

Bournemouth

Albert Road	C3-D3
Avenue Road	B3-C3
Bath Road	D2-E2-E3-E4-F4
Beacon Road	C1
Bodorgan Road	C4
Bourne Avenue	B3-C3
Braidley Road	B3-B4
Branksome Wood Road	A4
Cambridge Road	A2-A3
Central Drive	B4
Chine Crescent	A1-A2
Chine Crescent Road	A1-A2
Christchurch Road	F4
Cotlands Road	F4
Cranbourne Road	B2-C2
Crescent Road	A3-B3
Dean Park Crescent	C4-D4
Dean Park Road	C4
Durley Chine Road	A1-A2
Durley Gardens	A1-A2
Durley Road	A1-A2-B1
East Overcliff Drive	E2-F2-F3
Exeter Crescent	C2
Exeter Lane	C2-D2
Exeter Park Road	C2-D2
Exeter Road	C2-D2
Fir Vale Road	D3-D4
Gervis Place	C3-D3
Gervis Road	E3-F3
Glenfern Road	D3-E3-E4
Grove Road	E3-F3
Hahnemann Road	A1-B1-B2
Hinton Road	D2-D3-E2
Holdenhurst Road	F4
Lansdowne Road	E4-F4
Lorne Park Road	E4
Madeira Road	D4-E4
Marlborough Road	A2
Meyrick Road	F3-F4
Norwich Avenue	A2-A3-B3
Norwich Avenue West	A3
Old Christchurch Road	D3-D4-E4-F4
Parsonage Road	D3-E3
Poole Hill	A2-B2
Poole Road	A2
Priory Road	C1-C2

Richmond Hill	C3-C4
Russell Cotes Road	E2
St Michael's Road	B2-B1-C1
St Peter's Road	D3-E3
St Stephen's Road	B3-B4-C4-C3
Stafford Road	E4
Suffolk Road	A3-B3
Surrey Road	A3
Terrace Road	B2-C2
The Triangle	B2-B3
Tregonwell Road	B2-C2-C1
Undercliffe Drive	D1-D2-E1-E2-F2
Upper Hinton Road	D2-D3-E2
Upper Norwich Road	A2-B2
Upper Terrace Road	B2-C2
Wessex Way	A3-A4-B4-C4-D4-E4
West Cliff Gardens	B1
West Cliff Promenade	B1-C1-D1-C1
West Cliff Road	A1-B1
Westhill Road	A2-B2-B1-C1
Westover Road	D2-D3
West Promenade	C1-D1
Wimborne Road	C4
Wootton Gardens	E3-E4
Yelverton Road	C3-D3

Christchurch

Albion Road	A4
Arcadia Road	A4
Arthur Road	B3
Avenue Road	A3-B3-B4
Avon Road West	A3-A4-B4
Bargates	B2-B3
Barrack Road	A4-A3-B2-B3
Beaconsfield Road	B2-C3
Bridge Street	C2
Bronte Avenue	B4
Canberra Road	A4
Castle Street	B2-C2
Christchurch By-Pass	B2-C2-C3
Clarendon Road	A3-B3
Douglas Avenue	A2-B2
Endfield Road	A4
Fairfield	B3
Fairmile Road	A4-B4-B3
Flambard Avenue	B4
Gardner Road	A3-A4
Gleadowe Avenue	A2-B2
Grove Road East	A3-B3

Grove Road West	A3
High Street	B2
Iford Lane	A1
Jumpers Avenue	A4
Jumpers Road	A3-A4-B4
Kings Avenue	A2-B2
Manor Road	B2
Millhams Street	B2-C2
Mill Road	B3-B4
Portfield Road	A3-B3
Queens Avenue	B1
Quay Road	B1
St John's Road	A2
St Margarets Avenue	B1
Sopers Lane	B1-B2
South View Road	A1-B1
Stony Lane	C4-C3-C2
Stour Road	B3-B2-A1-A2
The Grove	A4
Tuckton Road	A1
Twynham Avenue	B2-B3
Walcott Avenue	A4-B4
Waterloo Place	C2
Wickfield Avenue	B1-B2
Wick Lane	A1-B1-B2
Willow Drive	A1-B1
Willow Way	A1-B1
Windsor Road	A3

Poole

Ballard Road	B1-C1
Church Street	A1
Dear Hay Lane	A2-B2
Denmark Road	C3
East Quay Road	B1
East Street	B1
Elizabeth Road	C3
Emerson Road	B1-B2
Esplanade	B3
Garland Road	C4
Green Road	B2-B1-C1
Heckford Road	C3-C4
High Street	A1-B1-B2
Hill Street	B2
Johns Road	C3-C4
Jolliffe Road	C4
Kingland Road	B2-C2
Kingston Road	C3-C4
Lagland Street	B1-B2

Longfleet Road	C3
Maple Road	C3-C4
Mount Pleasant Road	C2-C3
Newfoundland Drive	C1
New Orchard	A1-A2
North Street	B2
Old Orchard	B1
Parkstone Road	C3-C2
Perry Gardens	B1
Poole Bridge	A1
St Mary's Road	C3
Seldown Lane	C2-C3
Shaftesbury Road	C3
Skinner Street	B1
South Road	B2
Stanley Road	B1
Sterte Avenue	A4-B4
Sterte Road	B2-B3-B4
Stokes Avenue	B4-C4
Strand Street	A1-B1
Tatnam Road	B4-C4
The Quay	A1-B1
Towngate Bridge	B2-B3
West Quay Road	A1-A2-B2
West Street	A1-A2-B2
Wimborne Road	B3-C3-C4

LEGEND

Town Plan
AA Recommended route	▬▬
Other roads	▬▬
Restricted roads	----
Buildings of interest	◼ Town Hall
AA Centre	AA
Car Parks	P
Parks and open spaces	◢
One way streets	→

Area Plan
A roads	▬▬
B roads	▬▬
Locations	Mudeford O
Urban area	

Bournemouth

Until the beginning of the 19th century the landscape on which Bournemouth stands was open heath. Its rise began when a scattering of holiday villas were built by innovative trend-setters at a time when the idea of seaside holidays was very new. Soon a complete village had taken shape. In the next 50 years Bournemouth had become a major resort and its population catapulted to nearly 59,000.

Today's holidaymakers can enjoy Bournemouth's natural advantages – miles of sandy beaches, a mild climate and beautiful setting, along with a tremendous variety of amenities. These include some of the best shopping in the south – with shops ranging from huge departmental stores to tiny specialist places. Entertainments range from variety shows and feature films to opera, and the music of the world-famous Bournemouth Symphony Orchestra.

Poole has virtually been engulfed by the suburbs of Bournemouth, but its enormous natural harbour is still an attraction in its own right. At Poole Quay, some 15th-century cellars have been converted into a Maritime Museum, where the town's association with the sea from prehistoric times until the early 20th century is illustrated, and the famous Poole Pottery nearby offers guided tours of its workshops.

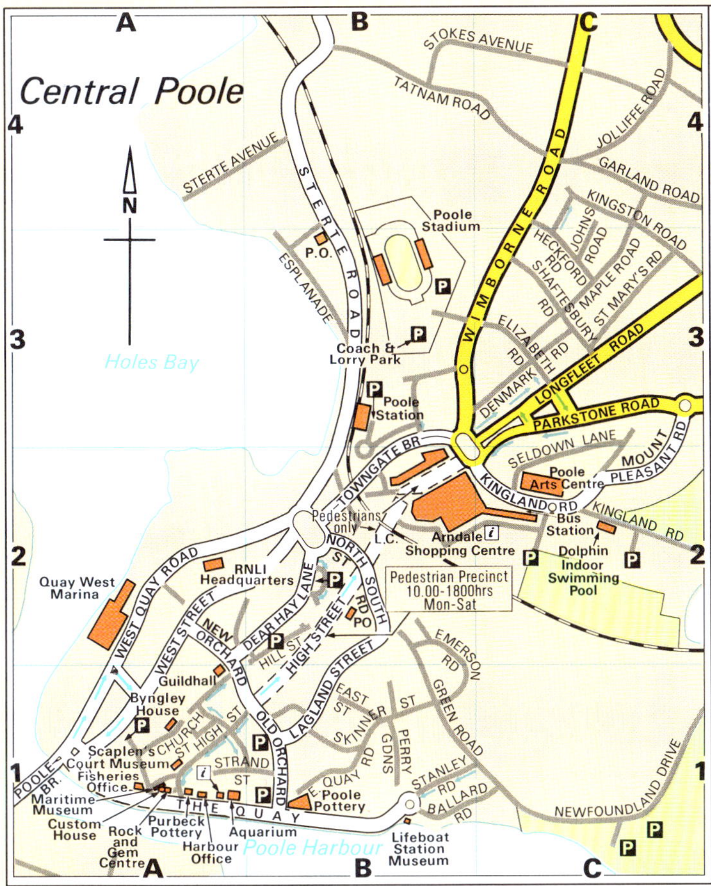

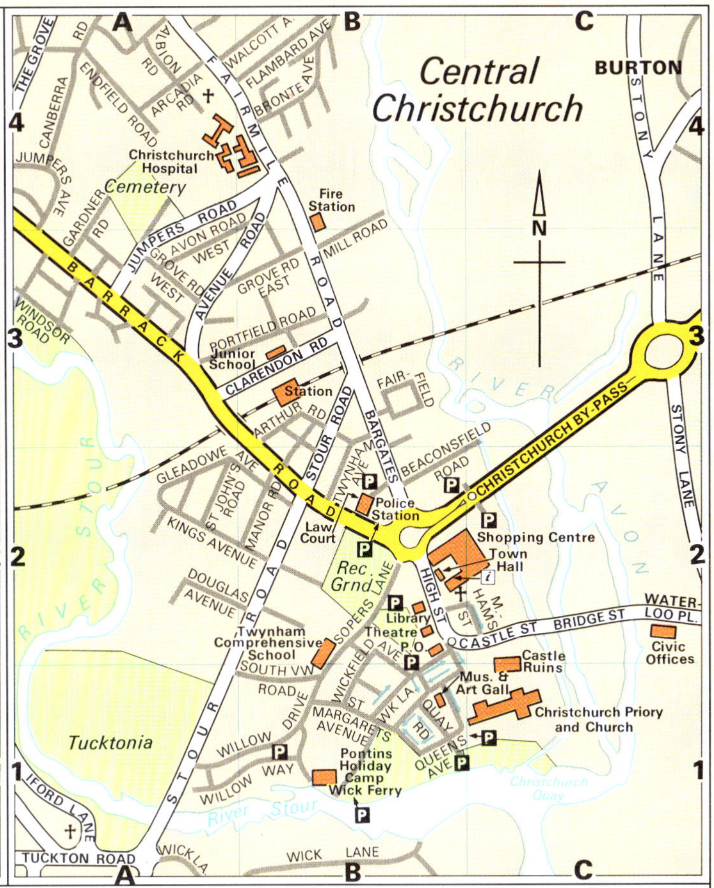

Central Poole

4

N

3

Holes Bay

2

Quay West Marina
West Quay Road
West Street
RNLI Headquarters
NEW ORCHARD
DEAR HAY LANE
HILL ST
Guildhall
Byngley House
Scaplen's Court Museum
Maritime Museum
Custom House
Rock and Gem Centre
Purbeck Pottery
Harbour Office
STRAND ST
POOLE BR
Fisheries Office
Poole Harbour
OLD ORCHARD
ST HIGH ST
LAGLAND STREET
EAST ST
SKINNER ST
PERRY GDNS
GREEN ROAD
EMERSON RD
STANLEY RD
BALLARD
THE QUAY
Aquarium
Poole Pottery
Lifeboat Station Museum
Newfoundland Drive

1

A B C

STOKES AVENUE
TATNAM ROAD
JOLLIFFE ROAD
GARLAND ROAD
STERTE AVENUE
STERTE ROAD
ESPLANADE
P.O.
Poole Stadium
P
Coach & Lorry Park
Poole Station
TOWNGATE BR
KINGLAND RD
NORTH RD
SOUTH RD
Pedestrians only
L.C.
Arndale Shopping Centre
Pedestrian Precinct 10.00-1800hrs Mon-Sat
WIMBORNE ROAD
HECKFORD RD
JOHNS RD
MAPLE RD
SHAFTESBURY RD
ST MARYS RD
ELIZABETH RD
DENMARK RD
KINGSTON ROAD
LONGFLEET ROAD
PARKSTONE ROAD
SELDOWN LANE
MOUNT PLEASANT RD
KINGLAND RD
Poole Arts Centre
Bus Station
Dolphin Indoor Swimming Pool
P

Central Christchurch

BURTON

4

THE GROVE
CANBERRA
FAIRMILE RD
WALCOTT A
ALBION RD
ARCADIA A
FLAMBARD AVE
BRONTE AVE
ENDFIELD ROAD
JUMPERS AVE
Christchurch Hospital
Cemetery
JUMPERS ROAD
AVON ROAD WEST
GARDNER RD
GROVE RD WEST
MILL ROAD
Fire Station
STONY LANE
RIVER
AVON

3

BARRACK ROAD
ARTHUR RD
WINDSOR ROAD
Junior School
Station
PORTFIELD ROAD
CLARENDON RD
STOUR ROAD
TWYNHAM AVE
GROVE RD EAST
FAIR-FIELD
BEACONSFIELD ROAD
CHRISTCHURCH BY-PASS
P

2

GLEADOWE AVE
MANOR ROAD
KINGS AVENUE
SOPERS LANE
Law Court
Police Station
HIGH ST
BARGATES
Shopping Centre
Town Hall
WATER-LOO PL
Library
P.O.
Twynham Theatre
Twynham Comprehensive School
SOUTH VW
Rec. Grnd
CASTLE ST
BRIDGE ST
Civic Offices
DOUGLAS AVENUE
WICKFIELD AVE
MARGARETS AVENUE
Mus. & Art Gall
Castle Ruins
QUAY RD
WK LA
Christchurch Priory and Church
P

1

IFORD LANE
Tucktonia
WILLOW WAY
WILLOW WAY
Pontins Holiday Camp
Wick Ferry
QUEENS AVE
Christchurch Quay
P
River Stour
TUCKTON ROAD
WICKLA
WICK LANE

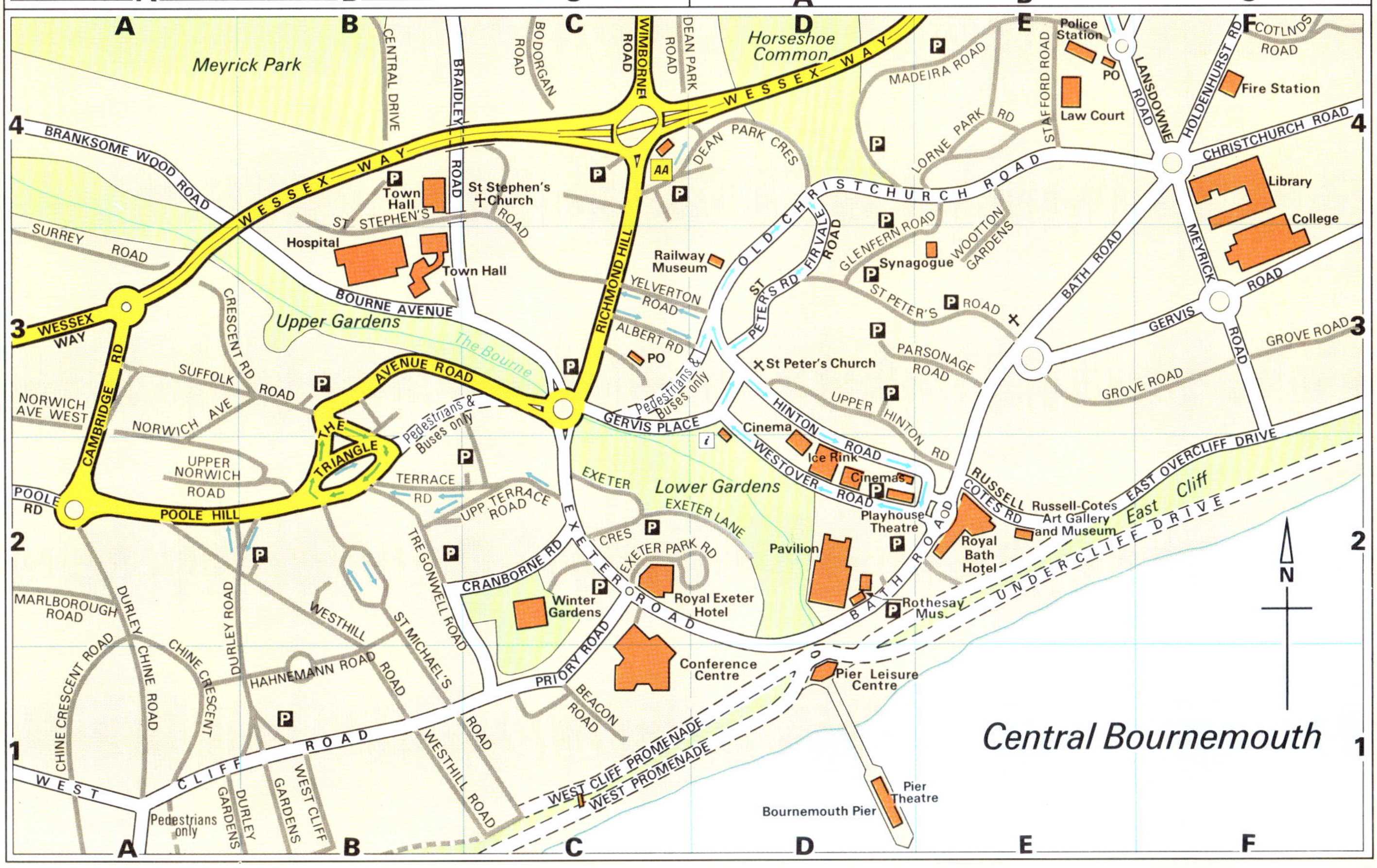

A B C

Central Bournemouth

4

Meyrick Park
CENTRAL DRIVE
BODORGAN ROAD
BRAIDLEY ROAD
DEAN PARK ROAD
WIMBORNE ROAD
DEAN PARK
Horseshoe Common
WESSEX WAY
MADEIRA ROAD
STAFFORD ROAD
Police Station
PO
COTLNDS ROAD
Fire Station
BRANKSOME WOOD ROAD
WESSEX WAY
Town Hall
St Stephen's Church
ST STEPHEN'S ROAD
AA
DEAN PARK CRES
LORNE PARK RD
Law Court
LANSDOWNE
HOLDENHURST RD
CHRISTCHURCH ROAD
Library
College
SURREY ROAD
Hospital
Town Hall
BOURNE AVENUE
Upper Gardens
The Bourne
Railway Museum
YELVERTON ROAD
RICHMOND HILL
OLD CHRISTCHURCH ROAD
GLENFERN ROAD
Synagogue
WOOTTON GARDENS
ST PETER'S RD
BATH ROAD
MEYRICK ROAD

3

WESSEX WAY
CAMBRIDGE RD
CRESCENT RD
NORWICH AVE
SUFFOLK RD
ALBERT RD
PO
St Peter's Church
PARSONAGE ROAD
UPPER HINTON RD
GROVE ROAD
GROVE ROAD
GERVIS ROAD

2

POOLE RD
NORWICH AVE WEST
UPPER NORWICH ROAD
POOLE HILL
THE TRIANGLE
AVENUE ROAD
Pedestrians & Buses only
TERRACE RD
UPP TERRACE RD
EXETER RD
GERVIS PLACE
Pedestrians & Buses only
Lower Gardens
HINTON ROAD
WESTOVER RD
Cinema
Ice Rink
Cinemas
Playhouse Theatre
Pavilion
Russell-Cotes Art Gallery and Museum
RUSSELL COTES RD
East Cliff
EAST OVERCLIFF DRIVE
UNDERCLIFF DRIVE
N

1

MARLBOROUGH ROAD
DURLEY ROAD
CHINE CRESCENT ROAD
CHINE CRESCENT ROAD
WESTHILL
ST MICHAEL'S ROAD
HAHNEMANN ROAD
CRANBORNE RD
EXETER PARK RD
EXETER LANE
EXETER CRES
PRIORY ROAD
BEACON ROAD
Winter Gardens
Royal Exeter Hotel
Conference Centre
Royal Bath Hotel
Rothesay Mus.
Pier Leisure Centre
WEST PROMENADE
WEST CLIFF PROMENADE
Pier Theatre
Bournemouth Pier
WEST CLIFF ROAD
WESTHILL ROAD
WEST CLIFF GARDENS
DURLEY CHINE ROAD
Pedestrians only
WEST

A B C D E F

BOURNEMOUTH
The pier, safe sea-bathing, golden sands facing south and sheltered by steep cliffs, and plenty of amenities for the holiday maker make Bournemouth one of the most popular resorts on the south coast of England.

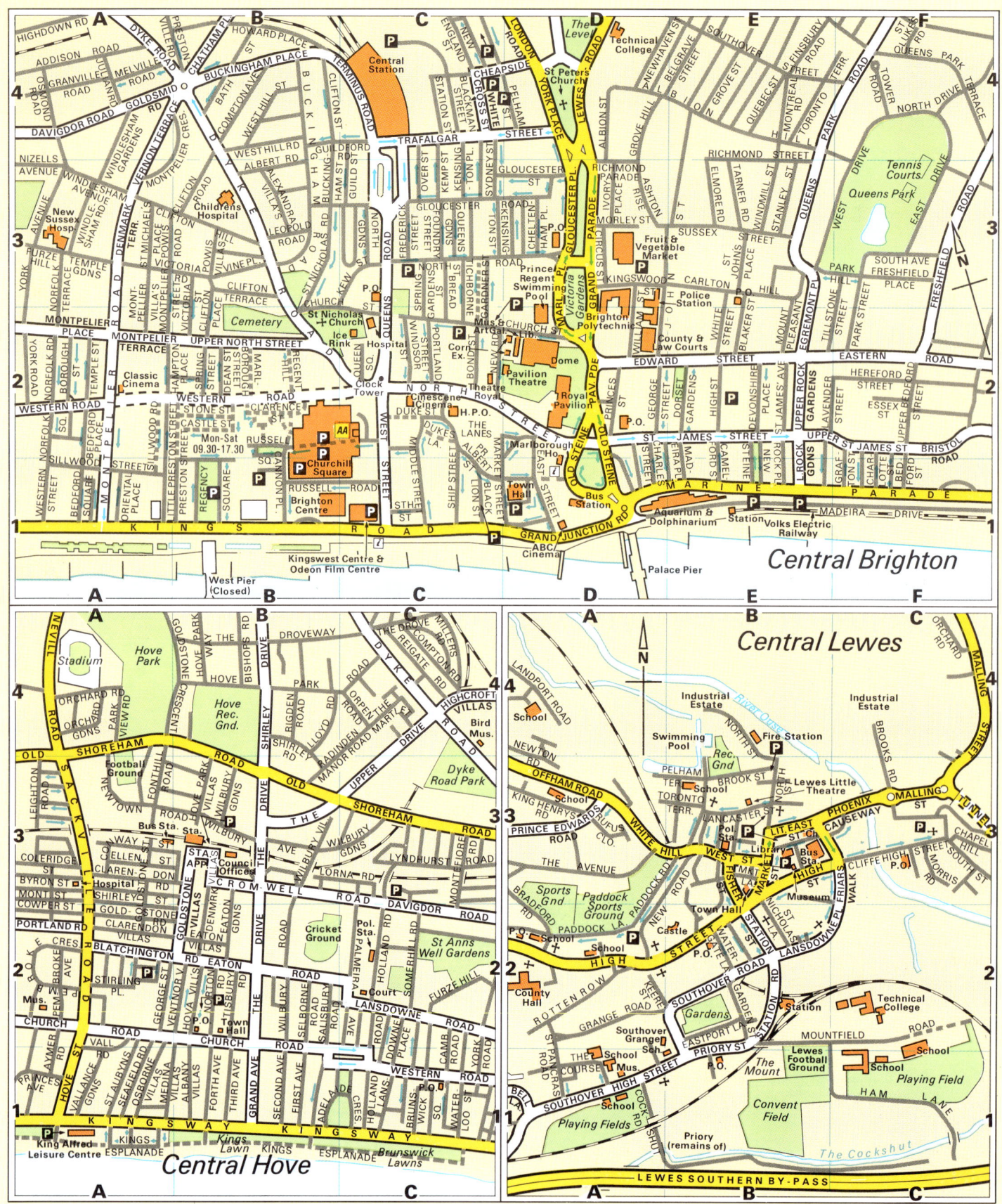

Central Brighton

Central Lewes

Central Hove

Brighton

Dr Richard Russell, from nearby Lewes, created the resort of Brighton almost singlehandedly. And he did it not by building houses or hotels, but by writing a book. His book, which praised the health-giving properties of sea-bathing and sea air, soon came to the attention of George, then Prince Regent and one day to become King George IV. He stayed at Brighthelmstone – as it was then known –

in 1783 and again in 1784. In 1786 the Prince rented a villa on the Steine – a modest house that was eventually transformed into the astonishing Pavilion. By 1800 – its popularity assured by royal patronage – the resort was described in a contemporary directory as 'the most frequented and without exception one of the most fashionable towns in the kingdom'.

Perhaps the description does not quite fit today, but Brighton is a perennially popular seaside

resort, as well as a shopping centre, university town and cultural venue. The Pavilion still draws most crowds, of course. Its beginnings as a villa are entirely hidden in a riot of Near Eastern architectural motifs, largely the creation of John Nash. Brighton's great days as a Regency resort *par excellence* are preserved in the sweeping crescents and elegant terraces, buildings which help to make it one of the finest townscapes in the whole of Europe.

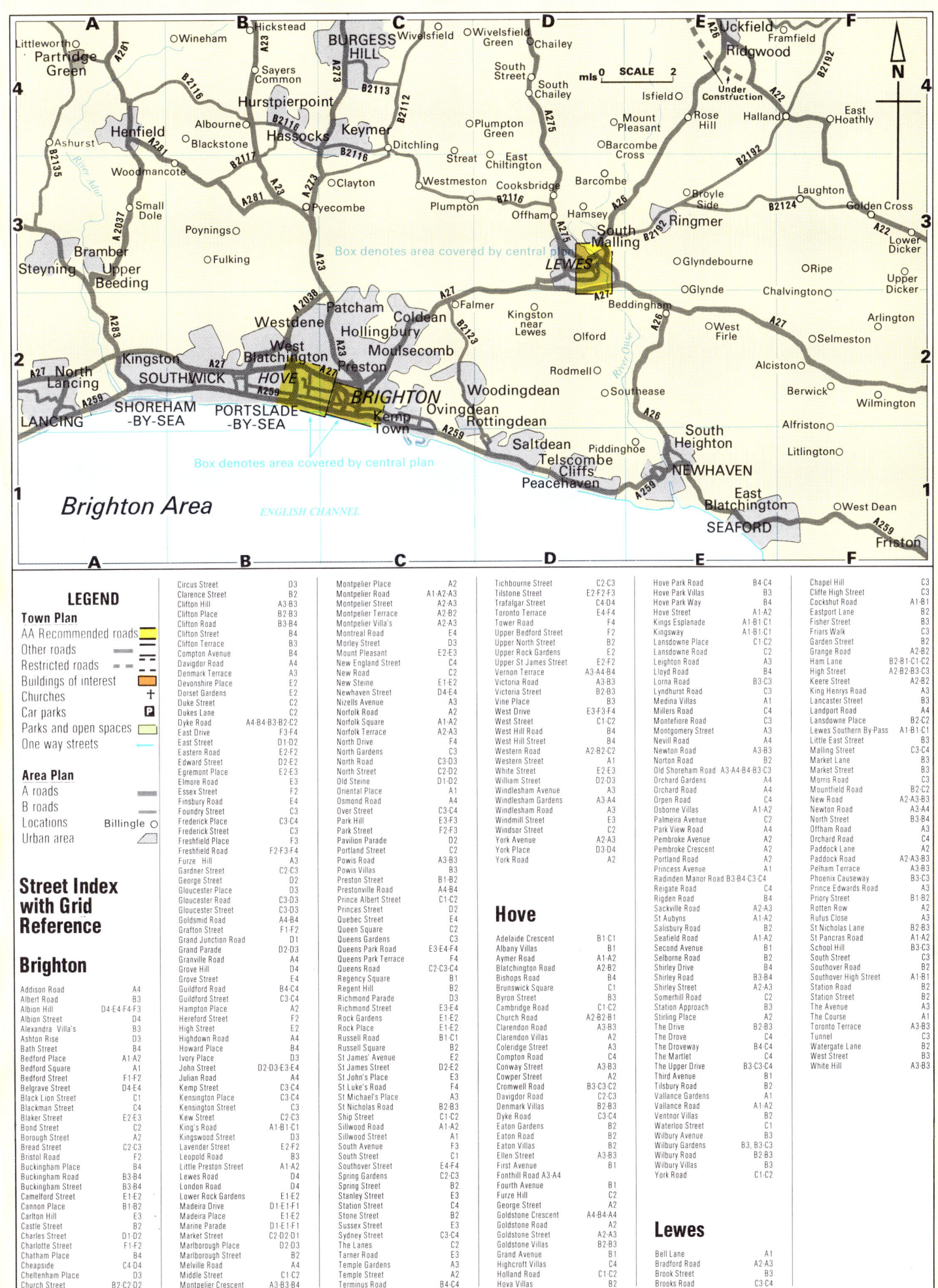

LEGEND

Town Plan

AA Recommended roads	
Other roads	
Restricted roads	
Buildings of interest	
Churches	†
Car parks	P
Parks and open spaces	
One way streets	

Area Plan

A roads	
B roads	
Locations	Billingle ○
Urban area	

Street Index with Grid Reference

Brighton

Addison Road	A4
Albert Road	B3
Albion Hill	D4-E4-F4-F3
Albion Street	D4
Alexandra Villa's	B3
Ashton Rise	D3
Bath Street	B4
Bedford Place	A1-A2
Bedford Square	A1
Bedford Street	F1-F2
Belgrave Street	D4-E4
Black Lion Street	C1
Blackman Street	C4
Blaker Street	E2-E3
Bond Street	C2
Borough Street	A2
Bread Street	C2-C3
Bristol Road	F2
Buckingham Place	B4
Buckingham Road	B3-B4
Buckingham Street	B3-B4
Camelford Street	E1-E2
Cannon Place	B1-B2
Carlton Hill	E3
Castle Street	B2
Charles Street	D1-D2
Charlotte Street	F1-F2
Chatham Place	B4
Cheapside	C4-D4
Cheltenham Place	D3
Church Street	B2-C2-D2

Circus Street	D3
Clarence Street	B2
Clifton Hill	A3-B3
Clifton Place	B2-B3
Clifton Road	B3-B4
Clifton Street	B4
Clifton Terrace	B3
Compton Avenue	B4
Davigdor Road	A4
Denmark Terrace	A3
Devonshire Place	E2
Dorset Gardens	E2
Duke Street	C2
Dukes Lane	C2
Dyke Road	A4-B4-B3-B2-C2
East Drive	F3-F4
East Street	D1-D2
Eastern Road	E2-F2
Edward Street	D2-E2
Egremont Place	E2-E3
Elmore Road	E3
Essex Street	F2
Finsbury Road	E4
Foundry Street	C3
Frederick Place	C3-C4
Frederick Street	C3
Freshfield Place	F3
Freshfield Road	F2-F3-F4
Furze Hill	A3
Gardner Street	C2-C3
George Street	D2
Gloucester Place	D3
Gloucester Road	C3-D3
Gloucester Street	C3-D3
Goldsmid Road	A4-B4
Grafton Street	F1-F2
Grand Junction Road	D1
Grand Parade	D2-D3
Granville Road	A4
Grove Hill	D4
Grove Street	E4
Guildford Road	B4-C4
Guildford Street	C3-C4
Hampton Place	A2
Hereford Street	F2
High Street	E2
Highdown Road	A4
Howard Place	B4
Ivory Place	D3
John Street	D2-D3-E3-E4
Julian Road	A4
Kemp Street	C3-C4
Kensington Place	C3-C4
Kensington Street	C3
Kew Street	C3
King's Road	A1-B1-C1
Kingswood Street	D3
Lavender Street	E2-F2
Leopold Road	B3
Little Preston Street	A1-A2
Lewes Road	D4
London Road	D4
Lower Rock Gardens	E1-E2
Madeira Drive	D1-E1-F1
Madeira Place	E1-E2
Marine Parade	D1-E1-F1
Market Street	C2-D2-D1
Marlborough Place	D2-D3
Marlborough Street	B2
Melville Road	A4
Middle Street	C1-C2
Montpelier Crescent	A3-B3-B4

Montpelier Place	A2
Montpelier Road	A1-A2-A3
Montpelier Street	A2-A3
Montpelier Terrace	A2-B2
Montpelier Villa's	A2-A3
Montreal Road	E4
Morley Street	D3
Mount Pleasant	E2-E3
New England Street	C4
New Road	C2
New Steine	E1-E2
Newhaven Street	D4-E4
Nizells Avenue	A3
Norfolk Road	A2
Norfolk Square	A1-A2
Norfolk Terrace	A2-A3
North Gardens	C3
North Road	C3-D3
North Street	C2-D2
Old Steine	D1-D2
Oriental Place	A1
Osmond Road	A4
Over Street	C3-C4
Park Hill	E3-F3
Park Street	F2-F3
Pavilion Parade	D2
Portland Street	C2
Powis Road	A3-B3
Powis Villas	B3
Preston Street	B1-B2
Prestonville Road	A4-B4
Prince Albert Street	C1-C2
Princes Street	D2
Quebec Street	E4
Queen Square	C2
Queens Gardens	C3
Queens Park Road	E3-E4
Queens Park Terrace	E4
Queens Road	C2-C3-C4
Regency Square	B1
Regent Hill	B2
Richmond Parade	D3
Richmond Street	E3-E4
Rock Gardens	E1-E2
Rock Place	E1-E2
Russell Road	B1-C1
Russell Square	B2
St James' Avenue	E2
St James Street	D2-E2
St John's Place	E3
St Luke's Road	F4
St Michael's Place	A2
St Nicholas Road	B2-B3
Ship Street	C1-C2
Sillwood Road	A1-A2
Sillwood Street	A1
South Avenue	F3
South Street	C1
Southover Street	E4-F4
Spring Gardens	C2-C3
Spring Street	B2
Stanley Street	E3
Station Street	C4
Stone Street	B2
Sussex Street	E3
Sydney Street	C3-C4
The Lanes	C2
Tarner Road	E3
Temple Gardens	A3
Temple Street	A2
Terminus Road	B4-C4

Tichbourne Street	C2-C3
Tilstone Street	E2-F2-F3
Trafalgar Street	C4-D4
Toronto Terrace	E4-F4
Tower Road	F4
Upper Bedford Street	F2
Upper North Street	B2
Upper Rock Gardens	E2
Upper St James Street	E2-F2
Vernon Terrace	A3-A4-B4
Victoria Road	A3-B3
Victoria Street	B2-B3
Vine Place	B3
West Drive	E3-F3-F4
West Street	C1-C2
West Hill Road	B4
West Hill Street	B4
Western Road	A2-B2-C2
Western Street	A1
White Street	E2-E3
William Street	D2-D3
Windlesham Avenue	A3
Windlesham Gardens	A3-A4
Windlesham Road	A3
Windmill Street	E3
Windsor Street	C2
York Avenue	A2-A3
York Place	D3-D4
York Road	A2

Hove

Adelaide Crescent	B1-C1
Albany Villas	B1
Aymer Road	A1-A2
Blatchington Road	A2-B2
Bishops Road	B4
Brunswick Square	C1
Byron Street	B3
Cambridge Road	C1-C2
Church Road	A2-B2-B1
Clarendon Road	A3-B3
Clarendon Villas	A2
Coleridge Street	A3
Compton Road	C4
Conway Street	A3-B3
Cowper Street	A2
Cromwell Road	B3-C3-C2
Davigdor Road	C2-C3
Denmark Villas	B2-B3
Dyke Road	C3-C4
Eaton Gardens	B2
Eaton Road	B2
Eaton Villas	B2
Ellen Street	A3-B3
First Avenue	B1
Fonthill Road	A3-A4
Fourth Avenue	B1
Furze Hill	C2
George Street	B2
Goldstone Crescent	A4-B4-A4
Goldstone Road	A2
Goldstone Street	A2-A3
Goldstone Villas	B2-B3
Grand Avenue	B1
Highcroft Villas	C4
Holland Road	C1-C2
Hova Villas	B2

Hove Park Road	B4-C4
Hove Park Villas	B3
Hove Park Way	B4
Hove Street	A1-A2
Kings Esplanade	A1-B1-C1
Kingsway	A1-B1-C1
Lansdowne Place	C1-C2
Lansdowne Road	C2
Leighton Road	A3
Lloyd Road	B4
Lorna Road	B3-C3
Lyndhurst Road	C3
Medina Villas	A1
Millers Road	C2
Montefiore Road	C3
Montgomery Street	A3
Nevill Road	A4
Newton Road	A3-B3
Norton Road	B2
Old Shoreham Road	A3-A4-B4-B3-C3
Orchard Gardens	A4
Orchard Road	A4
Orpen Road	C4
Osborne Villas	A1-A2
Palmeira Avenue	C2
Park View Road	A4
Pembroke Avenue	A2
Pembroke Crescent	A2
Portland Road	A2
Princess Avenue	A1
Radinden Manor Road	B3-B4-C3-C4
Reigate Road	C4
Rigden Road	B4
Sackville Road	A2-A3
St Aubyns	A1-A2
Salisbury Road	B2
Seafield Road	A1-A2
Second Avenue	B1
Selborne Road	B2
Shirley Drive	B4
Shirley Road	B3-B4
Shirley Street	A2-A3
Somerhill Road	C2
Station Approach	B3
Stirling Place	A2
The Drive	B2-B3
The Drove	C4
The Droveway	B4-C4
The Martlet	C4
The Upper Drive	B3-C3-C4
Third Avenue	B1
Tilsbury Road	B2
Vallance Gardens	A1
Vallance Road	A1-A2
Ventnor Villas	B2
Waterloo Street	C1
Wilbury Avenue	A3
Wilbury Gardens	B3-B3-C3
Wilbury Road	B2-B3
Wilbury Villas	B3
York Road	C1-C2

Lewes

Bell Lane	A1
Bradford Road	A2-A3
Brook Street	A2
Brooks Road	C3-C4

Chapel Hill	C3
Cliffe High Street	C3
Cockshut Road	A1-B1
Eastport Lane	B2
Fisher Street	B3
Friars Walk	C3
Garden Street	B2
Grange Road	A2-B2
Ham Lane	B2-B1-C1-C2
High Street	A2-B2-B3-C3
Keere Street	A2-B2
King Henrys Road	A2
Lancaster Street	B3
Landport Road	A4
Lansdowne Place	B2-C2
Lewes Southern By-Pass	A1-B1-C1
Little East Street	B3
Malling Street	C3-C4
Market Lane	B3
Market Street	B3
Morris Road	C3
Mountfield Road	B2-C2
New Road	A2-A3-B3
Newton Road	A3-A4
North Street	B3-B4
Offham Road	A3
Orchard Road	C4
Paddock Lane	A2
Paddock Road	A2-A3-B3
Pelham Terrace	A3-B3
Phoenix Causeway	B3-C3
Prince Edwards Road	A3
Priory Street	B1-B2
Rotten Row	A2
Rufus Close	A3
St Nicholas Lane	B2-B3
St Pancras Road	A1-A2
School Hill	B3-C3
South Street	C3
Southover Road	B2
Southover High Street	A1-B1
Station Road	B2
Station Street	B2
The Avenue	A3
The Course	A1
Toronto Terrace	A3-B3
Tunnel	C3
Watergate Lane	B2
West Street	B3
White Hill	A3-B3

17

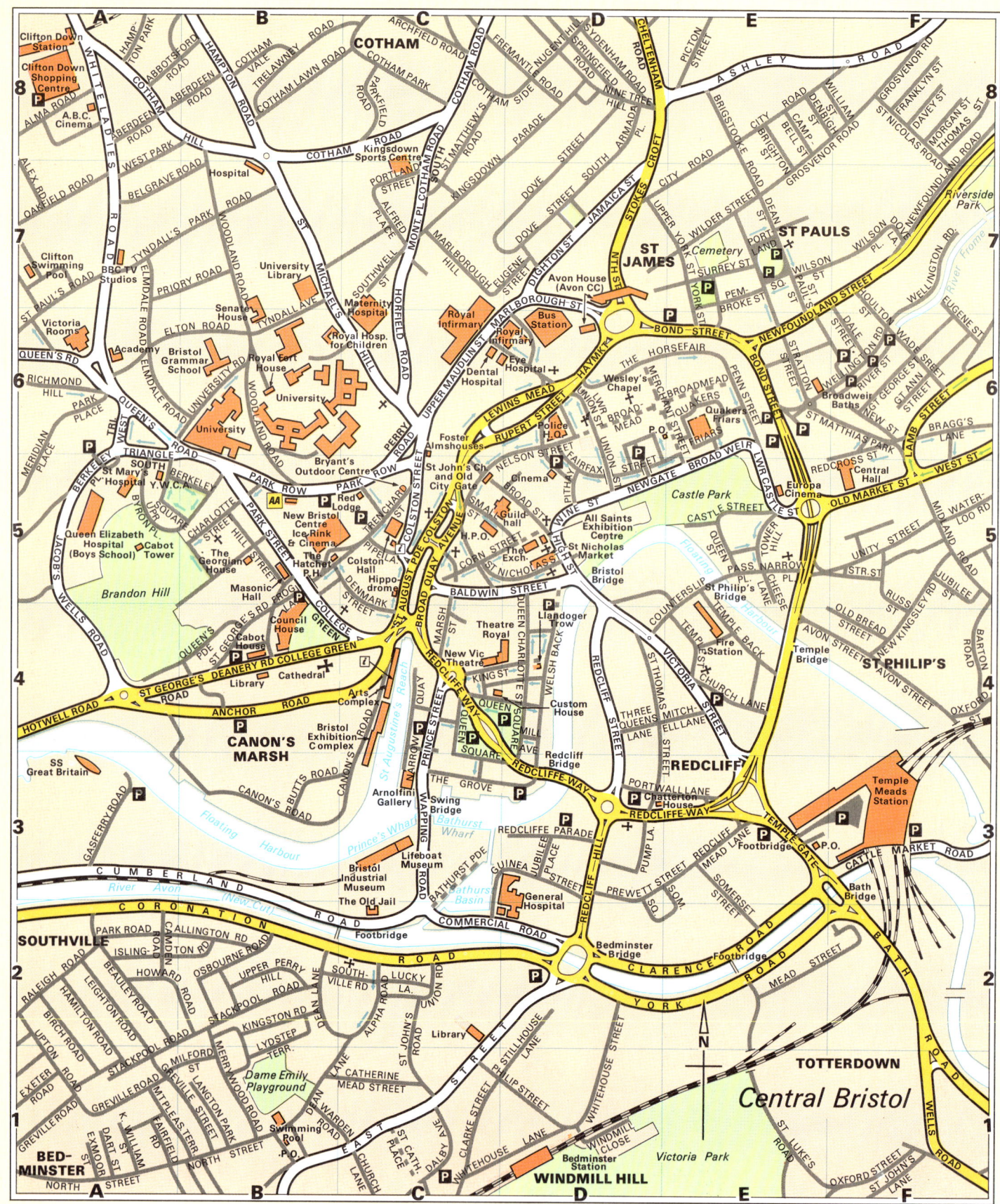

Bristol

One of Britain's most historic seaports, Bristol retains many of its visible links with the past, despite terrible damage inflicted during bombing raids in World War II. Most imposing is the cathedral, founded as an abbey church in 1140. Perhaps even more famous than the cathedral is the Church of St Mary Redcliffe. Ranking among the finest churches in the country, it owes much of

its splendour to 14th- and 15th-century merchants who bestowed huge sums of money on it.

The merchant families brought wealth to the whole of Bristol, and their trading links with the world are continued in today's modern aerospace and technological industries. Much of the best of Bristol can be seen in the area of the Floating Harbour – an arm of the Avon. Several of the old warehouses have been converted into museums, galleries and exhibition centres. Among them are

genuinely picturesque old pubs, the best-known of which is the Llandoger Trow. It is a timbered 17th-century house, the finest of its kind in Bristol. Further up the same street – King Street – is the Theatre Royal, built in 1766 and the oldest theatre in the country. In Corn Street, the heart of the business area, is a magnificent 18th-century corn exchange. In front of it are the four pillars known as the 'nails', on which merchants used to make cash transactions, hence 'to pay on the nail'.

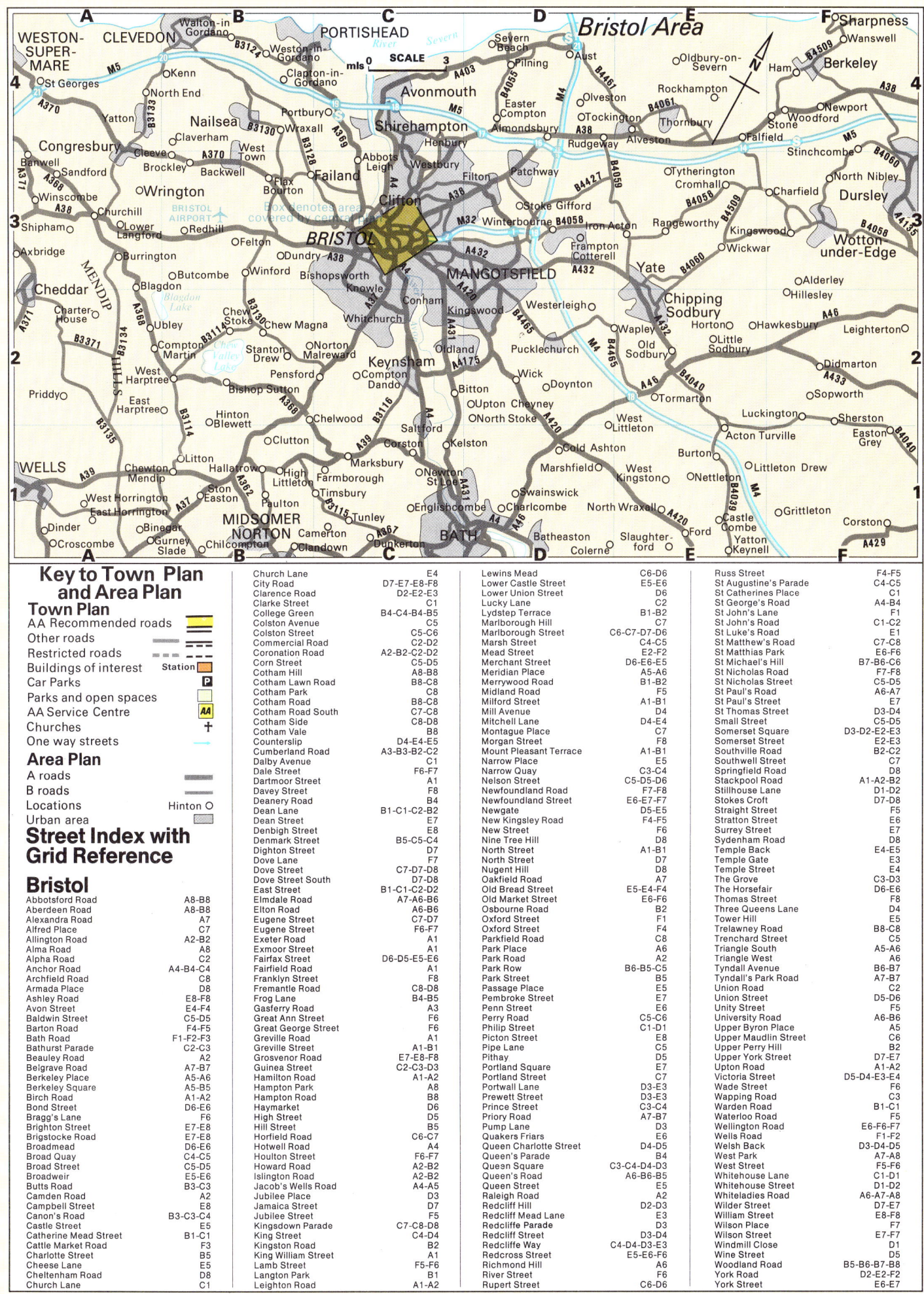

Key to Town Plan and Area Plan

Town Plan

AA Recommended roads	
Other roads	
Restricted roads	
Buildings of interest	Station
Car Parks	P
Parks and open spaces	
AA Service Centre	AA
Churches	+
One way streets	→

Area Plan

A roads	
B roads	
Locations	Hinton O
Urban area	

Street Index with Grid Reference

Bristol

Abbotsford Road	A8-B8
Aberdeen Road	A8-B8
Alexandra Road	A7
Alfred Place	C7
Allington Road	A2-B2
Alma Road	A8
Alpha Road	C2
Anchor Road	A4-B4-C4
Archfield Road	C8
Armada Place	D8
Ashley Road	E8-F8
Avon Street	E4-F4
Baldwin Street	C5-D5
Barton Road	F4-F5
Bath Road	F1-F2-F3
Bathurst Parade	C2-C3
Beauley Road	A2
Belgrave Road	A7-B7
Berkeley Place	A5-A6
Berkeley Square	A5-B5
Birch Road	A1-A2
Bond Street	D6-E6
Bragg's Lane	F6
Brighton Street	E7-E8
Brigstocke Road	E7-E8
Broadmead	D6-E6
Broad Quay	C4-C5
Broad Street	C5-D5
Broadweir	E5-E6
Butts Road	B3-C3
Camden Road	A2
Campbell Street	E8
Canon's Road	B3-C3-C4
Castle Street	E5
Catherine Mead Street	B1-C1
Cattle Market Road	F3
Charlotte Street	B5
Cheese Lane	E5
Cheltenham Road	D8
Church Lane	C1

Church Lane	E4
City Road	D7-E7-E8-F8
Clarence Road	D2-E2-E3
Clarke Street	C1
College Green	B4-C4-B4-B5
Colston Avenue	C5
Colston Street	C5-C6
Commercial Road	C2-D2
Coronation Road	A2-B2-C2-D2
Corn Street	C5-D5
Cotham Hill	A8-B8
Cotham Lawn Road	B8-C8
Cotham Park	C8
Cotham Road	B8-C8
Cotham Road South	C7-C8
Cotham Side	C8-D8
Cotham Vale	B8
Countership	D4-E4-E5
Cumberland Road	A3-B3-B2-C2
Dalby Avenue	C1
Dale Street	F6-F7
Dartmoor Street	A1
Davey Street	F8
Deanery Road	B4
Dean Lane	B1-C1-C2-B2
Dean Street	E7
Denbigh Street	E8
Denmark Street	B5-C5-C4
Dighton Street	D7
Dove Lane	F7
Dove Street	C7-D7-D8
Dove Street South	D7-D8
East Street	B1-C1-C2-D2
Elmdale Road	A7-A6-B6
Elton Road	A6-B6
Eugene Street	C7-D7
Eugene Street	F6-F7
Exeter Road	A1
Exmoor Street	A1
Fairfax Street	D6-D5-E5-E6
Fairfield Road	A1
Franklyn Street	F8
Fremantle Road	C8-D8
Frog Lane	B4-B5
Gasferry Road	A3
Great Ann Street	F6
Great George Street	F6
Greville Road	A1
Greville Road	A1-B1
Grosvenor Road	E7-E8-F8
Guinea Street	C2-C3-D3
Hamilton Road	A1-A2
Hampton Park	A8
Hampton Road	B8
Haymarket	D6
High Street	D5
Hill Street	B5
Horfield Road	C6-C7
Hotwell Road	A4
Houlton Street	F6-F7
Howard Road	A2-B2
Islington Road	A2-B2
Jacob's Wells Road	A4-A5
Jubilee Place	D3
Jamaica Street	D7
Jubilee Street	F5
Kingsdown Parade	C7-C8-D8
King Street	C4-D4
Kingston Road	B2
King William Street	A1
Lamb Street	F5-F6
Langton Park	B1
Leighton Road	A1-A2

Lewins Mead	C6-D6
Lower Castle Street	E5-E6
Lower Union Street	D6
Lucky Lane	C2
Lydstep Terrace	B1-B2
Marlborough Hill	C7
Marlborough Street	C6-C7-D7-D6
Marsh Street	C4-C5
Mead Street	E2-F2
Merchant Street	D6-E6-E5
Meridian Place	A5-A6
Merrywood Road	B1-B2
Midland Road	F5
Milford Street	A1-B1
Mill Avenue	D4
Mitchell Lane	D4-E4
Montague Place	C7
Morgan Street	F8
Mount Pleasant Terrace	A1-B1
Narrow Place	E5
Narrow Quay	C3-C4
Nelson Street	C5-D5-D6
Newfoundland Road	F7-F8
Newfoundland Street	E6-E7-F7
Newgate	D5-E5
New Kingsley Road	F4-F5
New Street	F6
Nine Tree Hill	D8
North Street	A1-B1
North Street	D7
Nugent Hill	D8
Oakfield Road	A7
Old Bread Street	E5-E4-F4
Old Market Street	E6-F6
Osbourne Road	B2
Oxford Street	F1
Oxford Street	F4
Parkfield Road	C8
Park Place	A6
Park Road	A2
Park Row	B6-B5-C5
Park Street	B5
Passage Place	E5
Pembroke Street	E7
Penn Street	E6
Perry Road	C5-C6
Philip Street	C1-D1
Picton Street	E8
Pipe Lane	C5
Pithay	D5
Portland Square	E7
Portland Street	C7
Portwall Lane	D3-E3
Prewett Street	D3-E3
Prince Street	C3-C4
Priory Road	A7-B7
Pump Lane	D3
Quakers Friars	E6
Queen Charlotte Street	D4-D5
Queen's Parade	B4
Queen Square	C3-C4-D4-D3
Queen's Road	A6-B6-B5
Queen Street	E5
Raleigh Road	A2
Redcliff Hill	D2-D3
Redcliff Mead Lane	E3
Redcliffe Parade	D3
Redcliff Street	D3-D4
Redcliffe Way	C4-D4-D3-E3
Redcross Street	E5-E6-F6
Richmond Hill	A6
River Street	F6
Rupert Street	C6-D6

Russ Street	F4-F5
St Augustine's Parade	C4-C5
St Catherines Place	C1
St George's Road	A4-B4
St John's Lane	F1
St John's Road	C1-C2
St Luke's Road	E1
St Matthew's Road	C7-C8
St Matthias Park	E6-F6
St Michael's Hill	B7-B6-C6
St Nicholas Road	F7-F8
St Nicholas Street	C5-D5
St Paul's Road	A6-A7
St Paul's Street	E7
St Thomas Street	D3-D4
Small Street	C5-D5
Somerset Square	D3-D2-E2-E3
Somerset Street	E2-E3
Southville Road	B2-C2
Southwell Street	C7
Springfield Road	D8
Stackpool Road	A1-A2-B2
Stillhouse Lane	D1-D2
Stokes Croft	D7-D8
Straight Street	F5
Stratton Street	E6
Surrey Street	E7
Sydenham Road	D8
Temple Back	E4-E5
Temple Gate	E3
Temple Street	E4
The Grove	C3-D3
The Horsefair	D6-E6
Thomas Street	F8
Three Queens Lane	D4
Tower Hill	E5
Trelawney Road	B8-C8
Trenchard Street	C5
Triangle South	A5-A6
Triangle West	A6
Tyndall Avenue	B6-B7
Tyndall's Park Road	A7-B7
Union Road	C2
Union Street	D5-D6
Unity Street	F5
University Road	A6-B6
Upper Byron Place	A5
Upper Maudlin Street	C6
Upper Perry Hill	B2
Upper York Street	D7-E7
Upton Road	A1-A2
Victoria Street	D5-D4-E3-E4
Wade Street	F6
Wapping Road	C3
Warden Road	B1-C1
Waterloo Road	F5
Wellington Road	E6-F6-F7
Wells Road	F1-F2
Welsh Back	D3-D4-D5
West Park	A7-A8
West Street	F5-F6
Whitehouse Lane	C1-D1
Whitehouse Street	D1-D2
Whiteladies Road	A6-A7-A8
Wilder Street	D7-E7
William Street	E8-F8
Wilson Place	F7
Wilson Street	E7-F7
Windmill Close	D1
Wine Street	D5
Woodland Road	B5-B6-B7-B8
York Road	D2-E2-F2
York Street	E6-E7

19

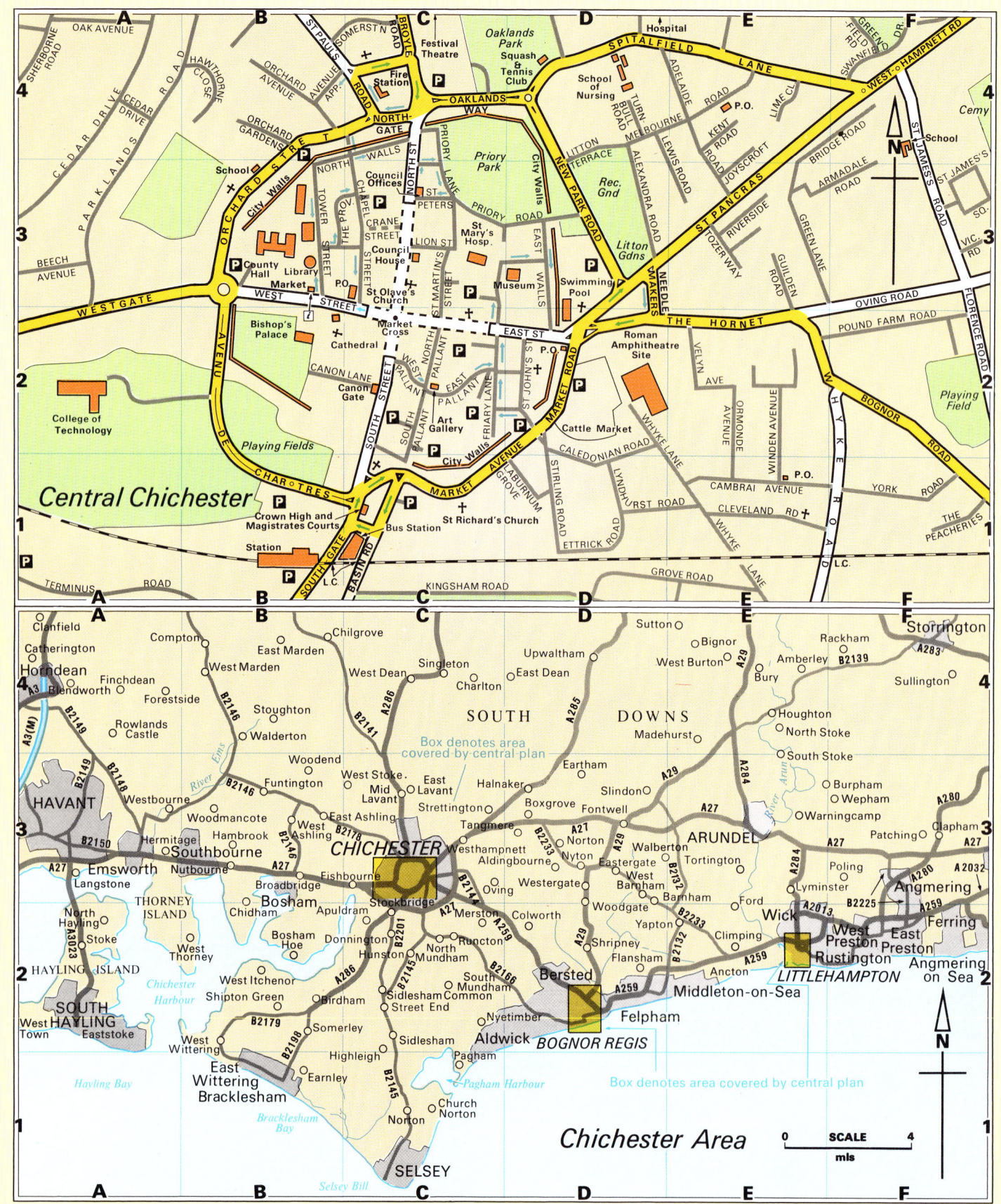

Chichester

The graceful spire of Chichester Cathedral, consecrated in 1184, rises over the rooftops to the west of this city, which dates back to Roman times and is one of Britain's oldest. Notable among its 18th-century streets are the Pallants and the Pallant House, and at Fishbourne Priory nearby, visitors can admire the mosaics, formal garden and other remains of the largest Roman residence found in Britain.

Chichester today gives pleasure to thousands with its Festival Theatre and its harbour — thronged with sailing enthusiasts throughout the summer and with a variety of wild birds during the winter. Other attractions are the Open Air Museum and West Dean Gardens.

Bognor Regis was plain Bognor until 1929 when George V granted the suffix Regis after convalescing there. A former fishing village, it began its transformation into a seaside town in the 1790s, and is now a favourite destination for family holidays. Elegant Hotham Park House is worth a visit.

Littlehampton at the mouth of the River Arun was once a busy port for passengers and cargo going to France; today it is a popular target for holidaymakers, who come here for the good fishing, bathing and sailing. The local museum concentrates on marine subjects.

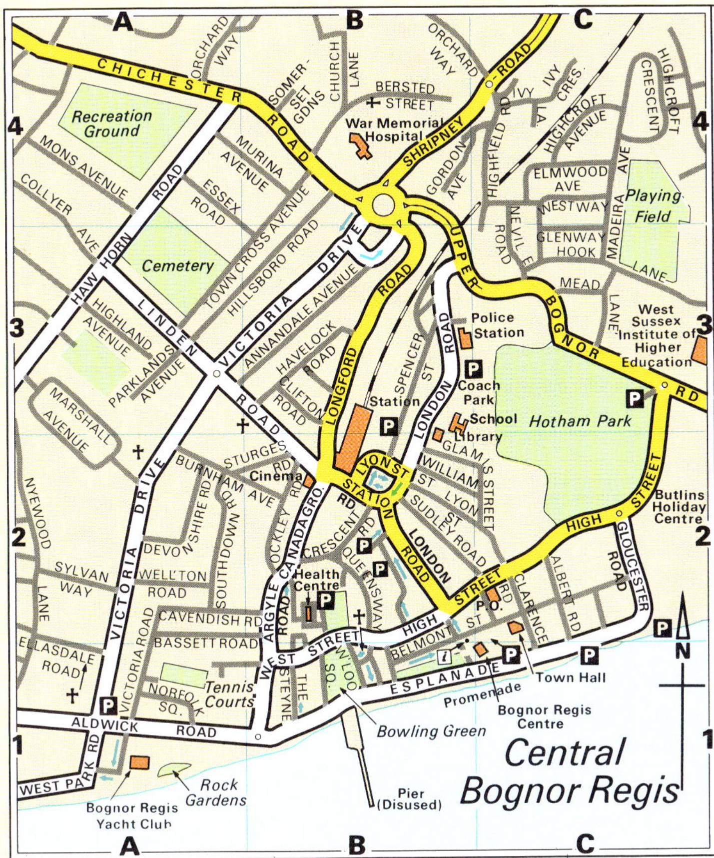

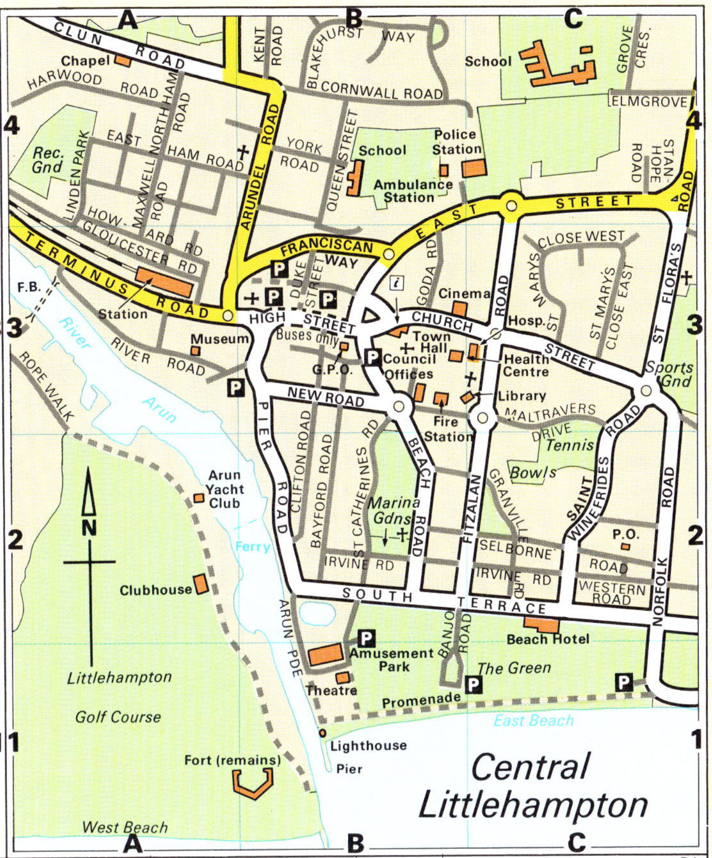

Central
Bognor Regis

Central
Littlehampton

LEGEND

Town Plan

AA Recommended roads	▬▬
Other roads	═══
Restricted roads	═ ═
Buildings of interest	■
Churches	+
Car parks	P
Parks and open spaces	▱
One way streets	←

Area Plan

A roads	▬▬
B roads	═══
Locations	Morton ○
Urban area	⬭

Street Index with grid reference

Chichester

Adelaide Road	D4-E4-E3
Alexandra Road	D3-D4
Armdale Road	E3-F3-F4
Avenue Approach	B4
Avenue de Chartres	B3-B2-B1-C1
Basin Road	C1
Beech Avenue	A3
Bognor Road	F1-F2
Bridge Road	E3-E4-F4
Broyle Road	C4
Caledonian Road	D2-D1-D2
Cambrai Avenue	E1-F1
Canon Lane	B2-C2
Cedar Drive	A3-A4
Chapel Street	C3-C4
Cleveland Road	E1
Crane Street	C3
East Pallant	C2
East Street	C2-D2
East Walls	D2-D3
Ettrick Road	D1
Florence Road	F2-F3
Friary Lane	C2
Greenfield Road	F4
Green Lane	E3
Greenfield Road	F4
Grove Road	D1-E1
Guilden road	E3
Hawthorne Close	B4
Joyscroft	E3-E4
Kent Road	E4
Kingsham Road	C1-D1
Laburnum Grove	D1
Lewis Road	D4-D3-E3-E4
Lime Cose	E4
Lion Street	C3
Litten Terrace	D3-D4
Lyndhurst Road	D1-E1
Market Avenue	C1-D1-D2
Market Road	D2
Melbourne Road	D4-D4
Needlemakers	D2-D3
New Park Road	D3-D4
Northgate	C4
North Pallant	C2
North Street	C3-C4
North Walls	B3-B4-C4
Oak Avenue	A4
Oaklands Way	C4-D4
Orchard Avenue	B4
Orchard Gardens	B4
Orchard Street	B3-B4-C4
Ormonde Avenue	E1-E2
Oving Road	E2-E3-F3
Parklands Road	A3-A4-B4
Pound Farm Road	E2-F2
Priory Lane	C3-C4
Priory Road	C3-D3
Riverside	E3
St James's Road	F3-F4
St James's Square	F3
St John's Street	D2
St Martin's Street	C2-C3
St Pancras	D2-D3-E3-E4-F4
St Paul's Road	B4-C4
St Peter's	C3
Sherbourne Road	A4
Somerston	B4-C4
South Pallant	C1-C2
South Street	C1-C2
Southgate	B1-C1
Spitalfield Lane	D4-E4-F4
Stirling Road	D1-D2
Swanfield Drive	F4
Terminus Road	A1-B1
The Preachers	F1
The Providence	B3-C3
The Hornet	D2-E2
Tower Street	B3
Tozer Way	E3
Turnbull Road	D4
Velyn Avenue	E2
Westgate	A2-A3-B3
Westhampnett Road	F4
West Pallant	C2
West Street	B3-C3-C2
Whyke Lane	D2-D1-E1
Whyke Road	E1-F1-F2-E2
Winden Avenue	E1-E2
York Road	F1

Bognor Regis

Albert Road	C2
Aldwick Road	A1-B1
Annandale Avenue	A3-B3
Argyle Road	B1-B2
Bassett Road	B2
Belmont Street	B1-B2-C2
Bersted Street	B4
Burnham Avenue	A2-B2
Canada Grove	B2
Cavendish Road	A2-B2
Chichester Road	A4-B4
Church Lane	B4
Clarence Road	C1-C2
Clifton Road	B3
Collyer Avenue	A3-A4
Crescent Road	B2
Devonshire Road	A2
Ellasdale Road	A1-A2
Elmwood Avenue	C4
Esplanade	B1-C1-C2
Essex Road	A4-A3-B3
Glamis Street	B2-C2
Glenway	C3
Gloucester Road	C2
Gordon Avenue	B4-C4
Havelock Road	B3
Hawthorn Close	A3-A4
Highcroft Avenue	C4
Highcroft Crescent	C4
Highfield Road	C3-C4
Highland Avenue	A3
High Street	B2-C2-C3
Hillsboro Road	A3-B3-B4
Hook Lane	C3
Ivy Crescent	C4
Ivy Lane	C4
Linden Road	A3-B3-B2
London Road	B2-B3
Longford Road	B2-B3
Lyon Street	B2-C2
Madeira Avenue	C3-C4
Marshall Avenue	A2-A3
Mead Lane	C3
Mons Avenue	A4
Murina Avenue	A4-B4
Neville Road	C3-C4
Norfolk Square	A1
Nyewood Lane	A1-A2-A3
Ockley Road	B2
Orchard Way	A4-B4-C4
Parklands Avenue	A3
Queensway	B2
Shripney Road	B4-C4
Somerset Gardens	B4
Southdown Road	A2
Spencer Street	B2-B3
Station Road	B2
Sturges Road	A2-B2
Sudley Road	B2-C2
Sylvan Way	A2
The Steyne	B1
Town Cross Road	A3-B3-B4
Upper Bognor Road	B4-B3-C3
Victoria Avenue	A1-A2-A3-B3-B4
Victoria Road	A1-A2
Waterloo Square	B1
Wellington Road	A2
West Park Road	A1
West Street	B1-B2
Westway	C4
William Street	B2-C2

Littlehampton

Arundel Road	A3-B3-B4
Arun Parade	B1-B2
Banjo Road	B1-B2
Bayford Road	B2-B3
Beach Road	B2-B3
Blakehurst Way	B4
Church Street	B3-C3
Clifton Road	B2-B3
Clun Road	A4-B4
Cornwall Road	B4
Duke Street	B3
East Ham Road	A4-B4
East Street	B3-B4-C4
Elmgrove	C4
Fitzalen Road	B2-C2-C3-C4
Franciscan Way	B3
Gloucester Road	A3-A4
Goda Road	B3
Granville Road	C2
Grove Crescent	C4
Harwood Road	A4
High Street	A3-B3
Howard Road	A3-A4
Irvine Road	B2-C2
Kent Road	B4
Linden Road	A4
Maltravers Drive	C3
Maxwell Road	A3-A4
New Road	B3
Norfolk Road	C1-C2-C3
North Ham Road	A4
Pier Road	B2-B3
Queen Street	B4
River Road	A3
Rope Walk	B4
Saint Winifredes Road	C2-C3
St Catherines Road	B1-B2-B3
St Flora's Road	C3-C4
St Mary's Close East	C3
St Mary's Close West	C3
Selbourne Road	B2-C2
South Terrace	B2-C2
Stanhope Road	C4
Terminus Road	A3-A4
Western Road	C2
York Road	B4

CHICHESTER
Opened in 1962 under the direction of Sir Laurence (later Lord) Olivier, the Festival Theatre draws an annual audience of half a million to its wide range of music and drama, both during the summer festival and throughout the year.

Central Falmouth

Central Penzance

Cornish towns

Falmouth Twin fortresses, St. Mawes and Pendennis, guard the harbour entrance and serve as a reminder of Falmouth's once vital strategic importance. Lying in the sheltered waters of the Carrick Roads and provided with one of the world's largest natural harbours, Falmouth prospered on trade until the 19th century. Today the town is popular with holidaymakers.

St Ives is one of the few British towns with a style of painting named after it, for both artists and holidaymakers are drawn to the port, with its charming old quarter known as Down-Long. Regular exhibitions of local painting, sculpture and pottery are held, and the work of sculptor Barbara Hepworth, who spent much of her creative life here, is displayed in the Hepworth Gallery.

Penzance is the first and last town in Britain — it lies at the western extremity of Mounts Bay and basks in a temperate climate and sub-tropical vegetation. Places of interest include the ornate Egyptian House (now a National Trust shop), and steamers and helicopters go to the Scilly Isles.

Newquay Favourite haunt of surfboarders for its Fistral and Watergate beaches, Newquay has a 'Huer's House' where lookouts once warned fishermen of approaching shoals of pilchards. There are fine beaches for holidaymakers, such as Towan, Lusty Glaze and Great Western.

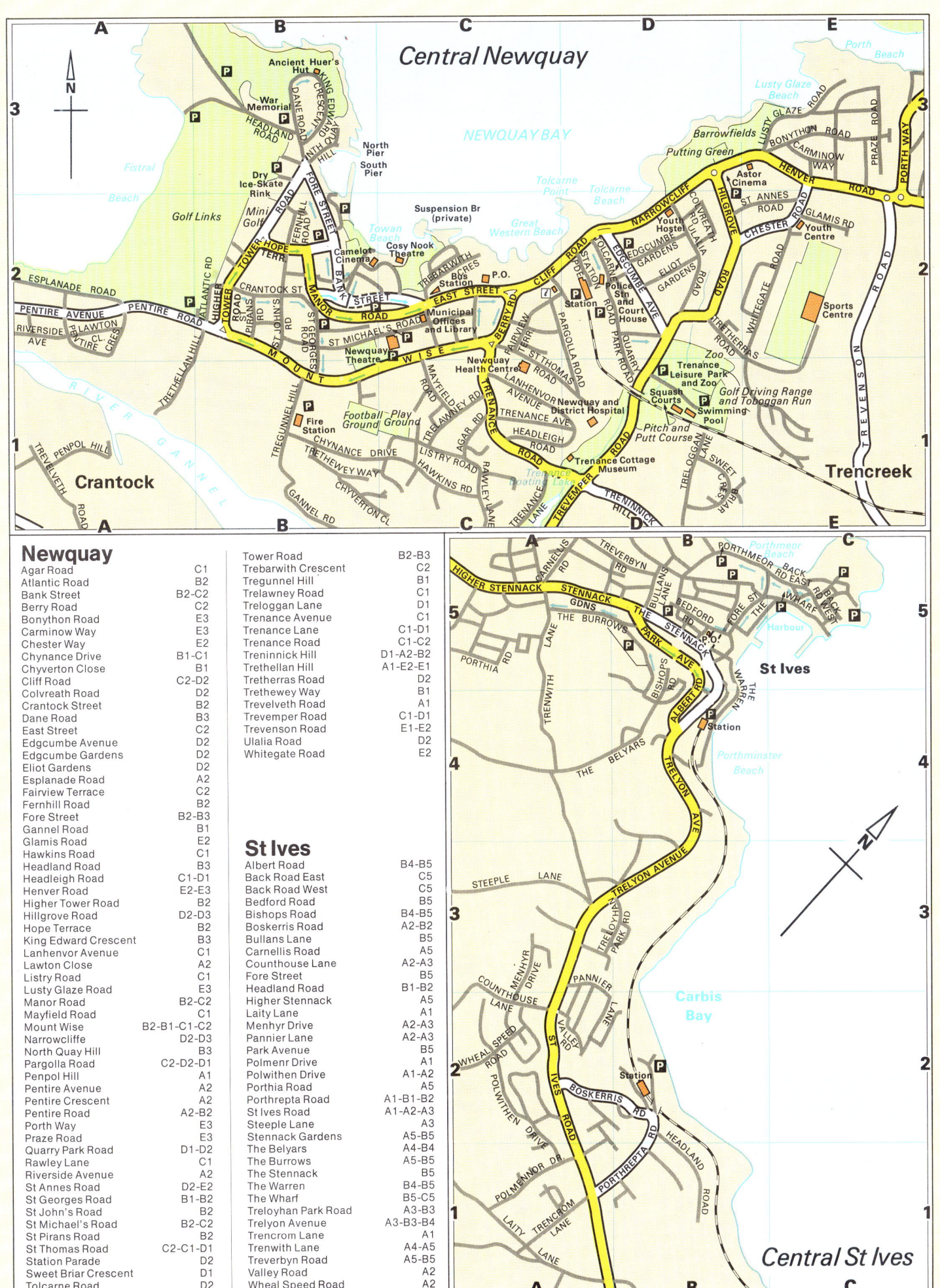

Central Newquay

Newquay

Agar Road	C1
Atlantic Road	B2
Bank Street	B2-C2
Berry Road	C2
Bonython Road	E3
Carminow Way	E3
Chester Way	E2
Chynance Drive	B1-C1
Chyverton Close	B1
Cliff Road	C2-D2
Colvreath Road	D2
Crantock Street	B2
Dane Road	B3
East Street	C2
Edgcumbe Avenue	D2
Edgcumbe Gardens	D2
Eliot Gardens	D2
Esplanade Road	A2
Fairview Terrace	C2
Fernhill Road	B2
Fore Street	B2-B3
Gannel Road	B1
Glamis Road	E2
Hawkins Road	C1
Headland Road	B3
Headleigh Road	C1-D1
Henver Road	E2-E3
Higher Tower Road	B2
Hillgrove Road	D2-D3
Hope Terrace	B2
King Edward Crescent	B3
Lanhenvor Avenue	C1
Lawton Close	A2
Listry Road	C1
Lusty Glaze Road	E3
Manor Road	B2-C2
Mayfield Road	C1
Mount Wise	B2-B1-C1-C2
Narrowcliffe	D2-D3
North Quay Hill	B3
Pargolla Road	C2-D2-D1
Penpol Hill	A1
Pentire Avenue	A2
Pentire Crescent	A2
Pentire Road	A2-B2
Porth Way	E3
Praze Road	E3
Quarry Park Road	D1-D2
Rawley Lane	C1
Riverside Avenue	A2
St Annes Road	D2-E2
St Georges Road	B1-B2
St John's Road	B2
St Michael's Road	B2-C2
St Pirans Road	B2
St Thomas Road	C2-C1-D1
Station Parade	D2
Sweet Briar Crescent	D1
Tolcarne Road	D2
Tower Road	B2-B3
Trebarwith Crescent	C2
Tregunnel Hill	B1
Trelawney Road	C1
Treloggan Lane	D1
Trenance Avenue	C1
Trenance Lane	C1-D1
Trenance Road	C1-C2
Treninnick Hill	D1-A2-B2
Trethellan Hill	A1-E2-E1
Tretherras Road	D2
Trethewey Way	B1
Trevelveth Road	A1
Trevemper Road	C1-D1
Trevenson Road	E1-E2
Ulalia Road	D2
Whitegate Road	E2

St Ives

Albert Road	B4-B5
Back Road East	C5
Back Road West	C5
Bedford Road	B5
Bishops Road	B4-B5
Boskerris Road	A2-B2
Bullans Lane	B5
Carnellis Road	A5
Counthouse Lane	A2-A3
Fore Street	B5
Headland Road	B1-B2
Higher Stennack	A5
Laity Lane	A1
Menhyr Drive	A2-A3
Pannier Lane	A2-A3
Park Avenue	B5
Polmenr Drive	A1
Polwithen Drive	A1-A2
Porthia Road	A5
Porthrepta Road	A1-B1-B2
St Ives Road	A1-A2-A3
Steeple Lane	A3
Stennack Gardens	A5-B5
The Belyars	A4-B4
The Burrows	A5-B5
The Stennack	B5
The Warren	B4-B5
The Wharf	B5-C5
Treloyhan Park Road	A3-B3
Trelyon Avenue	A3-B3-B4
Trencrom Lane	A1
Trenwith Lane	A4-A5
Treverbyn Road	A5-B5
Valley Road	A2
Wheal Speed Road	A2

Central St Ives

23

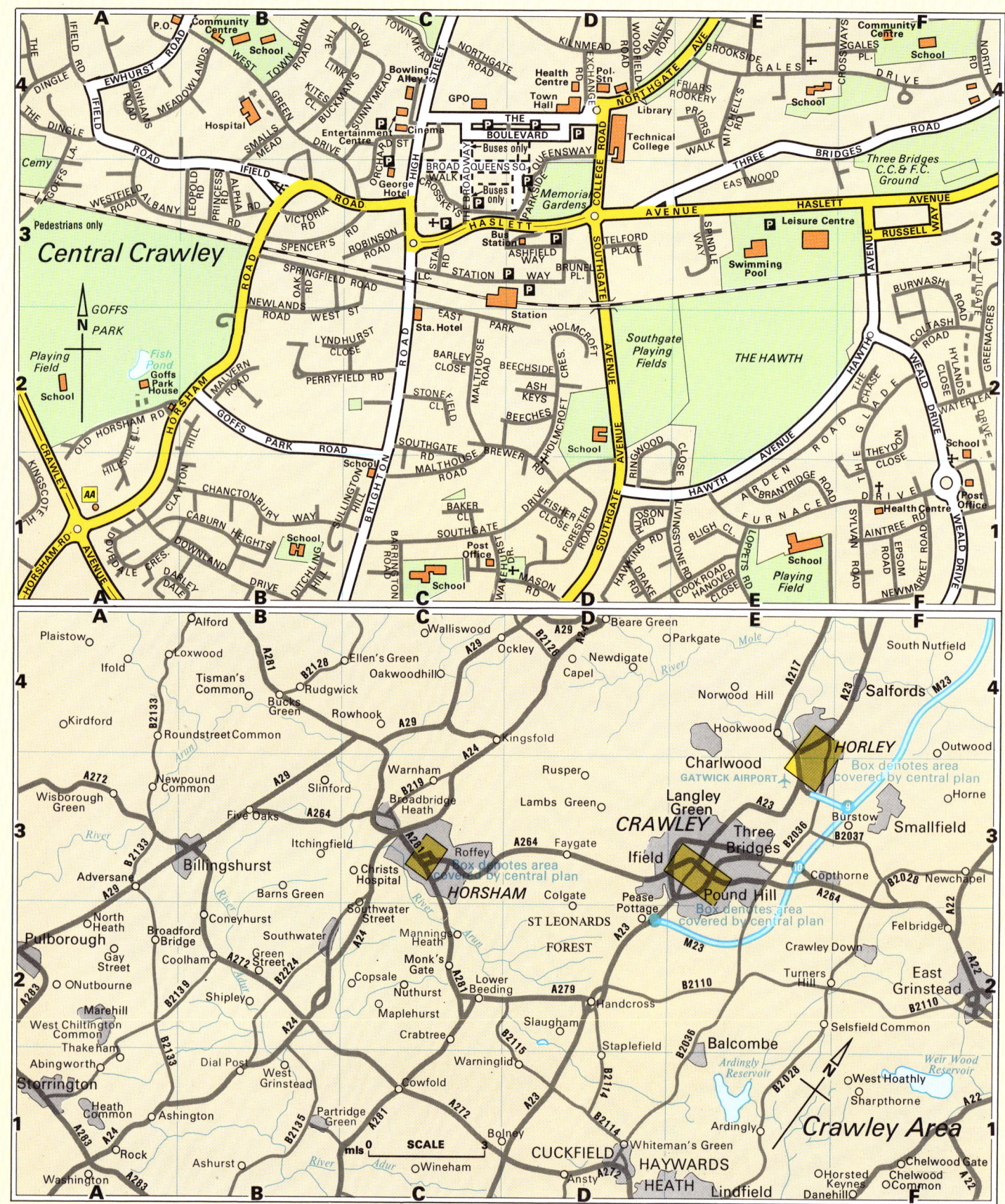

Crawley

Crawley New Town, the only one of that generation of post-war new towns to be built south of London, has been grafted on to the old Crawley where many ancient buildings resolutely survive. However, the new town does have its own examples of good architecture, including the bandstand in Queens Square which came from nearby Gatwick Racecourse – now the site of Gatwick Airport.

This, London's second largest airport, is expected to increase its passenger handling capacity from 16 million to 25 million passengers a year in the 1990s on completion of a second terminal.

Horsham is another town that has suffered from a rash of modern development as a result of being within striking distance of the capital. However, one or two corners of the original centre reveal some interesting old buildings. One of these

is a 16th-century black-and-white timbered house containing the local museum. Here, a period Sussex kitchen, a blacksmith's forge and a wheelwright's shop can be seen.

East Grinstead The well-heeled residential housing of commuter-land radiates from this old market town that has retained a number of Tudor buildings along its High Street. Sackville College, the 17th-century almshouses founded by the 2nd Earl of Dorset, forms an attractive group.

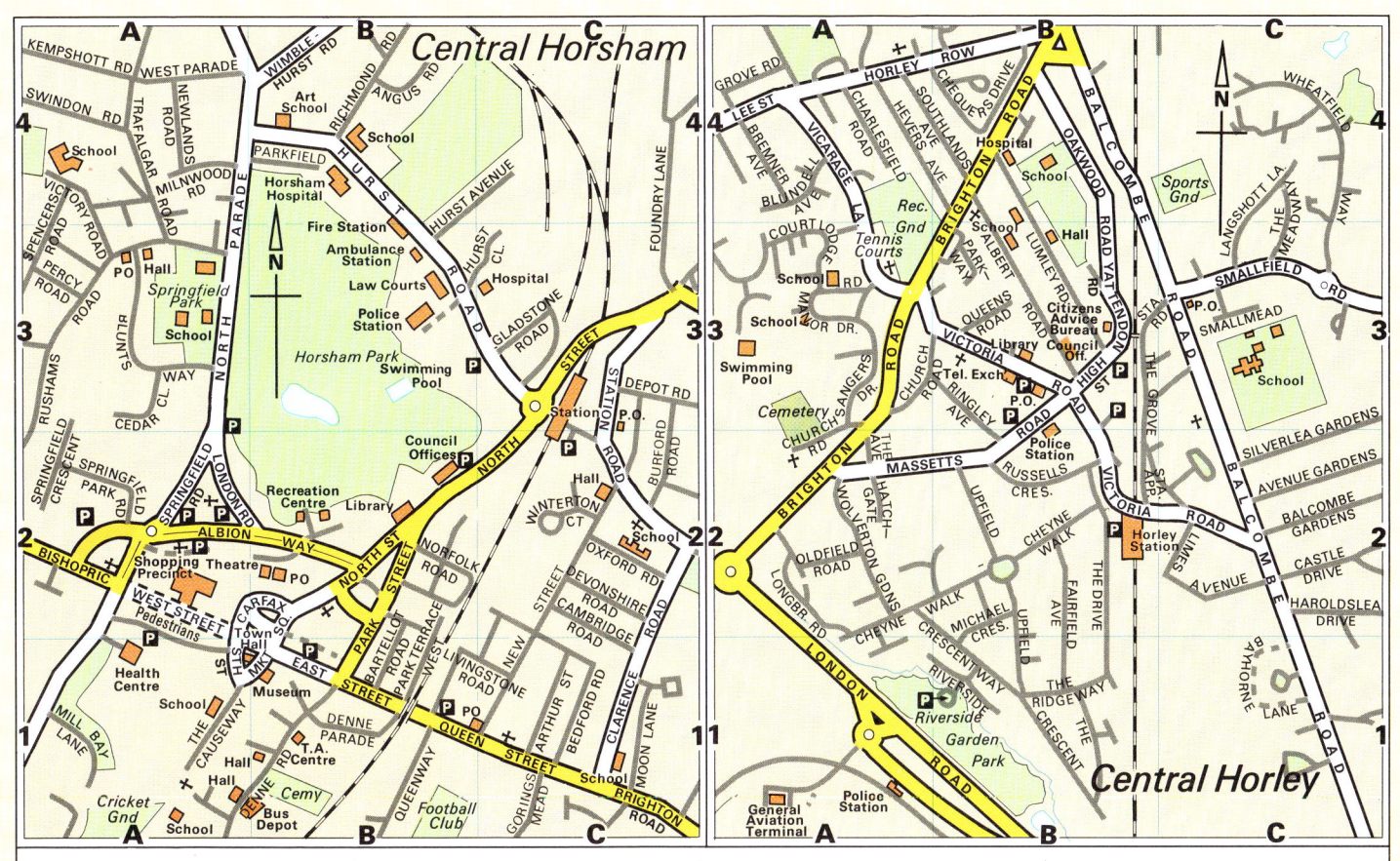

Key to Town Plan and Area Plan

Town Plan

A A Recommended roads
Other roads
Restricted roads
Buildings of interest — Mill
Car Parks — P
Parks and open spaces
A A Service Centre — AA

Area Plan

A roads
B roads
Locations — Lickey End○
Urban Area

Street Index with Grid Reference

Crawley

Aintree Road	F1
Albany Road	A4-A3-B3
Alpha Road	B3
Arden Road	E1-E2-F2
Ash Keys	D2
Ashfield Way	D3
Baker Close	C1
Barley Close	C2
Barrington Road	C1
Beeches	C2-D2
Beechside	D2
Bligh Close	E1
Brantridge Road	E1
Brewer Road	C2-D2-D1
Brighton Road	B1-C1-C2-C3
Broad Walk	C3
Brookside	E4
Brunel Place	D3
Buckman's Road	B4-C4-B4
Burwash Road	F2-F3
Caburn Heights	A1-B1
Chantonbury Way	A1-B1-C1
Clayton Hill	A1-B1-B2
College Road	D3-D4
Coltash Road	C3
Cook Road	D1-E1
Crawley Avenue	A1-A2
Crosskeys	C3
Crossways	E4-F4
Darley Dale	A1-B1
Ditchling Hill	B1
Dovedale Crescent	A1
Downland Drive	A1-B1
Drake Road	D1
East Park	C3-C2-D2
Eastwood	E3

Epsom Road	F1
Ewhurst Road	A4-B4
Exchange Road	D4
Fisher Close	D1
Forester Road	D1
Friars Rookery	E4
Furnace Drive	E1-F1
Gales Drive	E4-F4
Gales Place	F4
Ginhams Road	A4
Goffs Lane	A3-A4
Goffs Park Road	B2-C2-C1
Greenacres	F2-F3
Hanover Close	E1
Haslett Avenue	C3-D3-E3-F3
Hawkins Road	D1
Hawth Avenue	D1-E1-E2-F2-F3
High Street	C3-C4
Hillside Close	A1-A2
Holmcroft	D2
Holmcroft Crescent	D2
Horsham Road	A1-A2-B2-B3
Hudson Road	D1
Hylands Close	F2
Ifield Road	A4-A3-B3-C3
Kilnmead	D4
Kingscote Hill	A1
Kites Close	B4
Leopold Road	B3
Livingstone Road	D1-E1
Loppets Road	E1
Lyndhurst Close	B2-C2
Malthouse Road	C1-C2
Malvern Road	B2
Mason Road	C1-D1
Meadowlands	A4-B4
Mitchell's Road	E4
Newlands Road	B2-B3
Newmarket Road	F1
North Road	F4
Northgate Avenue	D4-E4
Northgate Road	C4-D4
Oak Road	B3
Old Horsham Road	A1-A2
Orchard Street	C3-C4
Parkside	D3
Perryfield Road	B2-C2
Princess Road	B3
Priors Walk	E4
Queens Square	C3-D3
Queensway	D3-D4
Railey Road	D4
Ringwood Close	D1-D2-E2-E1
Robinson Road	C3
Russell Way	F3
Smalls Mead	B3-B4
Southgate Avenue	D1-D2-D3
Southgate Drive	C1-D1
Southgate Road	C1-C2
Spencer's Road	B3-C3
Spindle Way	E3
Springfield Road	B3-C3
Station Road	C3
Station Way	C3-D3
Stonefield Close	C2
Sullington Hill	C1
Sunnymead	C4
Sylvan Road	F1
Telford Place	D3
The Boulevard	C4-D4
The Broadway	C3-C4

The Chase	F2
The Dingle	A4
The Glade	F1-F2
The Link	B4-C4
Theydon Close	F2
Three Bridges Road	D3-E3-E4-F4
Tilgate Drive	F1-F2-F3
Town Barn Road	B4
Town Mead	C4
Victoria Road	B3
Wakehurst Drive	C1
Waterlea	F2
Weald Drive	F1-F2
West Street	B2-B3-C3
Westfield Road	A3
West Green Drive	B4-B3-C3
Woodfield Road	D4

Horsham

Albion Way	A2-B2
Angus Road	B4
Arthur Street	C1
Bartellot Road	B1-B2
Bedford Road	C1
Bishopric	A2
Blunts Way	A3
Brighton Road	C1
Burford Road	C2-C3
Cambridge Road	C1-C2
Carfax	A2-B2
Cedar Close	A3
Clarence Road	C1-C2
Denne Parade	B1
Denne Road	A1-B1
Depot Road	C3
Devonshire Road	C2
East Street	B1
Foundry Lane	C3-C4
Gladstone Road	C3
Gorings Mead	C1
Hurst Avenue	B3-B4-C4
Hurst Close	B3-C3
Hurst Road	B4-B3-C3
Kempshott Road	A4
Livingstone Road	B1-C1
London Road	A2-B2
Market Square	A1-B1-B2
Mill Bay Lane	A1
Milnwood Road	A4
Moon Lane	C1
New Street	C1-C2
Newlands Road	A4
Norfolk Road	B2
North Parade	A3-A4-B4
North Street	B2-C2-C3
Oxford Road	C2
Park Street	B1-B2
Park Terrace West	B1-B2
Parkfield	B4
Percy Road	A3
Queen Street	B1-C1
Queenway	B1
Richmond Road	B4
Rushams Road	A2-A3
South Street	A1
Spencers Road	A3-A4
Springfield Crescent	A2-A3
Springfield Road	A2
Springfield Park Road	A2
Station Road	C2-C3

Swindon Road	A4
The Causeway	A1
Trafalgar Road	A3-A4
Victory Road	A3-A4
West Parade	A4
West Street	A2
Wimblehurst Road	B4
Winterton Court	C2

Horley

Albert Road	B3-B4
Avenue Gardens	C2
Balcombe Gardens	C2
Balcombe Road	B4-B3-C3-C2-C1
Bayhorne Lane	C1
Blundell Avenue	A4
Bremner Avenue	A4
Brighton Road	A2-A3-B3-B4
Castle Drive	C2
Charlesfield Road	A4
Chequers Drive	B4
Cheyne Walk	A2-B2
Church Road	A2-A3-B3
Court Lodge Road	A3
Crescent Way	A2-B2-B1
Fairfield Avenue	B1-B2
Grove Road	A4
Haroldslea Drive	A4
Hatchgate	C2
Hevers Avenue	A4-B4
High Street	B3
Horley Row	A4-B4
Langshott Road	C3-C4
Lee Street	A4
Limes Avenue	C2
London Road	A2-A1-B1
Longbridge Road	A2
Lumley Road	B3-B4
Manor Drive	A3
Massetts Road	A2-B2-B3
Michael Crescent	B1-B2
Oakwood Road	B3-B4
Oldfield Road	A2
Parkway	B3
Queens Road	B3
Ringley Avenue	B2-B3
Riverside	A1-B1
Russells Crescent	B2
Sangers Drive	A3
Silverlea Gardens	C2-C3
Smallfield Road	C3
Smallmead	C3
Southlands Avenue	A4-B4
Station Approach	B2
Station Road	B2-B3
The Avenue	A2
The Crescent	B1
The Drive	B1-B2
The Grove	B2-B3
The Meadway	C3-C4
The Ridgeway	B1
Upfield	B1-B2
Vicarage Lane	A3-A4
Victoria Road	A3-B3-B2-C2
Wheatfield Way	C3-C4
Wolverton Gardens	A2
Yattendon Road	B3

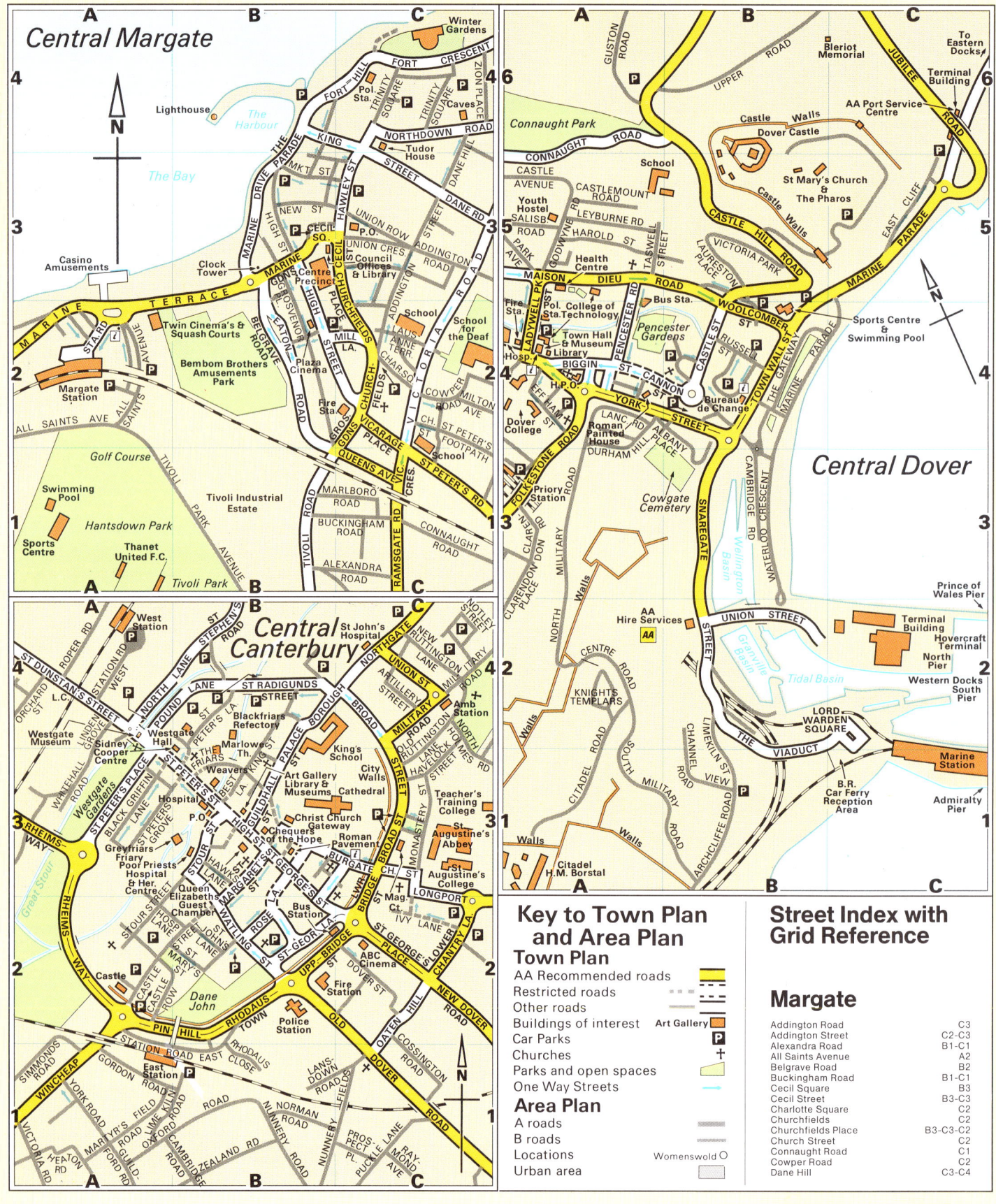

Key to Town Plan and Area Plan

Town Plan

AA Recommended roads	
Restricted roads	
Other roads	
Buildings of interest	Art Gallery
Car Parks	P
Churches	+
Parks and open spaces	
One Way Streets	

Area Plan

A roads	
B roads	
Locations	Womenswold O
Urban area	

Street Index with Grid Reference

Margate

Addington Road	C3
Addington Street	C2-C3
Alexandra Road	B1-C1
All Saints Avenue	A2
Belgrave Road	B2
Buckingham Road	B1-C1
Cecil Square	B3
Cecil Street	B3-C3
Charlotte Square	C2
Churchfields	C2
Churchfields Place	B3-C3-C2
Church Street	C2
Connaught Road	C1
Cowper Road	C2
Dane Hill	C3-C4

Dover

Travellers tend to rush through Dover – it is one of the busiest passenger ports in England – and by so doing miss an exciting town with much of interest. Outstanding is the castle. Its huge fortifications have guarded the town since the 12th century, but within its walls are even older structures – a Saxon church and a Roman lighthouse called the Pharos. In the town itself, the town hall is housed within the walls of a 13th-century guest house called the Maison Dieu. The Roman Painted House in New Street consists of substantial remains of a Roman town house and include the best-preserved Roman wall paintings north of the Alps.

Canterbury is one of Britain's most historic towns. It is the seat of the Church in England, and has been so since St Augustine began his mission here in the 6th century. The cathedral is a priceless work of art containing many other works of art, including superb displays of medieval carving and stained glass. Ancient city walls – partly built on Roman foundations – still circle parts of the city, and a wealth of grand public buildings as well as charming private houses of many periods line the maze of lanes in the shadow of the cathedral.

Margate and **Ramsgate** both grew as commercial ports, but for many years they have specialised in catering for holidaymakers who like safe, sandy beaches and excellent facilities.

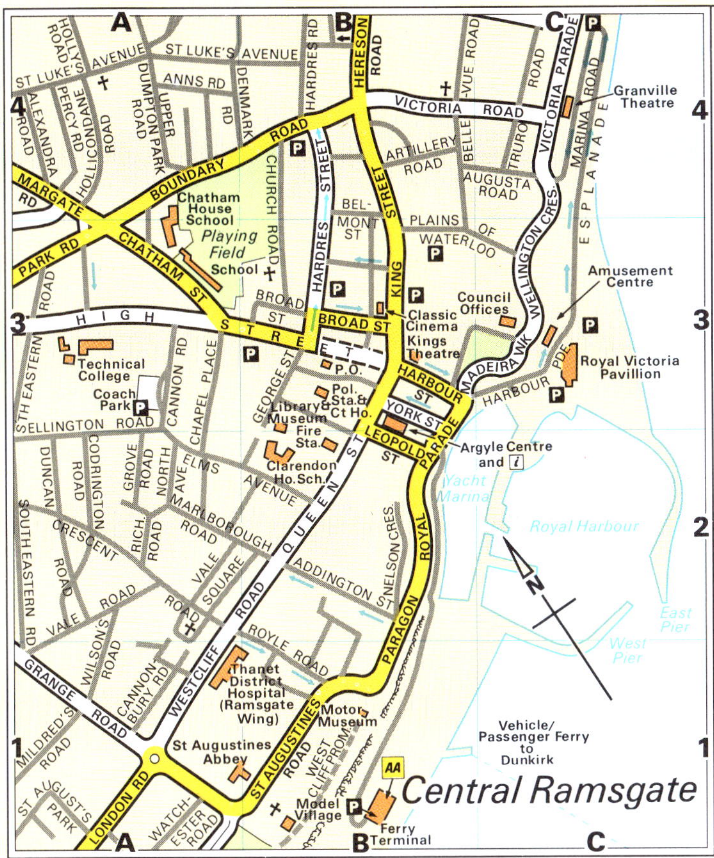

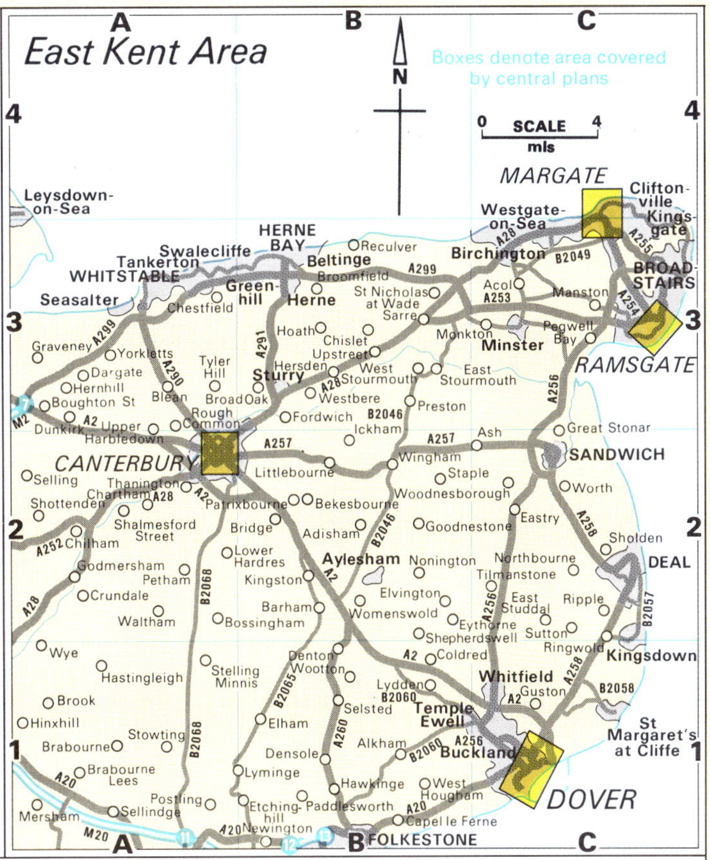

Central Ramsgate

Map labels include: ST LUKE'S AVENUE, ANNS RD, VICTORIA ROAD, HERESON ROAD, MARGATE RD, CHATHAM ST, BROAD ST, HIGH STREET, Chatham House School, Playing Field, Technical College, Coach Park, Clarendon Ho. Sch., Thanet District Hospital (Ramsgate Wing), St Augustines Abbey, Motor Museum, Model Village, Ferry Terminal, Library & Museum, Fire Sta., Council Offices, Kings Theatre, Classic Cinema, Granville Theatre, Amusement Centre, Royal Victoria Pavilion, Argyle Centre and i, Yacht Marina, Royal Harbour, East Pier, West Pier, Vehicle/Passenger Ferry to Dunkirk.

East Kent Area

Boxes denote area covered by central plans. SCALE 0–4 mls. Places include: MARGATE, Westgate-on-Sea, Cliftonville, Kingsgate, BROADSTAIRS, RAMSGATE, Minster, SANDWICH, DEAL, Kingsdown, St Margaret's at Cliffe, DOVER, FOLKESTONE, CANTERBURY, WHITSTABLE, HERNE BAY, Seasalter, Leysdown-on-Sea, and many villages.

Central Ramsgate	
Dane Road	C3
Eaton Road	B1-B2-B3
Fort Crescent	C4
Fort Hill	B4-C4
Grosvenor Gardens	C1-C2
Grosvenor Place	B2-B3
Hawley Street	C3
High Street	B3-B2-C2
King Street	B4-C4-C3
Lausanne Terrace	C2
Marine Drive	B3
Marine Gardens	B3
Marine Terrace	A2-A3-B3-B2
Market Street	B3-C3
Marlborough Road	B1-C1
Mill Lane	B2-C2
Milton Avenue	C2
New Street	B3
Northdown Road	C4
Queens Avenue	C1
Ramsgate Road	C1
St Peter's Footpath	C1-C2
St Peter's Road	C1
Station Road	A2
The Parade	B3-B4
Tivoli Park Avenue	A2-A1-B1
Tivoli Road	B1
Trinity Square	C4
Union Crescent	C3
Union Row	C3
Vicarage Crescent	C1
Vicarage Place	C1-C2
Victoria Road	C2-C3
Zion Place	C4

Canterbury

Street	Grid
Artillery Street	C4
Best Lane	B3
Black Griffin Lane	A3
Borough	B4-C4
Broad Street	C4-C3
Burgate	B3-C3
Cambridge Road	A1-B1
Castle Row	A2-B2
Castle Street	A2-B2
Church Street	C3
Cossington Road	C2-C1
Dover Street	C2
Gordon Road	A1-B1
Guildford Road	A1
Guildhall Street	B3
Havelock Street	C3-C4
Hawks Lane	B3
Heaton Road	A1
High Street	B3
Hospital Lane	A2-B2
Ivy Lane	C2
King Street	B3-B4
Lansdown Road	B1-C1
Lime Kiln Road	A1-B1
Linden Grove	A3-A4
Longport	C2-C3
Lower Bridge Street	C2-C3
Lower Chantry Lane	C2
Martyr's Field Road	A1
Military Road	C4
Monastery Street	C3
New Dover Road	C2
New Ruttington Lane	C4
Norman Road	B1
Northgate	C4
North Holmes Road	C4-C3
North Lane	A4-B4
Notley Street	C4
Nunnery Fields	B1-C1
Nunnery Road	B1
Oaten Hill	C1-C2
Old Dover Road	B2-C2-C1
Old Ruttington Lane	C3-C4
Orchard Street	A4
Oxford Road	A1-B1
Palace Street	B3-B4
Pin Hill	A2-B2
Pound Lane	A4-B4
Prospect Place	C1
Puckle Lane	C1
Raymond Avenue	C1
Rheims Way	A2-A3
Rhodaus Town	B1
Roper Road	A4
Rose Lane	B2-B3
St Dunstan's Street	A4
St Georges Lane	A4
St George's Place	C2
St George's Street	B3-B2
St John's Lane	B2
St Margaret's Street	B2-B3
St Mary's Street	A2-B2
St Peters Grove	A3-B3
St Peter's Lane	B4
St Peter's Place	A3
St Peter's Street	A3-B3
St Stephen's Road	B4
St Rudigunds Street	B4
Simmonds Road	A1-A2
Station Road East	A2-A1-B1
Station Road West	A4
Stour Street	A2-A3-B3
The Friars	B3
Union Street	C4
Upper Bridge Street	B2-C2
Victoria Road	A1
Watling Street	B2
Whitehall Road	A3
Wincheap	A1-A2
York Road	A1
Zealand Road	B1

Dover

Street	Grid
Albany Place	A4-B4-B3
Archcliffe Road	B1
Biggin Street	A4
Cambridge Road	B3
Cannon Street	A4-B4
Castle Avenue	A5
Castle Hill Road	B5
Castlemount Road	A5
Castle Street	B4
Centre Road	A2
Channel View Road	B1-B2
Citadel Road	A1-A2
Clarendon Place	A2-A3
Clarendon Road	A3
Connaught Road	A5-A6
Durham Hill	A3-A4
East Cliff	C5
Effingham Street	A2-A3
Folkestone Road	A3-A4
Godwyne Road	A5
Guston Road	A6
Harold Street	A5
Jubilee Road	C6
Knights Templars	A2
Ladywell Park Road	A4-A5
Lancaster Road	A4
Laureston Place	B5
Leyburne Road	A5
Limekiln Street	B1-B2
Lord Warden Square	C1-C2
Maison Dieu Road	A5-B5
Marine Parade	B4-C4-C5
North Military Road	A2-A3
Park Avenue	A5
Pencester Road	A4-A5
Russell Street	B4
Salisbury Road	A5
Snargate Street	B2-B3
South Military Road	A2-A1-B1
The Gateway	B4
The Viaduct	B1-B2
Taswell Street	A5
Town Hall Street	B4
Union Street	B2
Upper Road	A6-B6
Victoria Park	B5
Woolcomber Street	B4
York Street	A4-B4

Ramsgate

Street	Grid
Addington Street	B2
Alexandra Road	A4
Anns Road	A4
Artillery Road	B4
Augusta Road	B4-C4
Belle Vue Road	B4
Belmont Street	B4
Boundary Road	A3-A4-B4
Broad Street	B3
Cannonbury Road	A1
Canon Road	A3
Chapel Place	A2-A3
Chatham Street	A3
Church Road	B3-B4
Codrington Road	A2
Crescent Road	A2
Denmark Road	A4-B4
Duncan Road	A2
Ellington Road	A2-A3
Elms Avenue	A2-B2
Esplanade	C3-C4
George Street	B3
Grange Road	A1
Grove Road	A2
Harbour Parade	B3-C3
Harbour Street	B3
Hardres Street	B3-B4
Hereson Road	B4
High Street	A3-B3
Hollicondane Road	A4
Holly Road	A4
King Street	B3-B4
Leopold Street	B2-B3
London Road	A1
Madeira Walk	B3-C3
Margate Road	A3-A4
Marina Road	C4
Marlborough Road	A2-B2
Mildred's Road	A1
Nelson Crescent	B2
North Avenue	A2
Paragon Royal Parade	B1-B2-B3
Park Road	A3
Percy Road	A4
Plains of Waterloo	B3-C3
Queen Street	B2-B3
Richmond Road	A2
Royle Road	A2-B2-B1
St Augustines Road	A1-B1
St August's Park	A1
St Luke's Avenue	A4-B4
South Eastern Road	A1-A2-A3
Truro Road	C4
Upper Dumpton Park Road	A1-A2
Vale Road	A1-A2
Vale Square	A2-B2
Victoria Parade	C4
Victoria Road	B4-C4
Watchester Road	A1
Wellington Crescent	C3-C4
West Cliff Promenade	B1
Westcliff Road	A1-A2-B2
Wilson's Road	A1-A2
York Street	B2-B3

DOVER

The famous White Cliffs of Dover provide exhilarating coastal walks with views out across the Channel. Paths to the north-east lead to Walmer and to the south-east, to Folkestone.

Central Eastbourne

Eastbourne Area

Box denotes area covered by central plan

mls 0 SCALE 2

Eastbourne

Magnificent flower displays along the promenade combine with parks and gardens to provide a dazzling spectacle of colour from spring to autumn for this resort, which is one of the largest on the south coast and lies in the shelter of dramatic Beachy Head. Major sporting events take place throughout the year, including International and Championship tennis; on the

cultural side, Eastbourne's Towner Art Gallery, Lifeboat Museum and Redoubt Fortress are all worth visiting. The town also offers good shopping and a wide choice of theatres and cinemas. For children, the imaginative Playcentre is designed with paddling pools, slides and big models of jungle animals.

Seaford boasts a three mile long promenade, which leads down to the seashore and to the Martello Tower (at the eastern end of the Esplanade) which

houses the local museum. From Seaford Head a breathtaking view can be had of the coastline and the Seven Sisters, a line of cliffs stretching out along the shoreline. Between Cuckmere River and Seaford Head, a nature reserve supports a wide variety of plant and bird life.

Hailsham and ropemaking have gone together since the early 19th century, and another long-standing feature of the town is its cattle market, which has been operating on the same site since 1868.

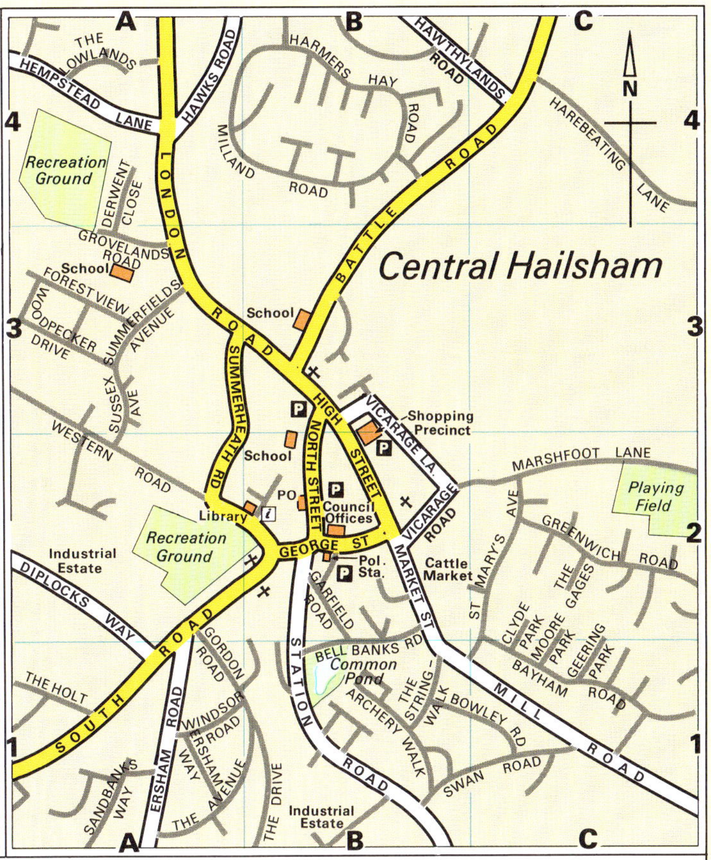

Key to Town Plan and Area Plan

Town Plan

A A Recommended roads
Other roads
Restricted roads
Buildings of interest
Car Parks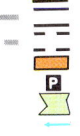
Parks and open spaces
One way streets

Area Plan

A roads
B roads
Locations   Ripe O
Urban Area

Street Index with Grid Reference

Eastbourne

Arundel Road	B2-C2-C3
Ashburnham Road	B3-C3
Ashford Road	C2-D2
Astaire Avenue	D4
Avondale Road	D3
Baldwin Avenue	A3-A4
Beach Road	E3
Bedfordwell Road	C3-D3
Belmore Road	D2
Beverington Road	A4-B4
Blackwater Road	C1-D1
Bourne Street	D2
Burton Road	B3-B4
Carew Road	B3-C3
Carlisle Road	C1-D1
Cavendish Avenue	D2-D3
Cavendish Place	D1-D2
Channel View Road	E3-E4
Church Street	A2-B2
Churchdale Road	D4-E4
Cobbold Avenue	A4

Compton Drive	A1
Compton Place Road	B2-B1-C1
Devonshire Place	D1
Dittons Road	B2-C2
East Dean Road	A2
Eldon Road	A3-B3
Enys Road	C2-C3
Firle Road	D2-D3
Furness Road	C1
Gildredge Road	C1-C2
Grand Parade	D1
Green Street	A2-A3
Grove Road	C1-C2
Hardwick Road	C1-D1
Hartfield Road	C2-C3
High Street	B2
Hurst Road	B3-B4
Kinfauns Avenue	D4
King's Avenue	B3-B4
King's Drive	B4-C4-C3
Latimer Road	E2-E3-E4
Lewes Road	C3
Lismore Road	D1-D2
Longland Road	A2-A3
Lottbridge Drive	E4-F4
Meads Road	B1-C1
Mill Gap Road	C2-C3
Mill Road	B3
Milton Road	A3
Marine Parade	D1-D2-E2
Motcombe Road	A2-A3-B3
Moy Avenue	D3-D4
Myrtle Road	E4-F4
Northbourne Road	E4
Northiam Road	A3
Ocklynge Road	B2-B3
Paradise Drive	A1-B1-B2
Pashley Road	A1-A2
Prideaux Avenue	B3-C3
Prideaux Road	C3
Ringwood Road	D4-D3-E3
Rodmill Drive	B4
Rodmill Road	B3-B4
Roselands Avenue	D4-E4-E3
Royal Parade	E2-E3-F3-F4
St Anne's Road	B3-C3-C2
St Leonard's Road	C2-D2
St Phillip's Avenue	D3-D4-E4
Saffrons Road	B2-C2-C1
Seaside	D2-E2-E3-E4
Selwyn Road	B3-B2-C2
Sidley Road	E3-E4
South Street	C1
Southbourne Road	D4-E4
Southfields Road	C2
Stuart Avenue	A1-A2
Susan's Road	D2
The Avenue	C2
The Goffs	B2
Trinity Trees	D1-D2
Upper Avenue	C2-D2-D3
Upperton Road	B2-C2
Vicarage Drive	A2
Vicarage Road	A2-B2
Victoria Drive	A2-A3-A4
Wartling Road	E4
Watts Lane	B3
Whitley Road	D3-E3
Willingdon Road	A4-B4-B3
Woodgate Road	D4-D3-E3

Seaford

Alfriston Road	B4-C4
Arundel Road	C3-C4
Avondale Road	A2-B2-A3
Blatchington Hill	A3
Blatchington Road	A2-A3
Bramber Road	B2-C2
Broad Street	A2-B2
Brooklyn Road	A2
Buckland Road	A4
Chichester Road	A2
Church Street	A2-A1-B1
Chyngton Road	C2
Claremont Road	A2
Cliff Close	C1
Cliff Road	C1
Clinton Place	A2
College Road	B1-C1
Cornfield Road	B2-B3
Corsica Close	C1-C2
Corsica Road	C1-C2
Cricketfield Road	B1-C1
Croft Lane	B2
Crooked Lane	B2
Dane Road	A1
Downs Road	B3-C3
Downsview Road	B3-C3
East Street	B2
East Albany Road	B3
Eastbourne Road	C4
Esher Close	A4
Esplanade	A1-B1-C1
Fitzgerald Avenue	C1-C2
Gildredge Road	B3
Glebe Drive	A3
Green Lane	A1
Grove Road	B2-B3
Hartfield Road	B3-C3-C4
Haven Brow	B4
Head Road	B3
Headland Avenue	C2-C3
Heathfield Road	C3-B3-B2-C2
High Street	B1-B2
Homefield Road	A3-A4
Kendale Road	A2-A3
Lions Place	C2
Lower Road	A4
Marine Crescent	B1
Marison Road	B4-C4
Mason Road	A4
Middle Furlong	B2-B3
Milldown Road	B3
North Camp Lane	A4
North Way	A4
Pelham Road	A1
Ridgeway	A4
Ringmer Road	B1
Rose Walk	A3
Rother Road	C2-C3
St Peter's Road	A2
Salisbury Road	A2
Sandore Road	B4-C4
Saxon Lane	B1
Sherwood Road	A3-A4
Southdown Road	B3-C3-C2
Stafford Road	A2-A3-B3
Station Approach	A1-A2
Steyne Road	B1-B2-C2
Sutton Avenue	C2-C3

Sutton Drove	A3-B3-B4-C4
Sutton Road	A2-B2-B3-B4-C4
Sutton Park Road	A2-B2
Upper Belgrave Road	A3-A4
Upper Sherwood Road	A4-B4
Vale Road	A3-B3-B4
Valley Rise	A4
West Street	A1
West View	A1-B1

Hailsham

Archery Walk	B1
Battle Road	B3-B4-C4
Bayham Road	C1-C2
Bell Banks Road	B1-B2
Bowley Road	B1-C1
Clyde Park	C1-C2
Derwent Close	A3-A4
Diplocks Way	A1-A2
Ersham Road	A1
Ersham Way	A1
Forest View	A3
Garfield Road	B2
Geering Park	C1-C2
George Street	B2
Gordon Road	A1-A2
Greenwich Road	C2
Grovelands Road	A3
Harebeating Lane	C4
Harmers Hay Road	B4
Hawks Road	A4
Hawthylands Road	B4-C4
Hempstead Lane	A4
High Street	B2-B3
London Road	A4-A3-B3
Market Street	B1-B2
Marshfoot Lane	C3
Mill Road	B1-C1
Milland Road	A4-B4
Moore Park	C1-C2
North Street	B2-B3
St Mary's Avenue	C1-C2
Sandbanks Way	A1
South Road	A1-A2-B2
Station Road	B1-B2
Summerfields Avenue	A3
Summerheath Road	A2-A3-B3-B2
Sussex Avenue	A2-A3
Swan Road	B1-C1
The Avenue	A1-B1
The Drive	B1
The Gages	C2
The Lowlands	A4
The Holt	A1
The Stringwalk	B1
Vicarage Lane	B2-B3
Vicarage Road	B2-C2
Western Road	A2-A3
Windsor Road	A1
Woodpecker Drive	A3

Exeter

The cathedral is Exeter's greatest treasure. Founded in 1050, but rebuilt by the Normans during the 12th century and again at the end of the 13th century, it has many beautiful and outstanding features – especially the exquisite rib-vaulting of the nave. Most remarkable, perhaps, is the fact that it still stood after virtually everything around it was flattened during bombing raids in World War II.

There are still plenty of reminders of Old Exeter, which has been a city since Roman times. Roman and medieval walls encircle parts of the city; 14th-century underground passages can be explored; the Guildhall is 15th-century and one of the oldest municipal buildings in the country; and Sir Francis Drake is said to have met his explorer companions at Mol's Coffee House. Exeter is famous for its extensive Maritime Museum, with over 100 boats from all over the world. Other

museums include the Rougemont House and the Royal Albert Memorial Museum and Art Gallery.

Exmouth has a near-perfect position at the mouth of the Exe estuary. On one side it has expanses of sandy beach, on another a wide estuary alive with wildfowl and small boats, while inland is beautiful Devon countryside.

Newton Abbot lies on the River Teign. It is a busy market town and has been an important railway junction since the mid 19th century.

30

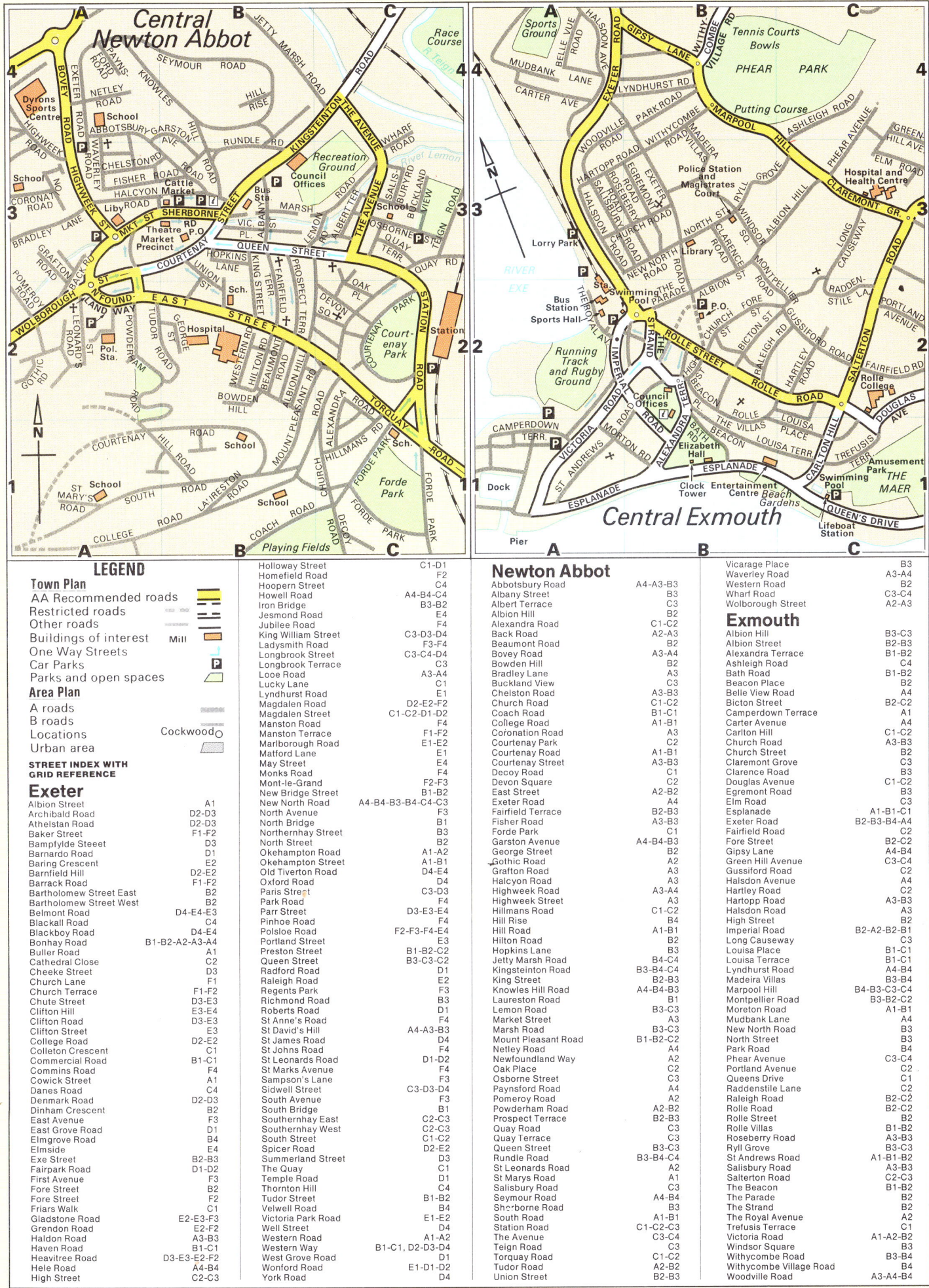

Central Newton Abbot / *Central Exmouth*

LEGEND

Town Plan
- AA Recommended roads
- Restricted roads
- Other roads
- Buildings of interest — Mill
- One Way Streets
- Car Parks — P
- Parks and open spaces

Area Plan
- A roads
- B roads
- Locations — Cockwood
- Urban area

STREET INDEX WITH GRID REFERENCE

Exeter

Albion Street	A1
Archibald Road	D2-D3
Athelstan Road	D2-D3
Baker Street	F1-F2
Bampfylde Steeet	D3
Barnardo Road	D1
Baring Crescent	E2
Barnfield Hill	D2-E2
Barrack Road	F1-F2
Bartholomew Street East	B2
Bartholomew Street West	B2
Belmont Road	D4-E4-E3
Blackall Road	C4
Blackboy Road	D4-E4
Bonhay Road	B1-B2-A2-A3-A4
Buller Road	A1
Cathedral Close	C2
Cheeke Street	D3
Church Lane	F1
Church Terrace	F1-F2
Chute Street	D3-E3
Clifton Hill	E3-E4
Clifton Road	D3-E3
Clifton Street	E3
College Road	D2-E2
Colleton Crescent	C1
Commercial Road	B1-C1
Commins Road	F4
Cowick Street	A1
Danes Road	C4
Denmark Road	D2-D3
Dinham Crescent	B2
East Avenue	F3
East Grove Road	D1
Elmgrove Road	B4
Elmside	E4
Exe Street	B2-B3
Fairpark Road	D1-D2
First Avenue	F3
Fore Street	B2
Fore Street	F2
Friars Walk	C1
Gladstone Road	E2-E3-F3
Grendon Road	E2-F2
Haldon Road	A3-B3
Haven Road	B1-C1
Heavitree Road	D3-E3-E2-F2
Hele Road	A4-B4
High Street	C2-C3

Holloway Street	C1-D1
Homefield Road	F2
Hoopern Street	C4
Howell Road	A4-B4-C4
Iron Bridge	B3-B2
Jesmond Road	E4
Jubilee Road	F4
King William Street	C3-D3-D4
Ladysmith Road	F3-F4
Longbrook Street	C3-C4-D4
Longbrook Terrace	C3
Looe Road	A3-A4
Lucky Lane	C1
Lyndhurst Road	E1
Magdalen Road	D2-E2-F2
Magdalen Street	C1-C2-D1-D2
Manston Road	F4
Manston Terrace	F1-F2
Marlborough Road	E1-E2
Matford Lane	E1
May Street	E4
Monks Road	F4
Mont-le-Grand	F2-F3
New Bridge Street	B1-B2
New North Road	A4-B4-B3-B4-C4-C3
North Avenue	F3
North Bridge	B1
Northernhay Street	B3
North Street	B2
Okehampton Road	A1-A2
Okehampton Street	A1-B1
Old Tiverton Road	D4-E4
Oxford Road	D4
Paris Street	C3-D3
Park Road	F4
Parr Street	D3-E3-E4
Pinhoe Road	F4
Polsloe Road	F2-F3-F4-E4
Portland Street	E3
Preston Street	B1-B2-C2
Queen Street	B3-C3-C2
Radford Road	D1
Raleigh Road	E2
Regents Park	F3
Richmond Road	B3
Roberts Road	D1
St Anne's Road	F4
St David's Hill	A4-A3-B3
St James Road	D4
St Johns Road	F4
St Leonards Road	D1-D2
St Marks Avenue	F4
Sampson's Lane	F3
Sidwell Street	C3-D3-D4
South Avenue	F3
South Bridge	B1
Southernhay East	C2-C3
Southernhay West	C2-C3
South Street	C1-C2
Spicer Road	D2-E2
Summerland Street	D3
The Quay	C1
Temple Road	D1
Thornton Hill	C4
Tudor Street	B1-B2
Velwell Road	B4
Victoria Park Road	E1-E2
Well Street	D4
Western Road	A1-A2
Western Way	B1-C1, D2-D3-D4
West Grove Road	D1
Wonford Road	E1-D1-D2
York Road	D4

Newton Abbot

Abbotsbury Road	A4-A3-B3
Albany Street	B3
Albert Terrace	C3
Albion Hill	B2
Alexandra Road	C1-C2
Back Road	A2-A3
Beaumont Road	B2
Bovey Road	A3-A4
Bowden Hill	B2
Bradley Lane	A3
Buckland View	C3
Chelston Road	A3-B3
Church Road	C1-C2
Coach Road	B1-C1
College Road	A1-B1
Coronation Road	A3
Courtenay Park	C2
Courtenay Road	A1-B1
Courtenay Street	A3-B3
Decoy Road	C1
Devon Square	C2
East Street	A2-B2
Exeter Road	A4
Fairfield Terrace	B2-B3
Fisher Road	A3-B3
Forde Park	C1
Garston Avenue	A4-B4-B3
George Street	B2
Gothic Road	A2
Grafton Road	A3
Halcyon Road	A3
Highweek Road	A3-A4
Highweek Street	A3
Hillmans Road	C1-C2
Hill Rise	B4
Hill Road	A1-B1
Hilton Road	B2
Hopkins Lane	B3
Jetty Marsh Road	B4-C4
Kingsteinton Road	B3-B4-C4
King Street	B2-B3
Knowles Hill Road	A4-B4-B3
Laureston Road	B1
Lemon Road	B3-C3
Market Street	A3
Marsh Road	B3-C3
Mount Pleasant Road	B1-B2-C2
Netley Road	A4
Newfoundland Way	A2
Oak Place	C2
Osborne Street	C3
Paynsford Road	A4
Pomeroy Road	A2
Powderham Road	A2-B2
Prospect Terrace	B2-B3
Quay Road	C3
Quay Terrace	C3
Queen Street	B3-C3
Rundle Road	B3-B4-C4
St Leonards Road	A2
St Marys Road	A1
Salisbury Road	C3
Seymour Road	A4-B4
Sherborne Road	B3
South Road	A1-B1
Station Road	C1-C2-C3
The Avenue	C3-C4
Teign Road	C3
Torquay Road	C1-C2
Tudor Road	A2-B2
Union Street	B2-B3

Vicarage Place	B3
Waverley Road	A3-A4
Western Road	B2
Wharf Road	C3-C4
Wolborough Street	A2-A3

Exmouth

Albion Hill	B3-C3
Albion Street	B2-B3
Alexandra Terrace	B1-B2
Ashleigh Road	C4
Bath Road	B1-B2
Beacon Place	B2
Belle View Road	A4
Bicton Street	B2-C2
Camperdown Terrace	A1
Carter Avenue	A4
Carlton Hill	C1-C2
Church Road	A3-B3
Church Street	B2
Claremont Grove	C3
Clarence Road	B3
Douglas Avenue	C1-C2
Egremont Road	C2
Elm Road	C3
Esplanade	A1-B1-C1
Exeter Road	B2-B3-B4-A4
Fairfield Road	C2
Fore Street	B2-C2
Gipsy Lane	A4-B4
Green Hill Avenue	C3-C4
Gussiford Road	C2
Halsdon Avenue	A4
Hartley Road	C2
Hartopp Road	A3-B3
Halsdon Road	A3
High Street	B2
Imperial Road	B2-A2-B2-B1
Long Causeway	C3
Louisa Place	B1-C1
Louisa Terrace	B1-C1
Lyndhurst Road	A4-B4
Madeira Villas	B3-B4
Marpool Hill	B4-B3-C3-C4
Montpellier Road	B3-B2-C2
Moreton Road	A1-B1
Mudbank Lane	A4
New North Road	B3
North Street	B3
Park Road	B4
Phear Avenue	C3-C4
Portland Avenue	C2
Queens Drive	C1
Raddenstile Lane	C2
Raleigh Road	B2-C2
Rolle Road	B2-C2
Rolle Street	B2
Rolle Villas	B1-B2
Roseberry Road	A3-B3
Ryll Grove	B3-C3
St Andrews Road	A1-B1-B2
Salisbury Road	A3-B3
Salterton Road	C2-C3
The Beacon	B1-B2
The Parade	B2
The Strand	B2
The Royal Avenue	A2
Trefusis Terrace	C1
Victoria Road	A1-A2-B2
Windsor Square	B3
Withycombe Road	B3-B4
Withycombe Village Road	B4
Woodville Road	A3-A4-B4

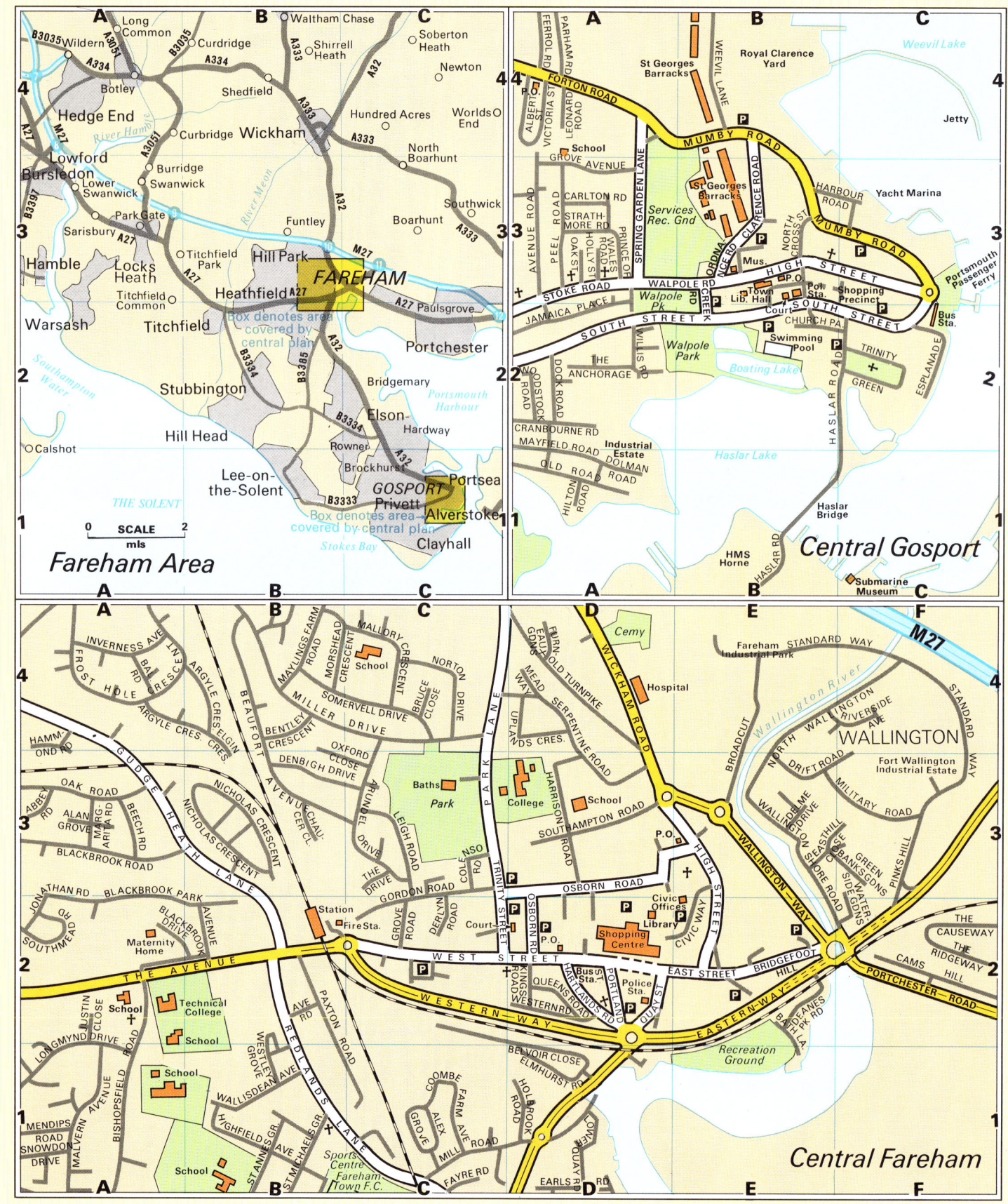

Fareham Area

SCALE
0   1   2
mls

Central Gosport

Central Fareham

Fareham

Naval connections have long been a feature of this old market town. A large number of its residents work at the Naval Base in Portsmouth, naval training establishment HMS Collingwood stands on the town's outskirts, and its pre-19th century importance as a boat-building centre is being recaptured today with the manufacture of small sailing craft.

The trade is centred mainly around the Lower Quay on Fareham Creek (which flows virtually into the town centre), and buildings used as a hospital for French prisoners during the Napoleonic Wars can also be seen in this part of town. The High Street has retained a distinctly Georgian flavour; neighbouring West Street reflects Fareham's popularity as a shopping centre and has seen a good deal of development.

Gosport is another town whose trade has always

been associated with the needs of the navy. Lying on the west side of Portsmouth Harbour and a major naval port since the 17th century, Gosport has probably the most extensive areas of military and naval housing in the country. HM Submarine Alliance, which houses a submarine museum, can be seen in Haslar Creek, and also of interest are Gosport Museum, 19th-century Fort Brockhurst, and the parish church, which dates from the 17th century and has an almost unchanged interior.

HM Submarine Alliance and Submarine Museum

Gosport's history as a submarine base goes back almost as far as submarines themselves, so this is a fitting home for the Royal Navy Submarine Museum and HM Submarine Alliance.

Submarines have come a long way since the days when a disgruntled Controller of the Navy said that "submariners should be hanged as pirates in wartime". In spite of early Admiralty misgivings, these sleek but lethal underwater travellers are the frontrunners of the Royal Navy today.

At the Submarine Museum in Gosport's Haslar Creek, visitors can see just how submarines have developed to become a crucial part of the modern fleet. Centrepiece of the museum is HM Submarine Alliance, which was intended for use in World War II but not ready in time to take part in any engagements. On her 'retirement' from service, she was presented to the Submarine Museum, and has been completely restored and raised up out of the water for easy access. Visitors enter through doors which have been cut in the pressure hull, and can walk right through the vessel. On the way, they are given a feel of the life and work of the submariners of World War II and they can also explore a more modern side to submarining, by looking at the new equipment which has been installed here. Guides are on hand to explain the functions of the various compartments, and to answer questions.

A recent arrival at the museum is HM Submarine Holland I — Britain's first submarine, newly salvaged from the seabed after the unlikely reprieve of sinking on her way to the breaker's yard. Named after her inventor John Philip Holland, she was launched in 1901, but has the porpoise-hull profile of the most up-to-date nuclear versions.

In the main body of the museum, models of all varieties of submarine are on display, coming right up to the advanced nuclear versions of today. Models featured in this section include HM Submarine Conqueror, while representing an earlier period in submarine development is the 1776 Turtle, built for American revolutionaries to launch an (unsuccessful) attack on Admiral Lord Howe's flagship in New York Harbour.

Visitors are advised to give themselves at least an hour and a half in order to do justice to all the museum has to offer, and to allow longer at busy times like the summer.

OPENING TIMES The Museum is open all year round, from 9.30am to 4.30pm, every day except Christmas Eve and Christmas Day.

TO GET THERE See town plan **Gosport**, grid squares B1 and C1. Cross Haslar Bridge and then turn left off Haslar Road. From here follow signs to the Submarine Museum.

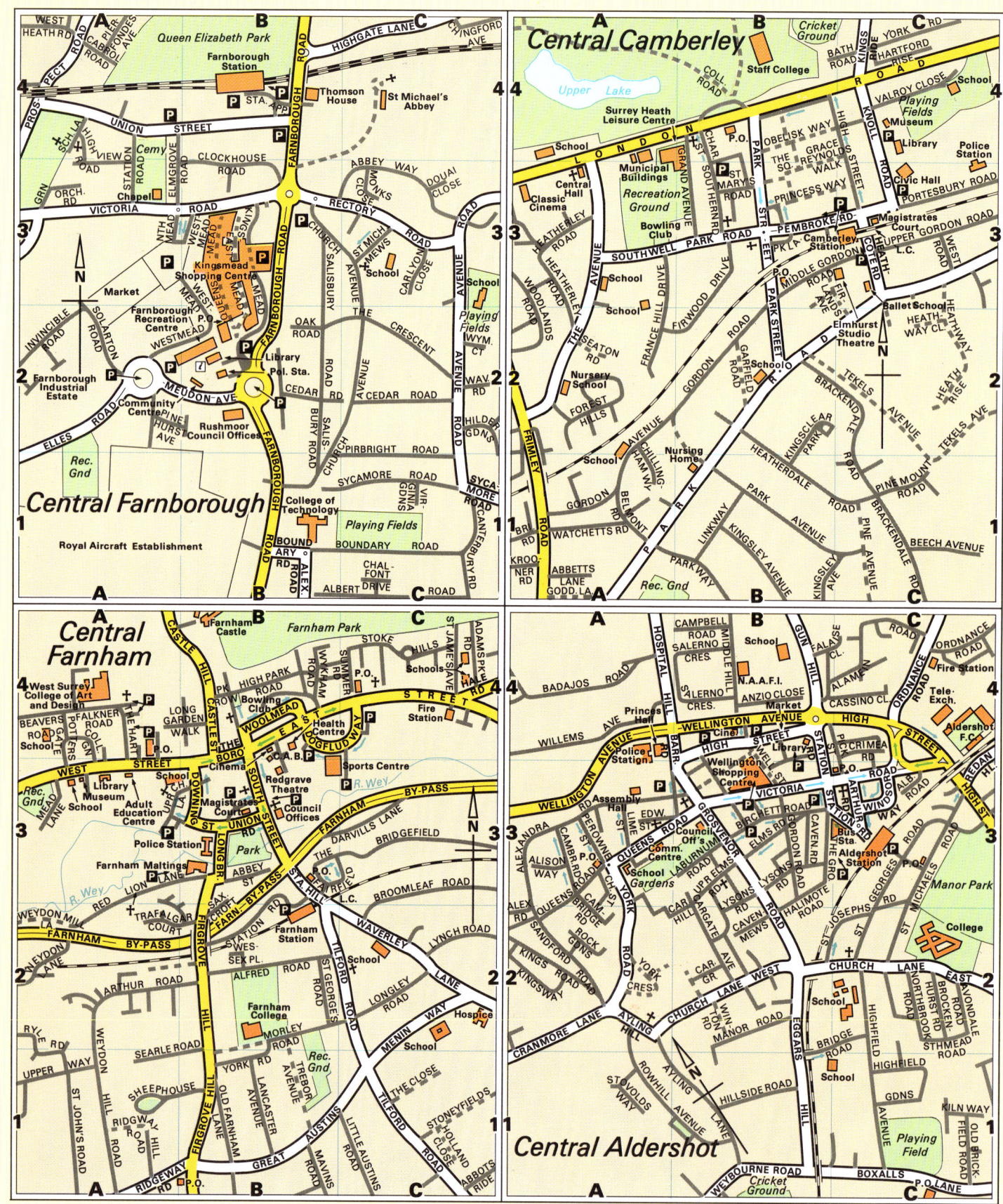

Farnborough

Dick Turpin is said to have been associated with Farnborough's Tumbledown Dick inn and the Ship Inn was once used by patrons of illegal prize fights — but today the town is synonymous with the high technology of aeronautical research, and with the army. This is the scene of the biennial Farnborough Air Show, and the town's growth really began in the mid-19th century, when large numbers of military personnel were moved into the area.

Aldershot is the appropriate home of the Wellington Monument, which was moved here from London's Hyde Park Corner in 1885. It stands near the 19th-century Royal Garrison Church — another symbol of Aldershot's military importance since the Army arrived here in 1885 and instigated the town's expansion. Every two years in June the Army Display is held in the Rushmoor Arena and in 1969, the Army combined with the council to found the Stainforth Ski Centre.

Camberley is mainly a residential town, close to the Royal Staff College and the Royal Military Academy at Sandhurst.

Farnham is the home of the thriving Redgrave Theatre, and its cultural life is also served by the Maltings, an Adult Education and community centre. Much of Farnham's character as an 18th-century market town has been retained, and the castle dates back to the 12th century.

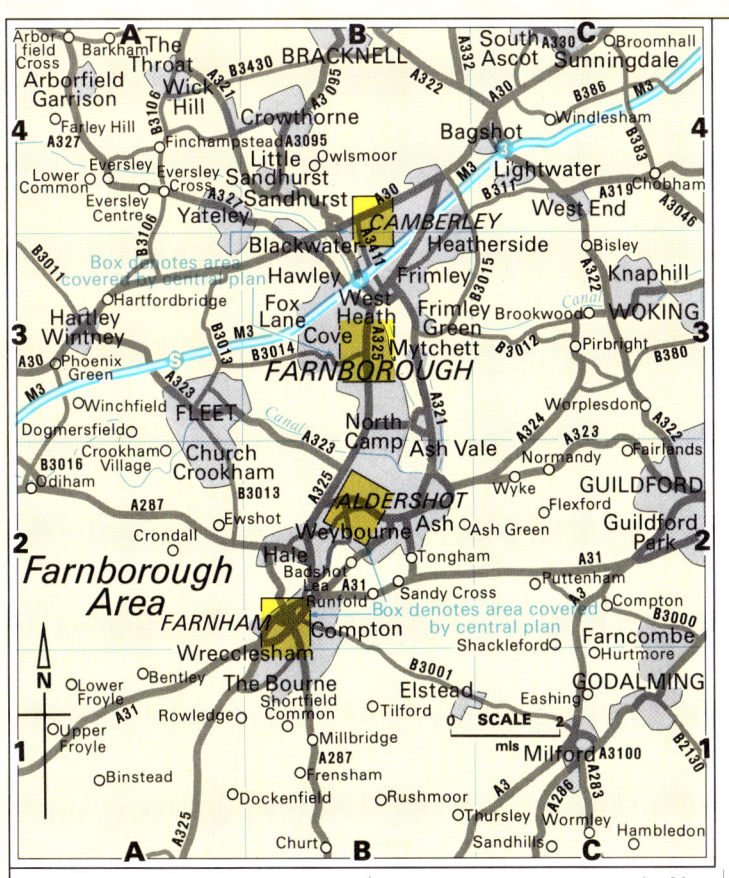

Key to Town Plan and Area Plan

Town Plan

AA Recommended roads
Other roads
Restricted roads
Buildings of interest   Cinema
Car Parks
Parks and open spaces
One Way Streets

Area Plan

A roads
B roads
Locations   Elstead○
Urban area

Street Index with Grid Reference

Farnborough

Abbey Way	B3-C3
Albert Road	B1-C1
Alexandra Road	B1
Avenue Road	C1-C2-C3
Boundary Road	B1-C1
Cabrol Road	A4
Canterbury Road	C1
Carlyon Close	C3
Cedar Road	B2-C2
Chalfont Drive	C1
Chingford Avenue	C4
Church Avenue	B1-B2-C2-C3-B3
Clockhouse Road	A3-B3
Eastmead	B2-B3
Elles Road	A1-A2
Elmgrove Road	A3-A4
Farnborough Road	B1-B2-B3-B4
Green School Lane	A3
Highgate Lane	B4-C4
Highview Road	A3-A4

Hilder Gardens	C1-C2
Invincible Road	A2
Kingsmead	B2-B3
Meudon Avenue	A2-B2
Monks Close	C3
Northmead	A3
Oak Road	B2
Orchard Road	A3
Pierfondes Avenue	A4
Pinehurst Avenue	A2-B2
Pirbright Road	B1-C1
Prospect Road	A4
Queensmead	B2-B3
Rectory Road	B3-C3
St Michaels Mews	C3
Salisbury Road	B1-B2-B3
Solatron Road	A2-A3
Station Approach	B4
Station Road	A3-A4
Sycamore Road	B1-C1
The Crescent	B2-C2
Union Street	A4-B4
Victoria Road	A3-B3
Virginia Gardens	C1
Waverley Road	C2
West Heath Road	A4
Westmead	A2-B2-B3-A3-B3
Wymering Court	C2

Camberley

Abbetts Lane	A1
Bath Road	B4-C4
Beech Avenue	C1
Belmont Road	A1
Brackendale Road	B2-C2-C1
Bridge Road	A1
Charles Street	B4
Chillingham Way	A1-A2
College Road	A4-B4
Firlands Avenue	B3-C3-C2
Firwood Drive	A2-B2-B3
Forest Hills	A2
France Hill Drive	A2-A3
Frimley Road	A1-A2
Garfield Road	B2
Goddards Lane	A1
Gordon Avenue	A1-A2
Gordon Road	A2-B2-B3
Grace Reynolds Walk	B3-B4-C4
Grand Avenue	B3-B4
Hartford Rise	C4
Heathcote Road	C3

Heatherdale Road	B2-B1-C1
Heatherley Road	A2-A3
Heath Rise	C2
Heathway	C2-C3
Heathway Close	C2
High Street	B4-C4-C3
Kingsclear Park	B1-B2
Kingsley Avenue	B1-C1
Kings Ride	C4
Knoll Road	C3-C4
Krooner Road	A1
Linkway	B1
London Road	A3-A4-B4-C4
Middle Gordon Road	B3-C3
Obelisk Way	B4
Park Avenue	B1-C1
Park Lane	B3
Park Road	A1-B1-B2-C2-C3
Park Street	B2-B3-B4
Parkway	A1-B1
Pembroke Road	B3-C3
Pine Avenue	C1
Pine Mount Road	C1
Portesbury Road	C3
Princes Way	B3-C3
St Mary's Road	B3
Seaton Road	A2
Southern Road	B3
Southwell Park Road	A3-B3
Tekels Avenue	B2-C2-C1-C2
Th Avenue	A2-A3
The Square	B3
Upper Gordon Road	C3
Valroy Close	C4
Watchetts Road	A1
West Road	C3
Woodlands Road	A2-A3
York Road	C4

Farnham

Abbey Street	B3
Abbots Ride	C1
Adams Park Road	C4
Alfred Road	B2
Arthur Road	A2-B2
Beavers Road	A4
Bridgefield	C3
Broomleaf Road	C2-C3
Castle Hill	A4-B4
Castle Street	B4
College Garden	A3-A4
Darvills Lane	B3-C3
Dogflud Way	B4-C4
Downing Street	B3
East Street	B4-C4
Falkner Road	A4
Farnham By-pass	A2-B2-B3-C3
Firgrove Hill	B1-B2-B3
Great Austins	B1-C1
Hale Road	C4
High Park Road	B4
Holland Close	C1
Lancaster Avenue	B1
Little Austins Road	C1
Long Bridge	B3
Long Garden Walk	A4-B4
Longley Road	C2
Lynch Road	C2
Mavins Road	B1
Mead Lane	A3
Menin Way	C1-C2
Morley Road	B1-B2-C2
Old Farnham Lane	B1
Park Row	B4
Potters Gate	A3-A4
Red Lion Lane	A2-A3-B3
Ridgway Hill Road	A1
Ridgway Road	A1-B1
Ryle Road	A1-A2
St George's Road	B2
St James's Avenue	C4
St John's Road	A1
Saxon Croft	B2-B3
Searle Road	A1-B1
Sheephouse	A1-B1
South Street	B3-B4
Station Hill	B2-B3
Station Road	B2-B3-B2-B3
Stoke Hills	C4
Stoneyfields	C1
Summer Road	C4
The Borough	B3-B4
The Close	C1
The Fairfield	B3-C3
The Hart	A3-A4
Tilford Road	B2-C2-C1
Trafalgar Court	A2-B2
Trebor Avenue	B1-B2
Union Road	B3
Upper Church Lane	A3-B3
Upper Way	A1
Waverley Lane	B2-C2
Wessex Place	B2
West Street	A3-B3-B2
Weydon Hill Road	A1-A2
Weydon Lane	A2
Weydon Mill Lane	A2
Woolmead	B4

Wykham Road	B4
York Road	B1-B2

Aldershot

Alamein Road	B4-C4
Albert Road	C3
Alexandra Road	A2-A3-B3
Alison Way	A3
Anzio Close	B4
Arthur Road	C3
Avondale Road	C2
Ayling Hill	A3
Ayling Lane	A2-A1-B1
Badajos Road	A3
Barrack Road	A4-A3-B3-B4
Birchett Road	B3
Boxalls Lane	B1-C1
Bridge Road	B1-B2-C2
Brockenhurst Road	C2
Cambridge Road	A2-A3
Campbell Road	B4
Cargate Avenue	B2-B3
Cargate Grove	B2
Cargate Hill	A2-B2-B3
Cassino Close	B4-C4
Cavendish Mews	B2
Cavendish Road	B3
Church Lane East	B2-C2
Church Lane West	A2-B2
Church Street	A2-A3
Cranmore Lane	A1-A2
Crimea Road	C4
Edward Street	A3-B3
Eggars Hill	B1-B2
Elms Road	B3
Falaise Close	B4-C4
Gordon Road	B3
Grosvenor Road	B2-B3
Gun Hill	B4
Halimote Road	B2-B3
Highfield Avenue	C1-C2
Highfield Gardens	C1
High Street	B4-C4-C3
Hillside Road	B1
Hospital Hill	A4-B4
Kilnway	C1
Kings Road	A2
Kingsway	A2
Laburnum Road	B3
Lime Street	A3
Lysons Road	B2-B3
Manor Road	B2
Middle Hill	B4
Northbrook Road	C2
Old Brickfield Road	C1
Ordnance Road	C4
Perowne Street	A3
Pickford Street	B4-C4-C3
Queens Road	A2-A3-B3
Redan Hill	C3-C4
Rock Gardens	A2
Rowhill Avenue	A2-A1-B1
St Georges Road	C2-C3
St Josephs Road	B2-C2-C3
St Michaels Road	C2-C3
Salerno Crescent	B4
Sandford Road	A2
Southmead Road	C2
Station Road	B4-B3-C3
Stovolds Way	A1
The Grove	B3
Upper Elms Road	B3
Victoria Road	B3-C3-C4
Wellington Avenue	A3-A4-B4
Wellington Street	B3-B4
Weybourne Road	B1
Willems Avenue	A4
Windsor Way	C3
Winton Road	B2
York Crescent	A2
York Road	A2-A3

FARNHAM
Attractive shops and houses line the broad thoroughfare of Castle Street, which is overlooked by the castle itself. Founded in the 12th century, this was once the seat of the bishops of Winchester and of Guildford.

Guildford

Guildford's impressive modern redbrick Anglican cathedral, consecrated in 1961, looks down on the county town of Surrey from its hill-top setting on the outskirts. Nearby are the differently-styled modern buildings of the University of Surrey. Another example of modern architecture is the Yvonne Arnaud Theatre, which opened in 1958 on the banks of the River Wey. Despite being a busy modern shopping centre the town retains many old buildings and its steep, partly-cobbled High Street has an unchanging Georgian character. Most prominent is the Guildhall with its hexagonal bell-turret and gilded clock overhanging the pavement. All that remains of the city's castle, just off the High Street, is the 12th-century keep built by Henry II, but close by the Castle Museum has a comprehensive range of local antiquities.

Godalming An important staging post on the London to Portsmouth road in stagecoach days, this attractive North Downs town still has several old coaching inns as well as a number of other 16th-century buildings. Local artefacts can be found in the Borough Museum.

Woking A residential and commuter town on the disused Basingstoke Canal, Woking developed as a direct result of the arrival of the railway in the 1830s. Its most distinctive feature is its large Mosque, built in 1889.

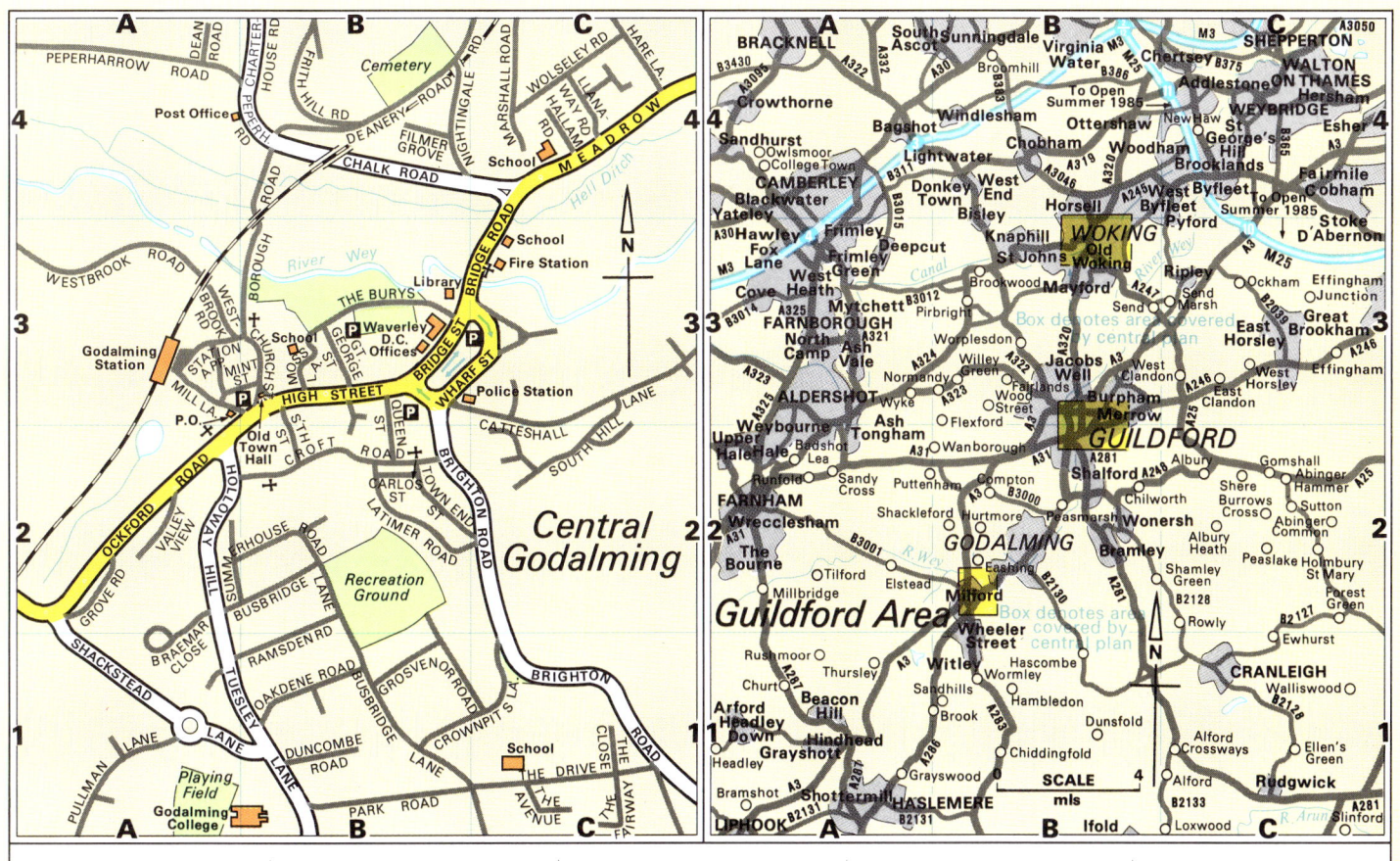

LEGEND

Town Plan

AA recommended route
Restricted roads
Other roads
Buildings of interest Station
Car parks P
Parks and open spaces
One way streets

Area Plan

A roads
B roads
Locations Fairlands ○
Urban area

Street Index with Grid Reference

Guildford

Abbot Road	C1
Addison Road	E2-F2-F1
Albury Road	F2-F3
Aldersey Road	F2-F3
Alexandra Terrace	D3
Artillery Road	B4-C4
Artillery Terrace	C4
Austen Road	E3-F3-F2
Baillie Road	E2-E3
Bedford Road	B2
Bridge Street	B2-B3
Bright Hill	D2
Brodie Road	D2
Buryfields	B1
Bury Street	B1-B2
Castle Hill	C1
Castle Street	C2
Chapel Street	C2
Chertsey Street	C3
Cheselden Road	D2-D3
Chesham Road	E2-E3
Church Road	B3-B4-C4
Clandon Road	D4-E4
Cline Road	E2-F2
College Road	B3-C3
Copper Road	E2
Cranley Road	E4-F4
Cross Lanes	E4-F4-F3-F2
Dapdune Road	B4-C4
Dene Road	D3
Denzil Road	A2-A3

Drummond Road	B4-C4
Eagle Road	C4
Eastgate Gardens	D3
Epsom Road	D3-E3-F3
Falcon Road	C4
Farnham Road	A2-B2
Flower Walk	B1
Foxenden Road	D4
Friary Bridge	A2-B2
Friary Street	B2
George Road	B4-C4
Guildford Park Avenue	A3
Guildford Park Road	A2-A3
Harvey Road	D2-E2-E3
Haydon Place	C3
High Street	B2-C2-D2-D3
Hillier Road	F4
Jenner Road	D2-D3
Laundry Road	B3
Lawn Road	B1
Leapale Lane	C3
Leapale Road	C3
Leas Road	B4
London Road	D3-D4-E4
Lower Edgeborough Road	E4-E3-F3
Ludlow Road	A2-A3
Maori Road	F4-F3
Mareschal Road	A1-A2
Margaret Road	B3-B4
Markenfield Road	B4-C4
Market Street	C2
Martyr Road	C3
Mary Road	B3-B4
Millbrook	B2-C2-C1
Millmead	B1-B2
Millmead Terrace	B1
Mount Pleasant	B1-B2
Mountside	A1
Nightingale Road	D4
North Street	C2-C3
Onslow Road	C4-D4
Onslow Street	B3
Park Road	C4
Park Street	B2
Pewley Bank	D2-E2-E1
Pewley Hill	C2-D2-D1-E1
Pewley Way	D2-E2-E1-F1
Portsmouth Road	B1-B2
Poyle Road	D1
Quarry Street	C2-B3-C3
Queens Road	C4-D4
Rupert Road	A3
Sandfield Terrace	C3
Semaphore Road	D1-D2
South Hill	C2-C1-D1
Springfield Road	D4
Stoke Fields	C4
Stoke Road	C3-C4
Sydenham Road	C2-D2-D3
Sydney Road	E3-F3-E2
Testard Road	A2
The Bars	C3
The Mount	A1-B1-B2
Tunsgate	C2
Upper Edgeborough Road	F2-F3
Upperton Road	A2
Walnut Treet Close	B2-B3-A3-A4
Ward Street	C3
Warren Road	E3-E2-F2
Waterden Road	D3-E3

Watford Close	F4
Wherwell Road	A2
Woodbridge Road	B4-B3-C3-C2
Wodeland Avenue	A1-A2-B2
York Road	B3-C3-C4-D3-D4

Woking

Abbey Road	A3
Arthurs Bridge Road	A3-B4
Ashwood Road	D2-E2
Beaufort Road	F4
Beta Road	F4
Birch Hill	A1
Boundary Road	D4
Bracken Close	D2
Brewery Road	B3-C3-C4
Brooklyn	B1-C1
Broomhill Lane	C4
Broomhill Road	C4
Bulbeggars Lane	A3
Bury Lane	A3-A4
Bylands	D1
Cavendish Road	A1-B1
Cawsey Way	C3
Cherry Street	B2
Chertsey Road	C3-D3-D4
Chobham Road	D2
Church Close	B4
Church Hill	B3-B4
Church Street	C2-C3
Church Street East	C3-D3
Cleardown	E1-E2
Coley Avenue	D2-D3
College Lane	A1
College Road	F4
Commercial Way	C3
Constitution Hill	C1
Courteney Road	D4-E4
Elm Road	A2-A1
East Hill	F3-F4
Fairview Avenue	C1-C2
Ferndale Road	C4
Frailey Hill	F4
Goldsworth Road	A1-A2-B2-C2
Guildford Road	B1-C1-C2
Heathfield Road	E2
Heathside Crescent	C2-D2-D3
Heathside Gardens	D2
Heathside Park Road	C2-D2-E2
Heathside Road	C1-D1-E1
Heathside Road	E2
High Street	A3-B4
High Street	C3
Hill Close	A4
Hill View Road	C2-D2
Hockering Gardens	E2
Hockering Road	E2-F2
Hopfields	B4
Horsell Moor	A3-B3-C3
Horsell Park	B3-B4-C4
Horsell Park Close	B3-B4
Horsell Vale	B4-C4
Ivy Lane	E2-F2
Kent Road	F4
Kings Road	E4
Kings Way	A1-A2-B2
Kirby Road	A3
Knowl Hill	F1-F2

Lavender Road	F3
Lych Way	B4
Lytton Road	E3-F3
Mabel Street	A2-B2
Manor Road	A4
Maybury Hill	E4-F4-F3-F2
Maybury Road	D3-D4-E4
Mayhurst Avenue	F4
Meadway Drive	A4
Midhope Road	B1
Mount Hermon Road	B1-C1
North Road	D4-E4
Oaks Road	B2-B3
Ockenden Road	D1-D2
Old Malt Way	B3
Old Woking road	F1-F2-F3
Omega Road	E4
Onslow Crescent	D3-E3
Oriental Road	C2-C3-D2-D3-E3-E4
Ormonde Road	A3-A4
Pares Close	A4-B4
Park Drive	C1-C2
Park Road	D3-E3-E2-F2
Parley Drive	A1-A2
Pembroke Road	E2-E3-E4
Pollard Road	F4
Poole Road	B2-C2
Poplar Grove	C1
Port Road	D3-D4
Princes Road	F4
Rosehill Avenue	A4
Royal Oak Road	A1
St Johns Road	A3
St Marys Road	A3
St Pauls Road	E3
Sandy Lane	F2-F3-F4
Sandy Way	F3
School Road	D4
Shaftesbury Road	E3-F3
Silversmiths Way	A2
South Close	A4
Stanley Road	D3
Station Approach	C2-C3-D3
Station Road	C2
The Broadway	D3
The Grove	C4-D4
The Ridge	E3-F3
Trigg's Close	A1
Trigg's Lane	A1
Vale Farm Road	B2-B3-C3
Victoria Way	C2-C3-C4-D4
Waldens Park Road	A3
Waldens Road	A3
Walton Road	D3-D4-E4
Well Lane	A3
Wendella Close	D1
West Hill Road	B1
White Rose Lane	D2-D1-E1-F1
Winnington Way	A1-A2
Wilson Way	B4
Wolsey Way	C3
York Road	B1-B2-C2

Godalming

Borough Road	B3-B4
Braemar Close	A1-A2
Bridge Road	B3-C3-C4
Bridge Street	B3

Brighton Road	B3-B2-C2-C1
Busbridge Lane	A2-B2-B1
Carlos Street	B2
Catteshal Lane	B3-C3-C2-C3
Chalk Road	B4-C4
Charterhouse Road	B4
Church Street	B3
Croft Road	B2
Crownpits Lane	B1-C1
Dean Road	B4
Deanery Road	B4
Duncombe Road	B1
Filmer Grove	B4
Frith Hill Road	B4
Great George Street	B3
Grosvenor Road	B1-C1
Grove Road	A2
Hallam Road	C4
Hare Lane	C4
High Street	B3
Holloway Hill	A2
Latimer Road	B2
Llanaway Road	C4
Marshall Road	C4
Meadrow	C4
Mill Lane	A3
Mint Street	A3-B3
Moss Lane	B3
Nightingale Road	B4-C4
Oakdene Road	B1
Ockford Road	A2-A3-B2-B3
Park Road	B1
Peperharow Road	A4-B4
Pullman Lane	A1
Queen Street	B3-B2
Ramsden Road	A1-B1-B2
Shackstead Lane	A2-A1-B1
South Hill	C2-C3
South Street	B2-B3
Station Approach	A3
Summerhouse Road	A2-B2
The Avenue	C1
The Burys	B3
The Close	C1
The Drive	C1
The Fairway	C1
Town End Street	B2-C2
Tuesley Lane	A2-A1-B1
Valley View	A2
Westbrook Road	A3
Wharf Street	B3-C3
Wolseley Road	C4

Central Hastings

Hastings Area

mls 0 SCALE 4

Hastings

Overlooking the beach of this popular resort are the remains of a castle established by William the Conqueror; Battle Abbey, the actual site of the great conflict of 1066, lies to the north of the town on the A2100. The Hastings Embroidery, which was commissioned in 1966 to commemorate the battle's 900th anniversary and depicts 81 memorable events in British history, can be seen at the Town Hall.

Rich in historical associations, Hastings also has a historic Old Town — a pleasant jumble of ancient buildings and narrow streets, and site of the local fish market and Fisherman's Museum. Theatres, pubs and amusement areas fill the main resort, which has all the amenities expected of a major holiday centre.

Bexhill offers the entertainment facilities of the De La Warr Pavilion, which overlooks the sands, and a good range of outdoor activities can be enjoyed in nearby Egerton Park. Manor Gardens, in the older part of the town, contains the Manor Costume Museum and the ruins of the manor house.

Rye is an atmospheric town of cobbled streets and half-timbered houses. A gang of smugglers had its headquarters at the 15th-century Mermaid Inn, and other places of interest include the Baddings Tower Museum, the Rye Town Model and the old harbour, which is now a nature reserve.

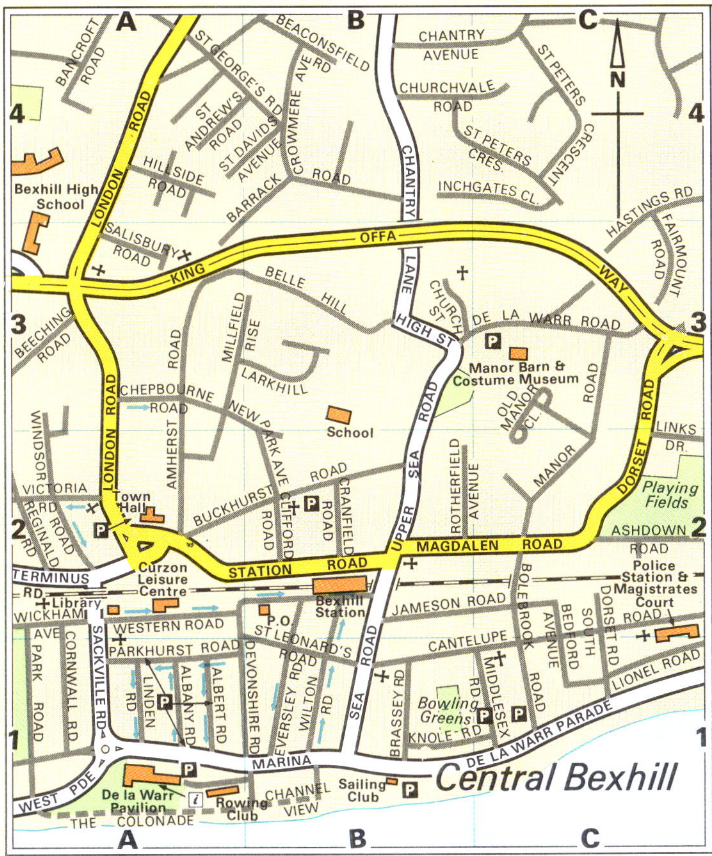

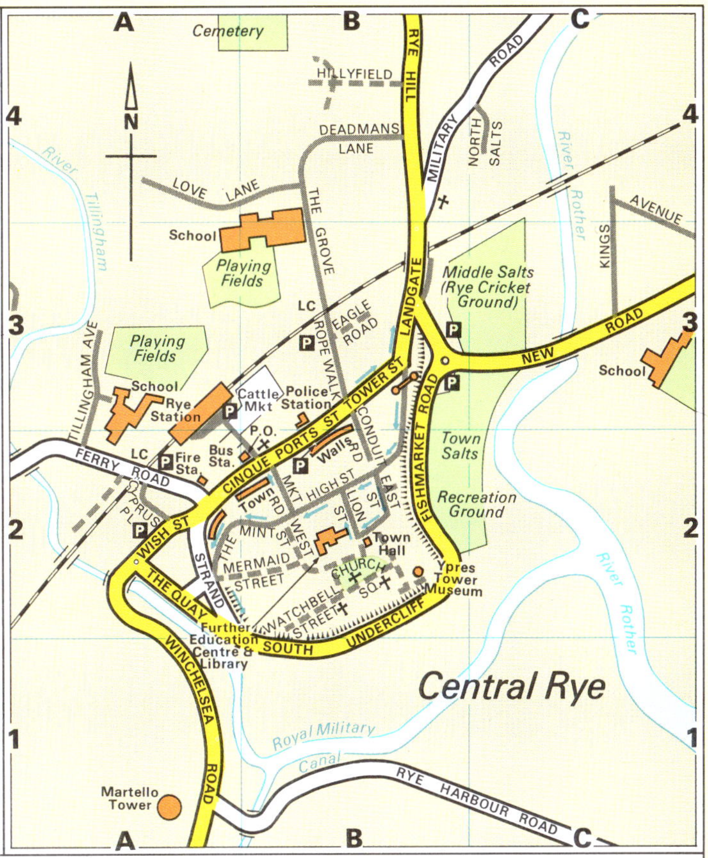

Central Bexhill

Central Rye

Key to Town Plan and Area Plan

Town Plan
AA Recommended roads
Restricted roads
Other roads
Buildings of interest — Castle
Car Parks — P
Churches
Parks and open spaces
One Way Streets

Area Plan
A roads
B roads
Locations — Kingston ○
Urban area

Street Index with Grid Reference

Hastings

Amherst Road	B4
All Saints Street	F2-F3
Bembrook Road	F4
Bethune Way	D4
Bohemia Road	A3-A2-B2
Braybrooke Road	B3-C3-C4-D4
Brook Street	C3-D3
Cambridge Road	B2-C2
Carlisle Parade	C2
Castlehill Road	D2-E2-E3
Castle Street	D2
Collier Road	E3-E4-F4
Cornwallis Gardens	B3-B2
Cornwallis Street	C3-D3
Cornwallis Terrace	B3-C3
Courthouse Street	E2
Croft Road	E4-F4-F3-E3
Crown Lane	F2
Denmark Place	C2-D2
Devonshire Road	C3
Dorset Place	B2
Earl Street	C3
East Parade	E2
East Street	E2
Emmanuel Road	E4
Eversfield Place	A1
Falaise Road	A2
George Street	D2-E2
Harold Place	C2
Havelock Road	C2
High Street	E2-F2-F3
Hill Street	E2
Hillyglen Close	B3
Hopsgarden Close	B3-B4
Linton Road	B4-B3
Lower Park Road	C4-D4
Mann Street	C3-D3
Marine Parade	D2-E2
Middle Street	C2
Milward Crescent	D3
Milward Road	D3-D4-E4
Nelson Road	D4
Pelham Arcade	D2
Pelham Place	D2
Plynlimmon Road	E3-E4
Priory Avenue	B4-C4-C3
Priory Close	C4
Priory Road	E3-E4-F4
Priory Street	C2
Prospect Place	B2
Queens Road	C2-D2-D3-D4
Robertson Street	B2-C2
Rock-a-Nore Road	F2
St Helens Road	D4
St Margaret's Road	A2
St Mary's Terrace	E3-E4
South Terrace	C3-D3
Stanley Road	B3-C3-C4
Station Road	C2-C3
Stonefield Road	D3-D4
Tackleway	F2-F3
The Coppice	B4-C4
The Bourne	E2-F2
Vicarage Road	E4
Waterworks Road	D4
Wellington Place	C2-D2
Wellington Road	D3-D2-E2
Wellington Square	D2
White Rock	B1-B2
White Rock Road	A2-B2
Whitefriars Road	E4
Winterbourne Close	A3-A4
Wykeham Road	B4-B3-C3

Bexhill

Albany Road	A1
Albert Road	A1
Amherst Road	A2-A3
Ashdown Road	C2
Bancroft Road	A4
Barrack Road	A3-B4
Beaconsfield Road	B4
Bedford Avenue	C2-C1
Beeching Road	A3
Belle Hill	B3
Bolebrook Road	C2-C1
Brassey Road	B1
Buckhurst Road	A2-B2
Cantelupe Road	B1-C1-C2
Channel View	B1
Chantry Avenue	B4-C4
Chantry Lane	B4-B3
Chelsea Close	C2
Chepbourne Road	A3
Church Street	B3
Churchvale Road	B4-C4
Clifford Road	B2
Cornwall Road	A2-A1
Cranfield Road	B2
Crowmere Avenue	B4
De la Warr Parade	B1-C1
De la Warr Road	C3
Devonshire Road	A1-B1
Dorset Road	C2-C3
Dorset Road South	C2-C1
Eversley Road	B1
Fairmount Road	C3-C4
Hastings Road	C4-C3
High Street	B3
Hillside Road	A4
Inchgates Close	B4-C4
Jameson Road	B2-C2
King Offa Way	A3-B3-C3
Knole Road	B1-C1
Larkhill	A3-B3
Linden Road	A1
Links Drive	C2
Lionel Road	C1
London Road	A4-A3-A2
Magdalen Road	B2-C2
Manor Road	C2-C3
Marina	A1-B1
Middlesex Road	C1
Millfield Rise	A3-B3
New Park Avenue	A3-B3-B2
Old Manor Close	C2-C3
Park Road	A1-A2
Parkhurst Road	A1
Reginald Road	A2
Rotherfield Avenue	B2
St Andrew's Road	A4-B4
St Davids Avenue	A4-B4
St George's Road	A4-B4
St Leonard's Road	B2-B1
St Peters Crescent	B4-C4
Sackville Road	A2-A1
Salisbury Road	A3
Sea Road	B1-B2
Station Road	A2-B2
Terminus Road	A2
The Colonade	A1
Upper Sea Road	B2-B3
Victoria Road	A2
West Parade	A1
Western Road	A2
Wickham Avenue	A2
Wilton Road	B1
Windsor Road	A3-A2

Rye

Church Square	B2
Cinque Ports Street	A2-B2-B3
Conduit Road	B3-B2
Cyprus Place	A2
Deadmans Lane	B4
Eagle Road	B3
East Street	B2
Ferry Road	A2
Fishmarket Road	B2-B3
High Street	B2
Hillyfield	B4
Kings Avenue	C3-C4
Landgate	B3
Lion Street	B2
Love Lane	A4-B4
Market Road	B2
Mermaid Street	A2-B2
Military Road	B3-C3
New Road	B3-C3
North Salts	B3
Rope Walk	B3
Rye Harbour Road	B1-C1
Rye Hill	B4
South Undercliff	B1-B2
Strand	A2
The Grove	B4-B3
The Mint	A2-B2
The Quay	A2
Tillingham Avenue	A2-A3
Tower Street	B3
Watchbell Street	B2
West Street	B2
Winchelsea Road	A1-A2
Wish Street	A2

HASTINGS
Although the harbour of this one-time Cinque Port silted up centuries ago, fishing boats are still winched up on the shingle beach, and fishermen's net-drying huts at the foot of the cliff railway are a distinctive feature.

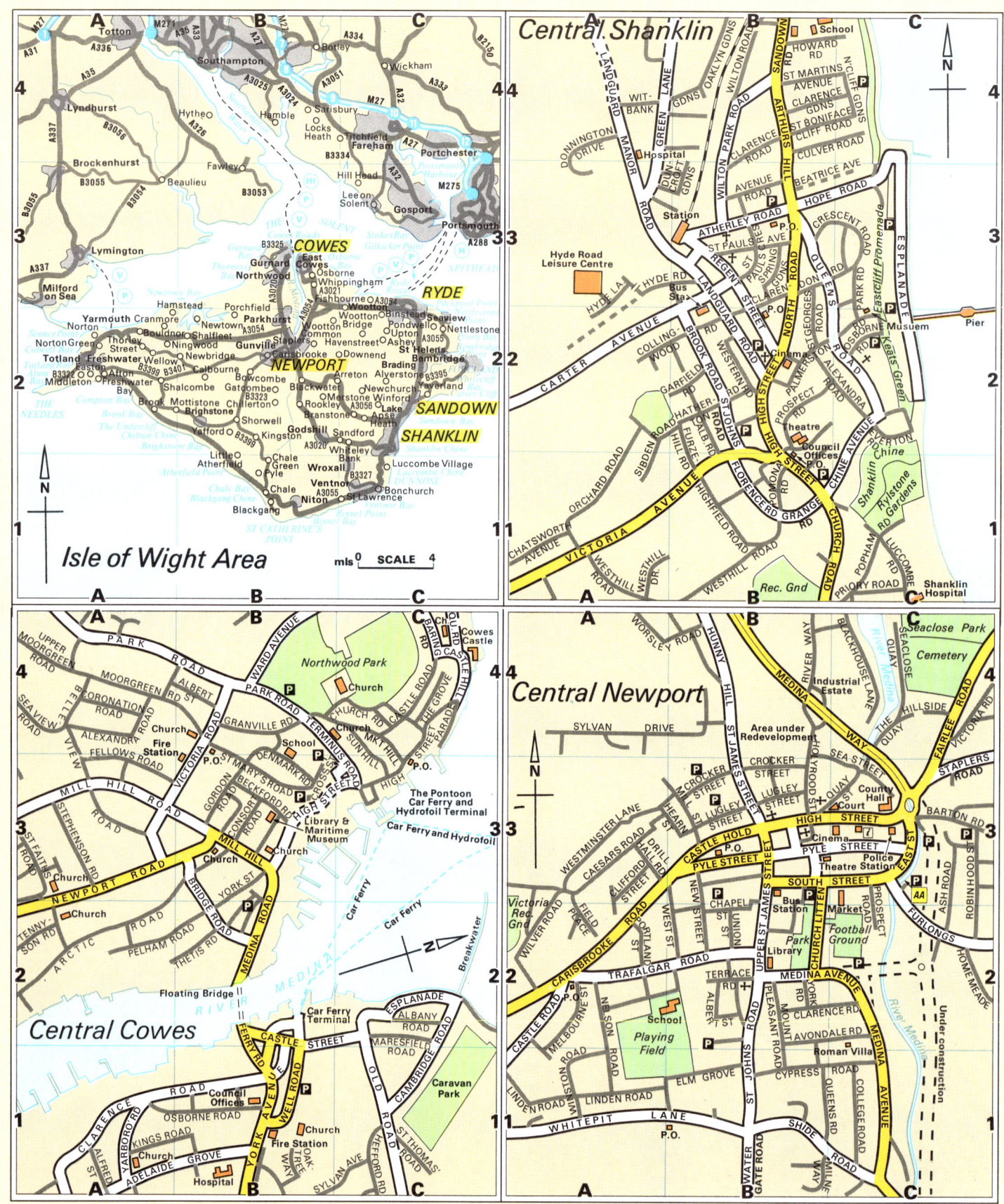

Isle of Wight

Most visitors to the island arrive at Ryde so its streets are always busy throughout the summer months. During the 19th century it was turned from a small village into a fashionable holiday resort which is as popular as ever today; sandy beaches, a pier with an electric railway, a boating lake and pleasant gardens are its main attractions.

Sandown lies at the centre of Sandown Bay on the south-east side of the island and as the largest resort, its holiday facilities are numerous. The Museum of Isle of Wight Geology houses, among other exhibits, over 5000 fossils from the island.

Shanklin Here attractions range from the excitement of the pier to the seclusion of Hope Beach. The old village has thatched cottages festooned with roses, and the natural gorge called Shanklin Chine has lovely gardens and a waterfall.

Newport, capital of the island, occupies a conveniently central position. Just south-west of the town is the 12th-century Carisbrooke Castle where Charles I was imprisoned for a year before his execution in London. Other places of interest include the Roman Villa in Cypress Road.

Cowes is the headquarters of the Royal Yacht Squadron and Cowes Week, held during the first week of August, is the fashionable event of the yachting calendar. The club house stands on the site of a castle built by Henry VIII.

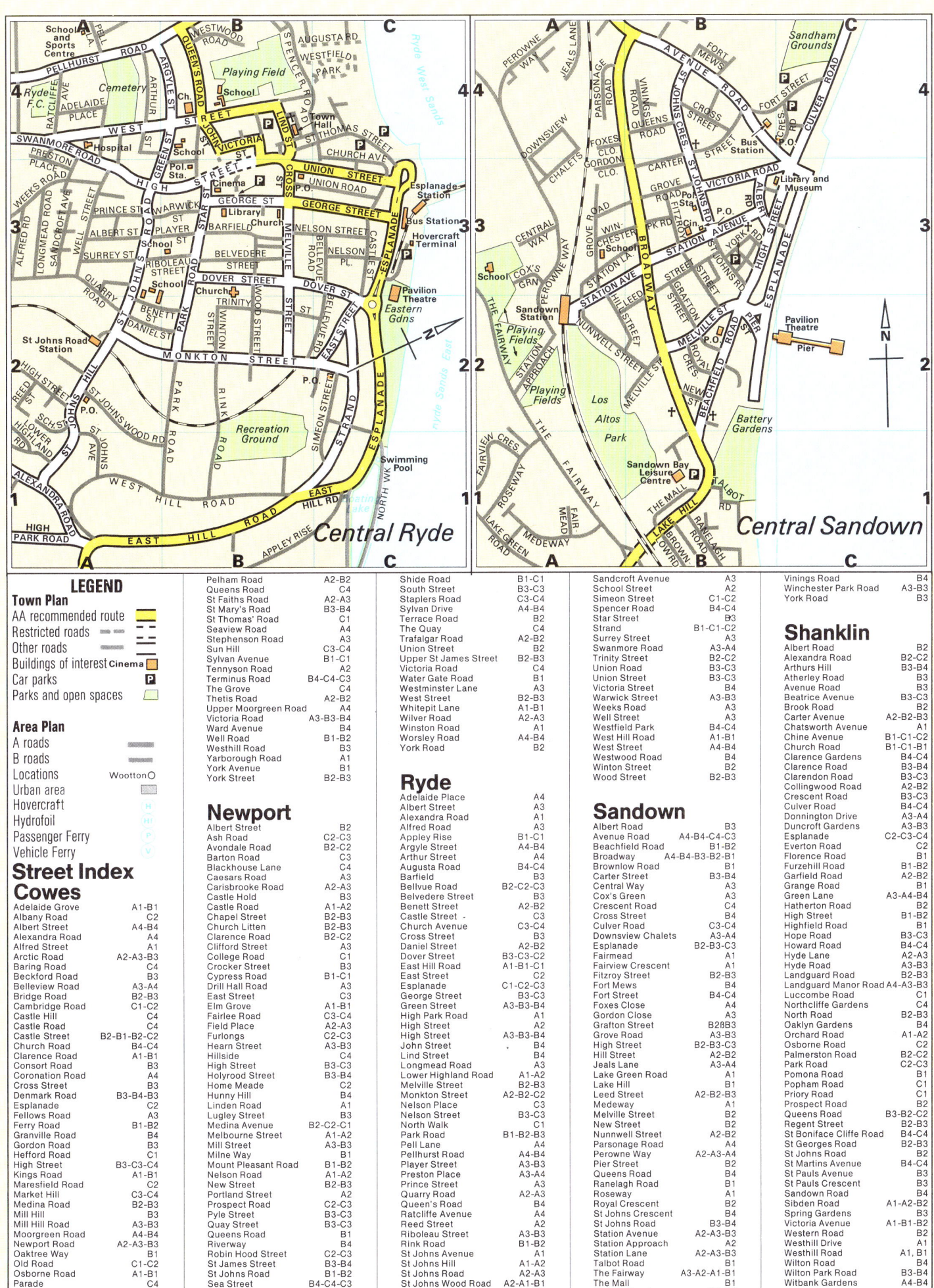

Central Ryde

Central Sandown

LEGEND

Town Plan
- AA recommended route
- Restricted roads
- Other roads
- Buildings of interest Cinema
- Car parks P
- Parks and open spaces

Area Plan
- A roads
- B roads
- Locations Wootton O
- Urban area
- Hovercraft
- Hydrofoil
- Passenger Ferry
- Vehicle Ferry

Street Index

Cowes

Adelaide Grove	A1-B1
Albany Road	C2
Albert Street	A4-B4
Alexandra Road	A4
Alfred Street	A1
Arctic Road	A2-A3-B3
Baring Road	C4
Beckford Road	B3
Belleview Road	A3-A4
Bridge Road	B2-B3
Cambridge Road	C1-C2
Castle Hill	C4
Castle Road	C4
Castle Street	B2-B1-B2-C2
Church Road	B4-C4
Clarence Road	A1-B1
Consort Road	B3
Coronation Road	A4
Cross Street	B3
Denmark Road	B3-B4-B3
Esplanade	C2
Fellows Road	A3
Ferry Road	B1-B2
Granville Road	B4
Gordon Road	B3
Hefford Road	C1
High Street	B3-C3-C4
Kings Road	A1-B1
Maresfield Road	C2
Market Hill	C3-C4
Medina Road	B2-B3
Mill Hill	B3
Mill Hill Road	A3-B3
Moorgreen Road	B3
Newport Road	A2-A3-B3
Oaktree Way	C1-C2
Old Road	C1-C2
Osborne Road	A1-B1
Parade	C4
Park Road	A4-B4

Newport

Albert Street	B2
Ash Road	C2-C3
Avondale Road	B2-C2
Barton Road	C3
Blackhouse Lane	C4
Caesars Road	A3
Carisbrooke Road	A2-A3
Castle Hold	B3
Castle Road	A1-A2
Chapel Street	B2-B3
Church Litten	B2-B3
Clarence Road	B2-C2
Clifford Street	A3
College Road	C1
Crocker Street	B3
Cypress Road	B1-C1
Drill Hall Road	A3
East Street	C3
Elm Grove	A1-B1
Fairlee Road	C3-C4
Field Place	A2-A3
Furlongs	C2-C3
Hearn Street	A3-B3
Hillside	C4
High Street	B3-C3
Holyrood Street	B3-B4
Home Meade	C2
Hunny Hill	B4
Linden Road	A1
Lugley Street	B3
Medina Avenue	B2-C2-C1
Melbourne Street	A1-A2
Mill Street	A3-B3
Milne Way	B1
Mount Pleasant Road	B1-B2
Nelson Road	A1-A2
New Street	B2-B3
Portland Street	A2
Prospect Road	C2-C3
Pyle Street	B3-C3
Quay Street	B3-C3
Queens Road	B1
Riverway	B4
Robin Hood Street	C2-C3
St James Street	B3-B4
St Johns Road	B1-B2
Sea Street	B4-C4-C3
Seaclose Quay	C4

Pelham Road	A2-B2
Queens Road	C4
St Faiths Road	A2-A3
St Mary's Road	B3-B4
St Thomas' Road	C1
Seaview Road	A4
Stephenson Road	A3
Sun Hill	C3-C4
Sylvan Avenue	B1-C1
Tennyson Road	A2
Terminus Road	B4-C4-C3
The Grove	C4
Thetis Road	A2-B2
Victoria Road	A3-B3-B4
Ward Avenue	B4
Well Road	B1-B2
Westhill Road	B3
Yarborough Road	A1
York Avenue	B1
York Street	B2-B3

Shide Road	B1-C1
South Street	B3-C3
Staplers Road	C3-C4
Sylvan Drive	A4-B4
Terrace Road	B2
The Quay	C4
Trafalgar Road	A2-B2
Union Street	B2
Upper St James Street	B2-B3
Victoria Road	C4
Water Gate Road	B1
Westminster Lane	A3
West Street	B2-B3
Whitepit Lane	A1-B1
Wilver Road	A2-A3
Winston Road	A1
Worsley Road	A4-B4
York Road	B2

Ryde

Adelaide Place	A4
Albert Street	A3
Alexandra Road	A1
Alfred Road	A3
Appley Rise	B1-C1
Argyle Street	A4-B4
Arthur Street	A4
Augusta Road	B4-C4
Barfield	B3
Bellvue Road	B2-C2-C3
Belvedere Street	B3
Benett Street	A2-B2
Castle Street	C3
Church Avenue	C3-C4
Cross Street	B3
Daniel Street	A2-B2
Dover Street	B3-C3-C2
East Hill Road	A1-B1-C1
East Street	C2
Esplanade	C1-C2-C3
George Street	B3-C3
Green Street	A3-B3-B4
High Park Road	A1
High Street	A2
High Street	A3-B3-B4
John Street	B4
Lind Street	B4
Longmead Road	A3
Lower Highland Road	A1-A2
Melville Street	B2-B3
Monkton Street	A2-B2-C2
Nelson Place	C3
Nelson Street	B3-C3
North Walk	C1
Park Road	B1-B2-B3
Pell Lane	A4
Pellhurst Road	A4-B4
Player Street	A3-B3
Preston Place	A3-A4
Prince Street	A3
Quarry Road	A2
Queen's Road	B4
Ratcliffe Avenue	A4
Reed Street	A2
Riboleau Street	A3-B3
Rink Road	B1-B2
St Johns Avenue	A1
St Johns Hill	A1-A2
St Johns Road	B1-B2
St Johns Wood Road	A2-A1-B1
St Thomas Street	B4-C4-C3

Sandcroft Avenue	A3
School Avenue	A2
Simeon Street	C1-C2
Spencer Road	B4-C4
Star Street	B3
Strand	B1-C1-C2
Surrey Street	A3
Swanmore Road	A3-A4
Trinity Street	B2-C2
Union Road	B3-C3
Union Street	B3-C3
Victoria Street	B4
Warwick Street	A3-B3
Weeks Road	A3
Well Street	A3
Westfield Park	B4-C4
West Hill Road	A1-B1
West Street	A4-B4
Westwood Road	B2
Winton Street	B2
Wood Street	B2-B3

Sandown

Albert Road	B3
Avenue Road	A4-B4-C4-C3
Beachfield Road	B1-B2
Broadway	A4-B4-B3-B2-B1
Brownlow Road	A3
Carter Street	B3-B4
Central Way	A3
Cox's Green	A3
Crescent Road	C4
Cross Street	B4
Culver Road	C3-C4
Downsview Chalets	A3-A4
Esplanade	B2-B3-C3
Fairmead	A1
Fairview Crescent	A1
Fitzroy Street	B2-B3
Fort Mews	B4
Fort Street	B4-C4
Foxes Close	A4
Gordon Close	A3
Grafton Street	B2&B3
Grove Road	A3-B3
High Street	B2-B3-C3
Hill Street	A2-B2
Jeals Lane	A3-A4
Lake Green Road	A1
Lake Hill	B1
Leed Street	A2-B2-B3
Medeway	A1
Melville Street	B2
New Street	B2
Nunnwell Street	A2-B2
Parsonage Road	A2
Perowne Way	A2-A3-A4
Pier Street	B2
Queens Road	B4
Ranelagh Road	B1
Roseway	A1
Royal Crescent	B2
St Johns Crescent	A2
St Johns Road	B3-B4
Station Avenue	A2-A3-B3
Station Approach	A2
Station Lane	A2-A3-B3
Talbot Road	B1
The Fairway	A3-A2-A1-B1
The Mall	B1
Victoria Road	B3-C3

Shanklin

Albert Road	B2
Alexandra Road	B2-C2
Arthurs Hill	B3-B4
Atherley Road	B3
Avenue Road	B3
Beatrice Avenue	B3-C3
Brook Road	B2
Carter Avenue	A2-B2-B3
Chatsworth Avenue	A1
Chine Avenue	B1-C1-C2
Church Road	B1-C1-B1
Clarence Gardens	B4-C4
Clarence Road	B3-B4
Clarendon Road	B3-C3
Collingwood Road	A2-B2-B3
Crescent Road	B3-C3
Culver Road	B4-C4
Donnington Drive	A3-A4
Duncroft Gardens	B3-B3
Esplanade	C2-C3-C3
Everton Road	C2
Florence Road	B1
Furzehill Road	B1-B2
Garfield Road	A2-B2
Grange Road	B1
Green Lane	A3-A4-B4
Hatherton Road	B3-B3
High Street	B1-B2
Highfield Road	B1
Hope Road	B3-C3
Howard Road	B4-C4
Hyde Lane	A2-A3
Hyde Road	A3-B3
Landguard Road	B2-B3
Landguard Manor Road	A4-A3-B3
Luccombe Road	C1
Northcliffe Gardens	C4
North Road	B2-B3
Oaklyn Gardens	B4
Orchard Road	A1-A2
Osborne Road	C2
Palmerston Road	B2-C2
Park Road	C2-C3
Pomona Road	B1
Popham Road	C1
Priory Road	C1
Prospect Road	B2
Queens Road	B3-B2-C2
Regent Street	B2-B3
St Boniface Cliffe Road	B4-C4
St Georges Road	B2-B3
St Johns Road	B2
St Martins Avenue	B4-C4
St Pauls Avenue	B3
St Pauls Crescent	B3
Sandown Road	B4
Sibden Road	A1-A2-B2
Spring Gardens	B3
Victoria Avenue	A1-B1-B2
Western Road	B2
Westhill Drive	A1
Westhill Road	A1, B1
Wilton Road	B4
Wilton Park Road	B3-B4
Witbank Gardens	A4-B4
Vinings Road	B4
Winchester Park Road	A3-B3
York Road	B3

Maidstone

County town of Kent, Maidstone has long been a place of importance. The ruins of the 14th-century Archbishop's Palace overlook the River Medway, and Allington Castle dates from the 13th century. Maidstone Museum and Art Gallery explores the town's extensive history; also of interest is the Tyrwhitt-Drake Museum of Carriages, housed in the Palace stables.

Rochester Medieval walls enclose the Norman castle and cathedral of this attractive and historic town, but its quaint old shops, inns and tea shops give it a distinctly Victorian flavour. Charles Dickens spent much of his life in the area and featured Rochester in his novels: justly proud of its associations with the great man, the town boasts an award-winning Charles Dickens Centre.

Gillingham has been associated with the nearby Royal Naval Dockyard since Tudor times and it continues the tradition with the Royal Naval Barracks and the Royal School of Military Engineering, both situated in the Brompton area.

Chatham Home of the Royal Naval Dockyard since the 16th century, Chatham today is dominated by the office tower block which crowns the Pentagon Centre, a shopping and entertainments complex. Pleasant riverside gardens have been laid out on the site of the old Gun Wharf, and the Medway Heritage Centre is in Dock Road.

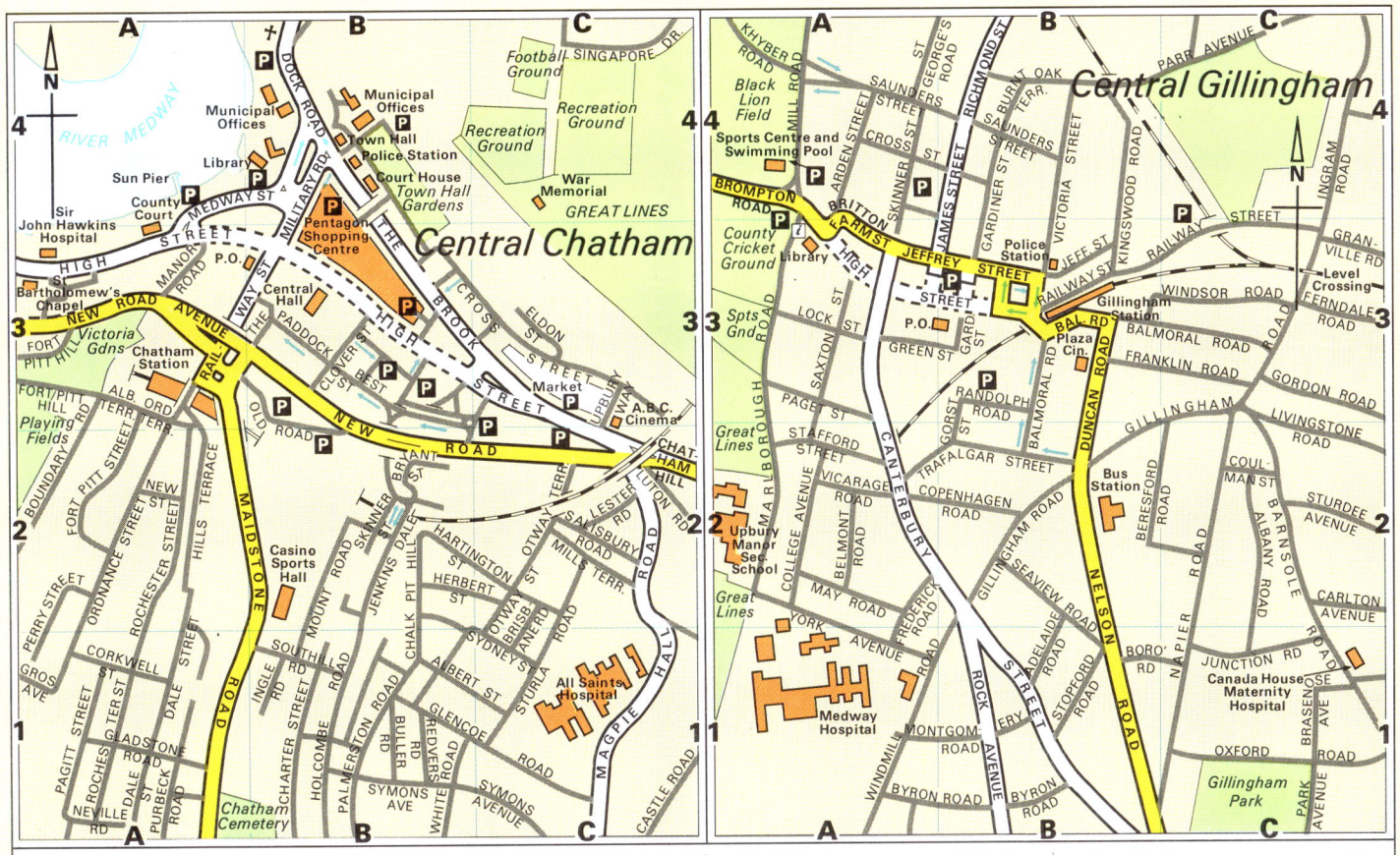

LEGEND

Town Plan

AA Recommended roads
Restricted roads
Other roads
Buildings of interest — Station ■
Churches — +
Parks and open spaces
Car Parks — P
One Way Streets — L

Area Plan

A roads
B roads
Locations — Muckingford ○
Urban area

Street Index with Grid Reference

Maidstone

Allen Street	C4
Bank Street	B2
Barker Road	A1-B1
Bishops Way	B1-B2
Boxley Road	B4-C4
Brewer Street	B3-C3
Broadway	A1-B1-B2
Brunswick Street	C1
Buckland Hill	A3
Buckland Road	A2-A3
Charles Street	A1
Church Street	C2-C3
College Avenue	B1
College Road	B1
County Road	B4-B3-C3-C4
Earl Street	B2-B3
Fairmeadow	B2-B3
Foley Street	C4
Foster Street	B1-C1
Gabriel's Hill	B2-C2
Hart Street	A1
Hastings Road	C1
Hedley Street	C3-C4
High Street	B2
Holland Road	C3-C4
James Street	C4
Kingsley Road	C1
King Street	B2-C2
Knightrider Street	B1-C1
Lower Stone Street	C1-C2
Market Buildings	B2
Market Street	B2-B3
Marsham Street	C2
Medway Street	B2
Melville Road	C1
Mill Street	B1-B2
Mote Road	C1
Museum Street	B2-B3
Padsole Lane	C1
Palace Avenue	B1-B2-C2
Priory Road	B1
Pudding Lane	B2
Queen Anne Road	C2
Reginald Road	A1
Rocky Hill	A1-A2
Romney Place	C1
St Faith's Street	B3
St Peter's Street	A2-A3
Sandling Road	B4
Station Road	B3
Terrace Road	A1-A2
Tufton Street	C3
Union Street	B3-C3
Upper Stone Street	C1
Waterlow Road	C4
Week Street	B2-B3
Well Road	B4-C4
Wheeler Street	C3-C4
Wyatt Street	C2-C3

Rochester

Bardell Terrace	B2-C2
Blue Boar Lane	B3
Boley Hill	A3
Castle Hill	A3-A4
Cazeneuve Street	B2
City Way	B2-B1-C1
Corporation Street	A4-B4-B3-B2
Crow Lane	B2-B3
Delce Road	B1-B2
Dunnings Lane	A2-B2
East Row	B2
Esplanade	A2-A3-A4
Ethelbert Avenue	A1
Foord Street	B1
Furrells Road	B2-C2
Gashouse Road	B4
Gordon Terrace	A1-A2
High Street	A4-A3-B3-B2-C2
Hoopers Road	A1-B1
James Street	B1
John Street	B2-B1-A1-B1
King Edward Road	A2
King Street	B2
Lockington Grove	A2-B2
Longley Road	A1-B1
Love Lane	A2-A3
Maidstone Road	A1-A2-B2
New Road	B1-C1
Rochester Avenue	A1-B1
Rochester Bridge	A4
Roebuck Road	A1-A2
St Margaret's Street	A1-A2-A3
South Avenue	A1
The Terrace	B2
Victoria Street	B2
Vines Lane	A3-B2
Watts Avenue	A1-A2

Gillingham

Adelaide Road	B1-B2
Albany Road	C1-C2
Arden Street	A4
Balmoral Road	B2-B3-C3
Barnsole Road	C1-C2-C3
Belmont Road	A2
Beresford Road	C2-B2-C2
Borough Road	B1-C1
Brasenose Avenue	C1
Britton Farm Street	A3-A4
Brompton Road	A4
Burnt Oak Terrace	B4
Byron Road	A1-B1
Canterbury Street	A3-A2-B2-B1
Carlton Avenue	C2
College Avenue	A2
Copenhagen Road	A2-B2
Coulman Street	C2
Cross Street	A4-B4
Duncan Road	B2-B3
Ferndale Road	C3
Franklin Road	B3-C3
Frederick Road	A1-A2
Gardiner Street	B3-B4
Gillingham Road	B2-B3-C3
Gordon Road	C3
Gorst Street	B2-B3
Granville Road	C3
Green Street	A3-B3
High Street	A3-B3
Ingram Road	C3-C4
James Street	A3-B3-B4
Jeffrey Street	A3-B3
Junction Road	C1
Kingswood Road	B3-B4
Khyber Road	A4
Livingstone Road	C2-C3
Lock Street	A3
Marlborough Road	A2-A3-A4
May Road	A2
Mill Road	A4
Montgomery Road	A1-B1
Napier Road	B1-C1-C2-C3
Nelson Road	B2-B1-C1
Oxford Road	C1
Paget Street	A3
Park Avenue	C1
Railway Street	B3-C3
Randolph Road	B3
Richmond Street	B4
Rock Avenue	B1-B2
St George's Road	A4-B4
Saunders Street	A4-B4
Saxton Street	A2-A3
Seaview Road	B1-B2
Skinner Street	A3-A4
Stafford Street	A2
Stopford Road	B1
Sturdee Avenue	C2
Trafalgar Street	A2-B2
Vicarage Road	B3-B4
Victoria Street	B3-B4
Windmill Road	A1-B1-B2
Windsor Road	B3-C3
York Avenue	A1-A2

Chatham

Albany Terrace	A3
Albert Street	B1-C1
Best Street	B3
Boundary Road	A2-A3
Brisbane Road	C1-C2
Bryant Street	B2
Buller Road	B1
Castle Road	C1
Chalk Pit Hill	B1-B2
Charter Street	B1
Chatham Hill	C2
Clover Street	B3
Corkwell Street	A1
Cross Street	B3-C3
Dale Street	A1-A2
Dock Road	B4
Eldon Street	C3
Fort Pitt Hill	A3
Fort Pitt Street	A2-A3
Gladstone Road	A1
Glencoe Road	B1-C1
Grosvenor Avenue	A1
Hartington Street	B2-C2
Herbert Street	B2-C2
High Street	A3-B3-C3
Hills Terrace	A2
Holcombe Road	B1-B2
Ingle Road	B1
Jenkins Dale	B2
Lester Road	C2
Luton Road	C2
Magpie Hall Road	C1-C2
Maidstone Road	A3-A2-B2-B1-A1
Manor Road	A3
Medway Street	A3-A4-B4
Military Road	B3-B4
Mills Terrace	C2
Mount Road	B1-B2
Neville Road	A1
New Road	B3-B2-C2
New Road Avenue	A3-B3
New Street	A2
Old Road	A3-B3-B2
Ordnance Street	A1-A2-A3
Ordnance Terrace	A3
Otway Street	C1-C2
Otway Terrace	C2
Pagitt Street	A1
Palmerston Road	B1
Perry Street	A1-A2
Purbeck Road	A1
Railway Street	A3-B3
Redvers Road	B1
Rochester Street	A1-A2
Salisbury Road	C2
Singapore Drive	C4
Skinner Street	B2
Southill Road	B1
Sturla Road	C1-C2
Sydney Street	B2-C2-C1
Symons Avenue	B1-C1
The Brook	B4-B3-C3
The Paddock	B3
Upbury Way	C2-C3
White Road	B1

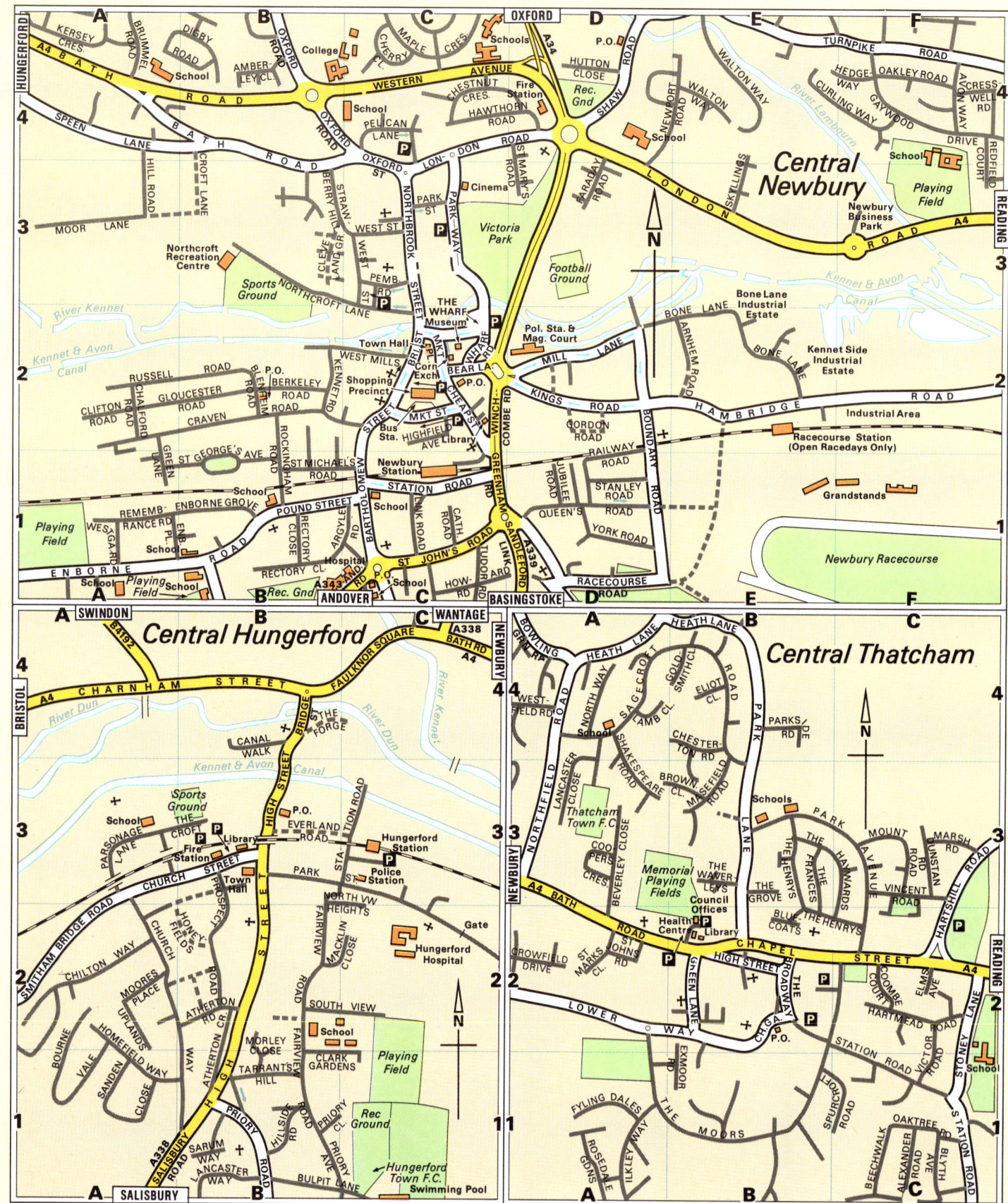

Newbury

Racegoers flock to Newbury's racecourse all the year round, but in the 15th century this principal town of West Berkshire was better known for broadcloth than for betting. The cloth manufacturing era is recalled in the Newbury District Museum, which is appropriately housed in the former Cloth Hall and lies near to the area known as the Wharf. A number of well preserved 17th- and 18th-century buildings can be seen here, including the 18th-century Granary.

Other places of interest include St. Nicholas' Church, built in the 16th century in the Perpendicular style.

Hungerford still retains a flavour of its years as a staging point on the Bath Road, notably in the Bear Inn and in the 17th- and 18th-century shops and houses of the High Street.

Two miles to the north west lies Littlecote

House, a charming Tudor manor which features 'Frontier City' (an authentic Wild West town), and excavations of a Roman villa in its grounds.

Thatcham has also kept several buildings from the 17th and 18th centuries in the midst of its industrial and residential expansion. Notable are two interesting old coaching inns, the King's Head and the White Hart. An early 14th-century chapel at the eastern end of town has been converted into an antiques shop.

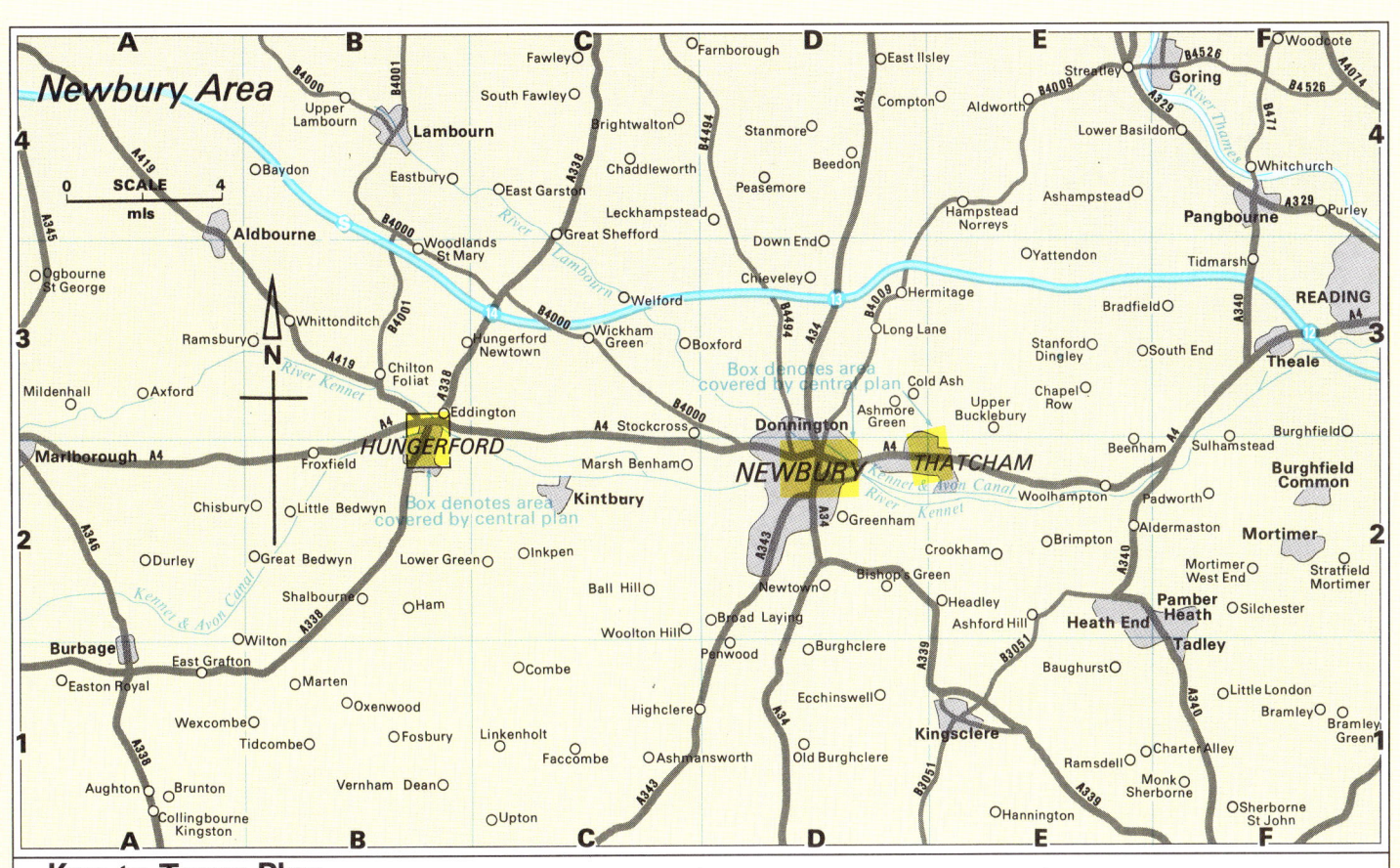

Newbury Area

Box denotes area covered by central plan

Key to Town Plan and Area Plan

Town Plan

AA Recommended roads
Restricted roads
Other roads
Buildings of interest · Station
Car Parks · P
Parks and open spaces
One Way Street

Area Plan

A roads
B roads
Locations · Bradfield○
Urban area

Street Index with Grid Reference

Newbury

Amberley Close	B4
Andover Road	B1-C1
Argyle Road	B1-C1
Arnhem Road	E2
Avon Way	F4
Bartholomew Street	C1-C2
Bath Road	A4-B4-B3-C3
Bear Lane	C2
Berkeley Road	B2
Blenheim Road	B2
Bone Lane	D2-E2
Boundary Road	D1-D2
Bridge Street	C2
Brummell Road	A4
Catherine Road	C1
Chalford Road	A2
Cheap Street	C2
Cherry Close	C4
Chestnut Crescent	C4-D4
Cleveland Grove	B3
Clifton Road	A2
Craven Road	A2-B2-C2
Cresswell Road	F4
Croft Lane	B3-B4
Curling Way	E4-F4
Digby Road	A4
Enborne Grove	A1-B1
Enborne Place	A1
Enborne Road	A1-B1
Faraday Road	D3-D4
Gaywood Drive	F4
Gloucester Road	A2-B2
Gordon Road	D2
Green Lane	A1-A2
Greenham Road	C2-C1-D1
Hambridge Road	D2-E2-F2
Hawthorn Road	C4-D4
Hedgeway	E4-F4
Highfield Avenue	C2
Hill Road	A3-A4
Howard Road	C1-D1
Hutton Close	D4
Jubilee Road	D1
Kennet Road	B2
Kersey Crescent	A4
Kings Road	D2
Link Road	C1
London Road	C3-C4-D4-D3-E3-F3
Maple Crescent	C4
Market Place	C2
Market Street	C2
Mill Lane	D2
Moor Lane	A3
Newport Road	D3-D4-E4
Northbrook Street	C2-C3
Northcroft Lane	B3-C3-C2
Oakley Road	F4
Oxford Road	B4-C4
Oxford Street	C3-C4
Park Street	C3
Park Way	C3
Pelican Lane	C4
Pembroke Road	C3
Pound Street	B1-C1
Queen's Road	D1
Racecourse Road	D1
Railway Road	D1-D2
Rectory Close	B1
Redfield Court	F3-F4
Remembrance Road	A1
Rockingham Road	B1-B2
Russell Road	A2-B2
St George's Avenue	A1-B1
St John's Road	C1
St Mary's Road	D3-D4
St Michael's Road	B1-C1
Sandleford Link	C1-D1
Shaw Road	D4
Skyllings	E3-E4
Speen Lane	A4-B4
Stanley Road	D1
Station Road	C1
Strawberry Hill	B3-C3
The Wharf	C2
Tudor Road	C1
Turnpike Road	E4-F4
Walton Way	E4
Western Avenue	B4-C4-D4
Westgate Road	A1
West Mills	B2-C2
West Street	C3
Wharf Road	C2
Winchcombe Road	C2
York Road	D1

Hungerford

Atherton Crescent	B1-B2
Atherton Road	B2
Bath Road	C4
Bourne Vale	A1-A2
Bridge Street	B4
Bulpit Lane	B1-C1
Canal Walk	B4
Charnham Street	A4-B4-C4
Chilton Way	A2
Church Street	A3-B3
Church Way	A3-A2-B2-B1
Clark Gardens	B1-C1
Everland Road	B3-C3
Fairview Road	B1-B2-B3
Faulknor Square	B4-C4
High Street	B1-B2-B3-B4
Hillside Road	B1
Homefield Way	A1-A2
Honeyfields	A2-B2
Lancaster Way	B1
Macklin Close	B2-C2
Moores Place	A2
Morley Close	B1-B2
North View Heights	B3-C3-C2
Park Street	B3-C3
Parsonage Lane	A3
Priory Avenue	B1-C1
Priory Close	B1
Priory Road	B1
Prospect Road	B2-B3
Salisbury Road	A1-B1
Sanden Close	A1
Sarum Way	B1
Smitham Bridge Road	A2-A3
South View	B2-C2
Station Road	C3
Tarrant's Hill	B1
The Croft	A3-B3
The Forge	B4-C4
Uplands	A2

Thatcham

Alexander Road	C1
Bath Road	A3-A2-B2
Beechwalk	C1
Beverley Close	A2-A3
Bluecoats	B2
Blyth Avenue	C1
Bowling Green Road	A4
Brown Close	A3-B3
Chapel Street	B2-C2
Chesterton Road	B4
Church Gate	B2
Coombe Court	C2
Coopers Crescent	A3
Crowfield Drive	A2
Dunstan Road	C3
Eliot Close	B4
Elms Avenue	C2
Exmoor Road	A1-B1-B2
Fyling Dales	A1
Goldsmith Close	B4
Green Lane	B2
Hartmead Road	C2
Hartshill Road	C2-C3
Heath Lane	A4-B4
High Street	B2
Ilkley Way	A1
Lamb Close	A4
Lancaster Close	A3-A4
Lower Way	A2-B2
Masefield Road	B3-B4
Marsh Road	C3
Mount Road	C3
Northfield Road	A3-A4
North Way	A4
Oaktree Road	C1
Park Avenue	B3-C3-C2
Park Lane	B2-B3-B4
Parkside Road	B4
Rosedale Gardens	A1
St Johns Road	A2
St Marks Close	A2
Sagecroft Road	A4-B4-B3
Shakespeare Road	A3-A4
Spurcroft Road	B1-C1
Station Road	B2-C2-C1
Stoney Lane	C1-C2
The Broadway	B2
The Frances	B2-B3
The Grove	B3
The Haywards	B3-C3-C2
The Henrys	B3-B2-C2
The Moors	A2-A1-B1
The Waverleys	B3
Victor Road	C1-C2
Vincent Road	C3
Westfield Road	A4

45

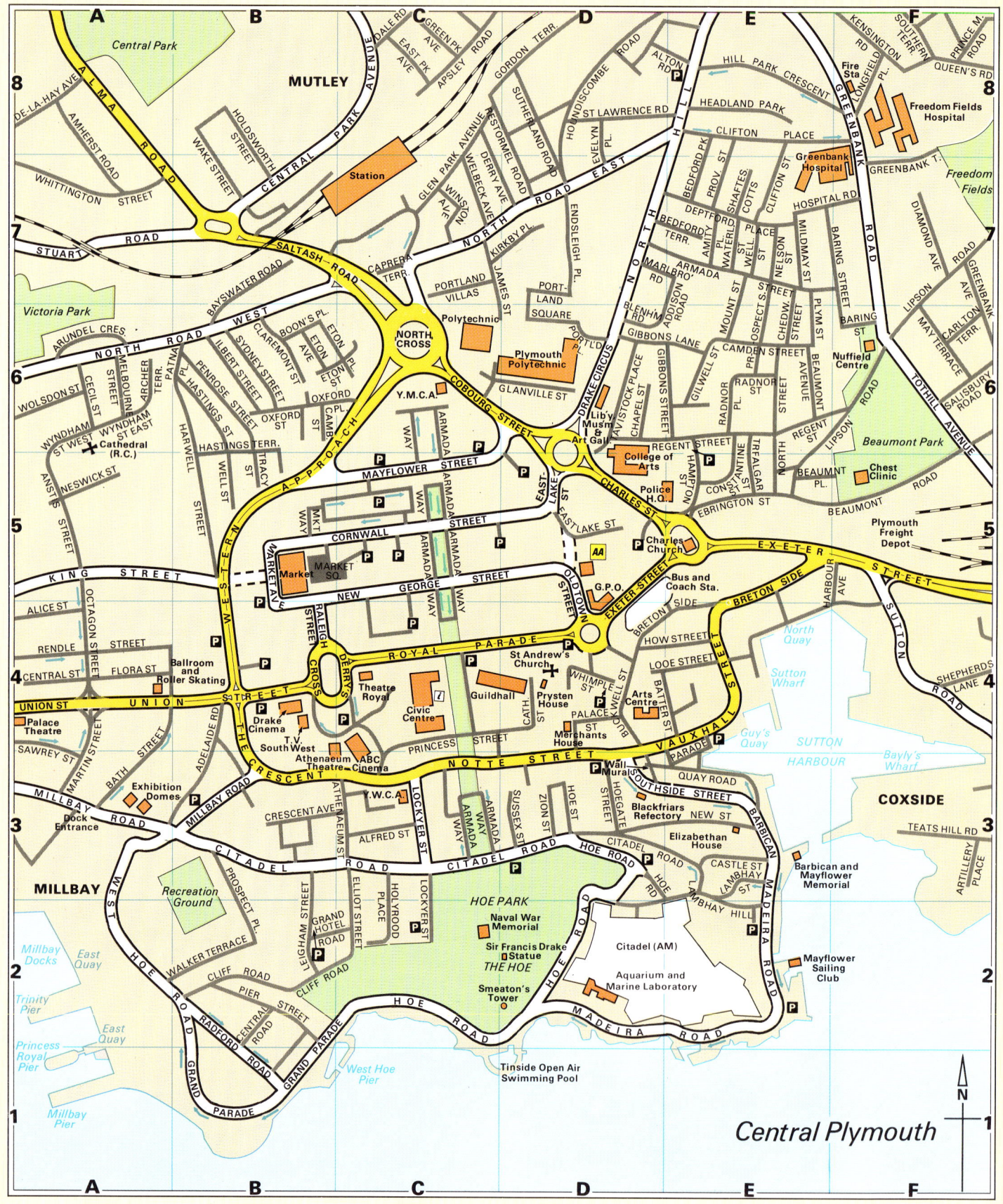

Central Plymouth

Plymouth

Ships, sailors and the sea permeate every aspect of Plymouth's life and history. Its superb natural harbour – Plymouth Sound – has ensured its importance as a port, yachting centre and naval base (latterly at Devonport) over many centuries. Sir Francis Drake is undoubtedly the city's most famous sailor. His statue stands on the Hoe – where he really did play bowls before tackling the

Spanish Armada. Also on the Hoe are Smeaton's Tower, which once formed the upper part of the third Eddystone Lighthouse, and the impressive Royal Naval War Memorial. Just east of the Hoe is the Royal Citadel, an imposing fortress built in 1666 by order of Charles II. North is Sutton Harbour, perhaps the most atmospheric part of Plymouth. Here fishing boats bob up and down in a harbour whose quays are lined with attractive old houses, inns and warehouses. One of the memorials on

Mayflower Quay just outside the harbour commemorates the sailing of the *Mayflower* from here in 1620. Plymouth's shopping centre is one of the finest of its kind, and was built after the old centre was badly damaged in World War II. Nearby is the 200ft-high tower of the impressive modern Civic Centre. Some buildings escaped destruction, including the Elizabethan House and the 500-year-old Prysten House. Next door is St Andrew's Church, with stained glass by John Piper.

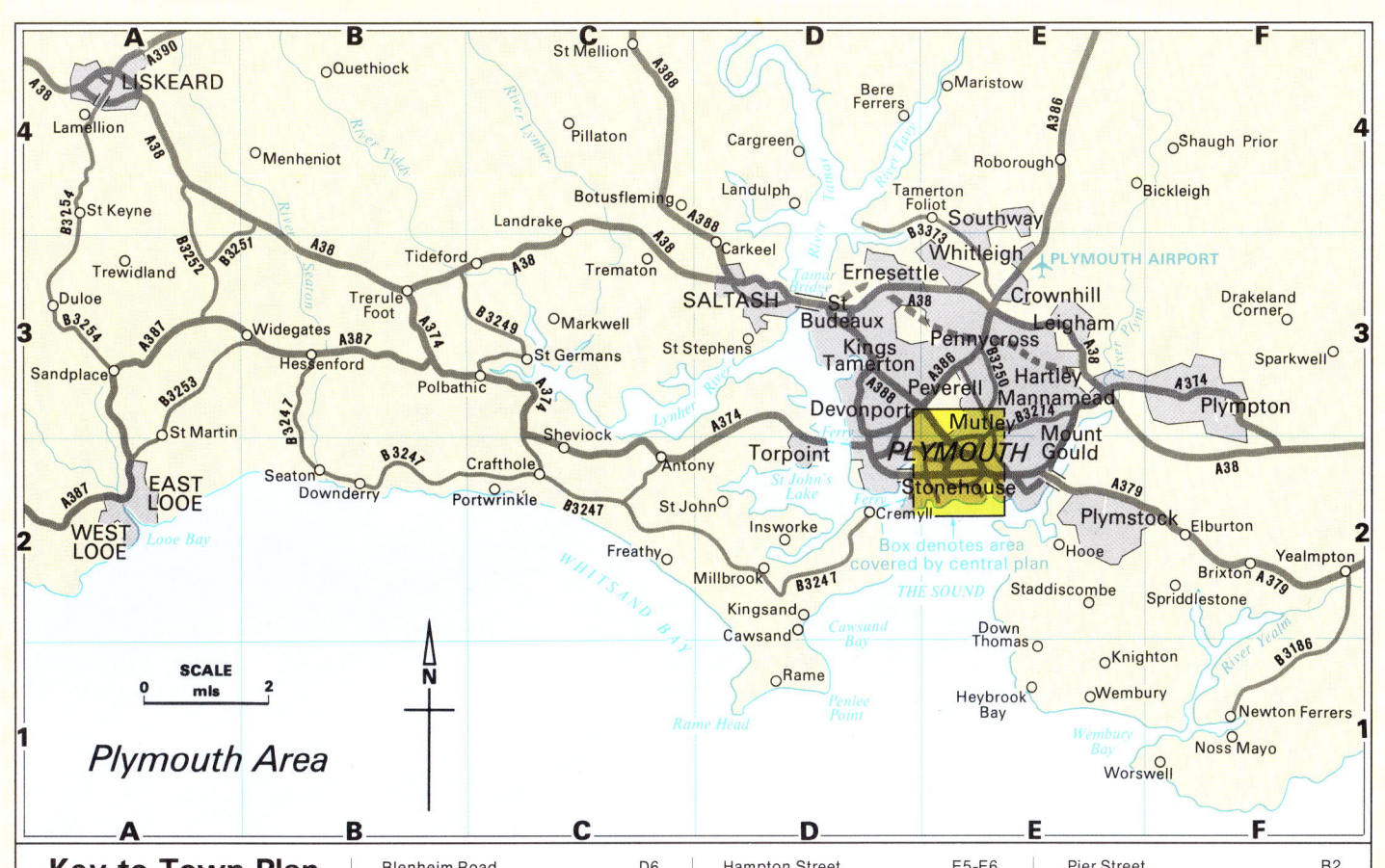

Plymouth Area

SCALE
mls
0   2

N

Key to Town Plan and Area Plan

Town Plan

AA Recommended roads
Other roads
Restricted roads
Buildings of interest
Car Parks   P
Parks and open spaces
One way streets

Area Plan

A roads
B roads
Locations   Sandplace O
Urban area

Street Index with Grid Reference

Plymouth

Addison Road	D6-D7-E7
Adelaide Road	B3-B4
Alfred Street	C3
Alice Street	A4
Alma Road	A8-A7-B7
Alton Road	D8-E8
Amherst Road	A7-A8
Amity Place	E7
Anstis Street	A5-A6
Apsley Road	C8
Archer Terrace	A6
Armada Street	D7-E7-F7
Armada Way	C3-C4-C5-C6
Artillery Place	F3
Arundel Crescent	A6
Athenaeum Street	C3
Barbican	E3
Baring Street	E7-F7-F6
Bath Street	A3-A4
Batter Street	D4-E4
Bayswater Road	B6-B7
Bedford Park	E7-E8
Bedford Terrace	D7-E7
Beaumont Avenue	E6
Beaumont Place	E5-F5
Beaumont Road	E5-F5-F6

Blenheim Road	D6
Boon's Place	B6
Breton Side	D4-E4-E5
Buckwell Street	D4
Cambridge Street	B6
Camden Street	E6
Caprera Terrace	C7
Carlton Terrace	F6
Castle Street	E3
Catherine Street	D4
Cecil Street	A6
Central Road	B2
Central Street	A4
Central Park Avenue	B7-B8-C8
Chapel Street	D6
Charles Street	D5
Chedworth Street	E6-E7
Citadel Road	B3-C3-D3-E3
Claremont Street	B6
Cliff Road	B2-C2
Clifton Place	E8-F8
Clifton Street	E7-E8
Cobourg Street	C6-D6
Constantine Street	E5-E6
Cornwall Street	B5-C5-D5
Crescent Avenue	B3-C3
Dale Road	C8
De-la-Hay-Avenue	A8
Deptford Place	D7-E7
Derry Avenue	C8-C7-D7
Derry's Cross	B4-C4
Diamond Avenue	F7
Drake Circus	D6
East Park Avenue	C8
Eastlake Street	D5
Ebrington Street	E5
Elliot Street	C2-C3
Endsleigh Place	D7
Eton Avenue	B6
Eton Place	B6-C6
Eton Street	B6-C6
Evelyn Place	D7-D8
Exeter Street	D4-D5-E5-F5
Flora Street	A4
Gibbons Lane	D6-E6
Gibbons Street	E6
Gilwell Street	E6
Glanville Street	C6-D6
Glen Park Avenue	C7-C8
Gordon Terrace	C8-D8
Grand Hotel Road	B2-C2
Grand Parade	B1-B2-C2
Great Western Road	B1-B2
Green Park Avenue	C8
Greenbank Avenue	F6-F7
Greenbank Road	F6-F7-F8-E8
Greenbank Terrace	F7-F8

Hampton Street	E5-E6
Harbour Avenue	E5-F5
Harwell Street	B5-B6
Hastings Street	B6
Hastings Terrace	B5-B6
Headland Park	E8
Hill Park Crescent	E8-F8
Hoe Road	C2-D2-D3
Hoe Street	D3
Hoegate Street	D3
Holdsworth Street	B7-B8
Holyrood Place	C2-C3
How Street	D4-E4
Hospital Road	E7-F7
Houndiscombe Road	D7-D8
Ilbert Street	B6
James Street	C6-C7
Kensington Road	F8
King Street	A5-B5
Kirkby Place	C7-D7
Lambhay Hill	E2-E3
Lambhay Street	E3
Leigham Street	B2-B3
Lipson Road	E5-E6-F6-F7
Lockyer Street	C2-C3
Longfield Place	F8
Looe Street	D4-E4
Madeira Road	D2-E2-E3
Marlborough Road	D7-E7
Market Avenue	B4-B5
Market Square	B5-C5
Market Way	B5
Martin Street	A3-A4
May Terrace	F6
Mayflower Street	B5-C5-C6-D5-D6
Melbourne Street	A6
Mildmay Street	E7
Millbay Road	A3-B3
Mount Street	E6-E7
Nelson Street	E7
Neswick Street	A5
New Street	D3-E3
New George Street	B4-B5-C5-D5
North Cross	C6
North Hill	D6-D7-E7-E8
North Road East	C7-D7-D8-E8
North Road West	A6-B6-B7-C7
North Street	E5-E6
Notte Street	C3-D3-D4
Octagon Street	A4-A5
Old Town Street	D4-D5
Oxford Place	B6-C6
Oxford Street	B6
Palace Street	D4
Parade	E3-E4
Patna Place	B6
Penrose Street	B6

Pier Street	B2
Portland Place	D6
Portland Square	D6-D7
Portland Villas	C7
Plym Street	E6-E7
Prince Maurice Road	F8
Princess Street	C3-C4-D4
Prospect Place	B2-B3
Prospect Street	E6-E7
Providence Street	E7-E8
Quay Road	D3-E3
Queen's Road	F8
Radford Road	B1-B2
Radnor Place	E6
Radnor Street	E6
Raleigh Street	B4
Regent Street	D6-E6-F6
Rendle Street	A4
Restormel Road	C8-D8-D7
Royal Parade	C4-D4
St Lawrence Road	D8-E8
Salisbury Road	F6
Saltash Road	B7-C7-C6
Sawrey Street	A3-A4
Shaftesbury Cottages	E7
Shepherds Lane	F4
Southern Terrace	F8
Southside Street	D3-E3
Southland Road	D7-D8
Stuart Road	A7-B7
Sussex Street	D3
Sutherland Road	D7-D8
Sutton Road	F4-F5
Syney Street	B6
Tavistock Place	D6
Teats Hill Road	F3
The Crescent	B4-B3-C3
Tothill Avenue	F5-F6
Tracy Street	B5
Trafalgar Street	E5-E6
Union Street	A4-B4
Vauxhall Street	D3-D4-E4
Wake Street	B7-B8
Walker Terrace	A2-B2
Waterloo Street	E7
Welbeck Avenue	C7
Well Street	B5
Well Street	E7
West Hoe Road	A3-A2-B2
Western Approach	B4-B5-B6-C6
Whimple Street	D4
Whittington Street	A7
Winston Lane	C7
Wolsdon Street	A6
Wyndham Street East	A6
Wyndham Street West	A6
Zion Street	D3

47

Central Portsmouth

Portsmouth

Richard the Lionheart first recognised the strategic importance of Portsea Island and subsequently ordered the first docks, and later the town of Portsmouth, to be built. Over the centuries, succeeding monarchs improved the defences and extended the docks which now cover some 300 acres – as befits Britain's premier naval base. Of the defensive fortifications, Fort Widley and the

Round Tower are the best preserved remains. Two famous ships rest in Portsmouth; HMS Victory and the Mary Rose. The former, Lord Nelson's flagship, has been fully restored and the adjacent Royal Naval museum houses numerous relics of Trafalgar. The Mary Rose, built by Henry VIII, lay on the sea bed off Southsea until she was spectacularly raised in 1982. She has now been put on display and there is an exhibition in Southsea Castle of artefacts that have been recovered from

her. Portsmouth suffered greatly from bombing in World War II and the centre has been almost completely rebuilt. However, the old town, clustered around the harbour mouth, escaped severe damage and, now restored, forms an attractive and fashionable area of the city.

Southsea, Portsmouth's near neighbour, developed in the 19th century as an elegant seaside resort with fine houses and terraces, an esplanade and an extensive seafront common.

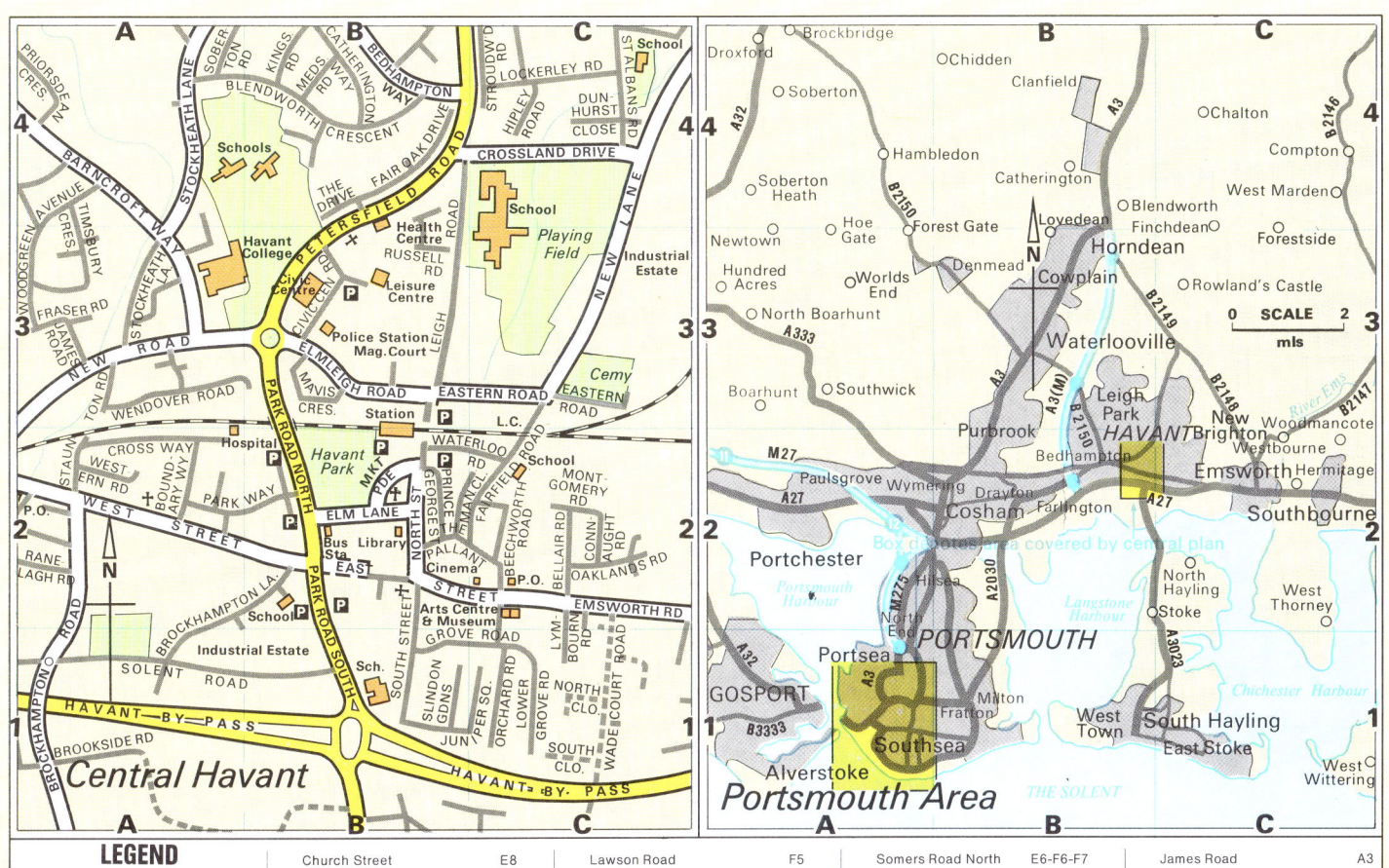

Central Havant

Portsmouth Area

49

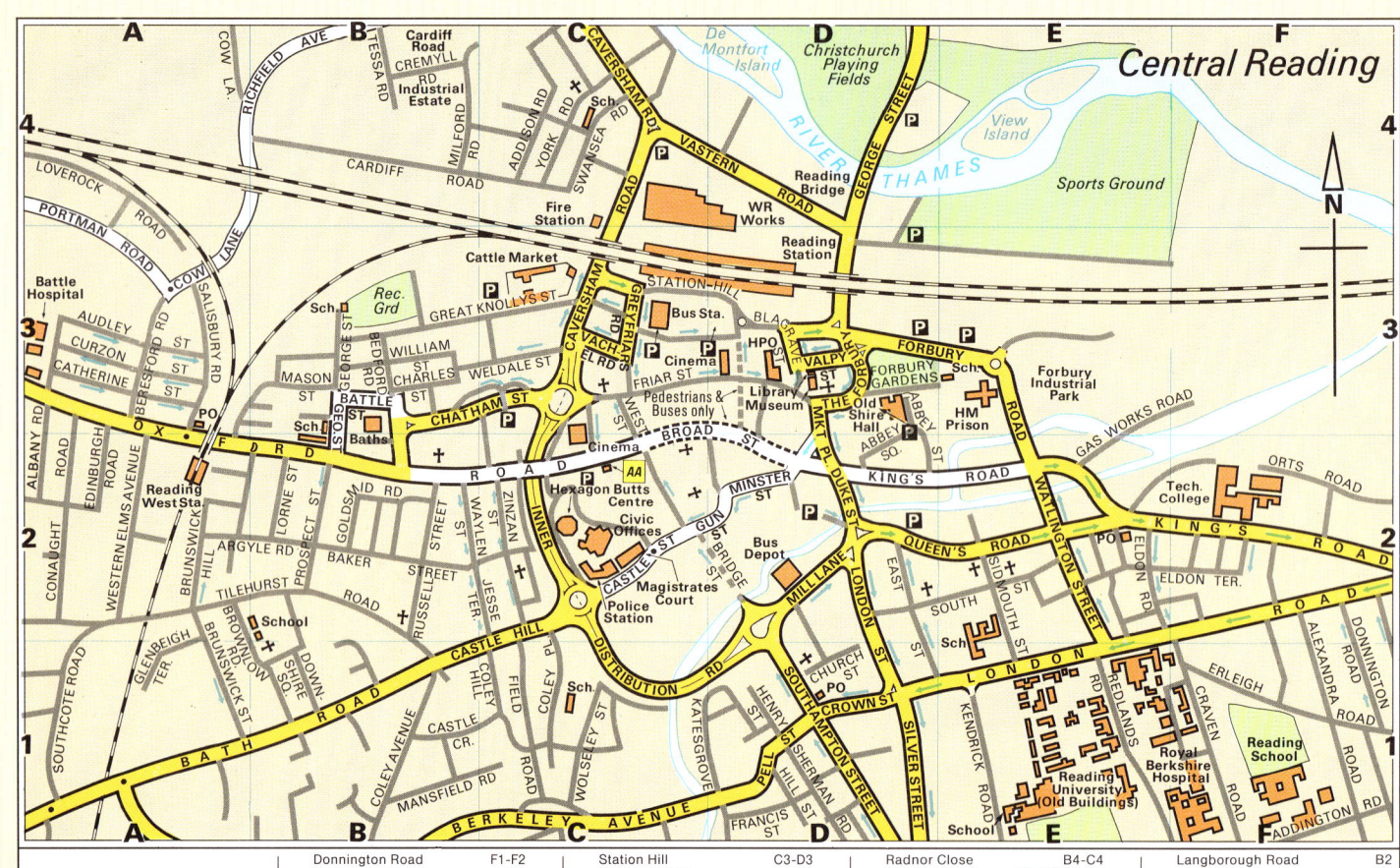

Central Reading

Street Index with Grid Reference

Reading

Abbey Square	D2-D3
Abbey Street	D2-D3
Addington Road	F1
Addison Road	C4
Alexandra Road	F1-F2
Argyle Road	A2-B2
Audley Street	A3
Baker Street	A2
Bath Road	A1-B1
Battle Street	B3
Bedford Road	B3
Beresford Road	A3
Berkeley Avenue	B1-C1-D1
Blagrave Street	D3
Bridge Street	C2-D2
Broad Street	C2-C3-D3-D2
Brownlow Road	A2-B2-B1
Brunswick Hill	A2
Brunswick Street	A1-A2
Cardiff Road	B4-C4
Castle Crescent	B1-C1
Castle Hill	B1-B2-C2
Castle Street	C2
Catherine Street	A3
Caversham Road	C3-C4
Charles Street	B3
Chatham Street	B3-C3
Church Street	D1
Coley Avenue	B1
Coley Hill	C1
Coley Place	C1-C2
Conaught Road	A2-A3
Cow Lane	A3-A4
Craven Road	F1-F2
Cremyll Road	B4
Crown Street	D1
Curzon Street	A3
Donnington Road	F1-F2
Downshire Square	B1
Duke Street	D2
East Street	D1-D2
Edinburgh Road	A2-A3
Eldon Road	E2
Eldon Terrace	E2-F2
Elm Park Road	A2-A3
Erleigh Road	F1
Field Road	C1
Forbury Gardens	D3-E3
Forbury Road	D3-E3-E2
Francis Street	D1
Friar Street	C3-D3
Gas Works Road	E2-E3-F3
George Street	B2-B3
George Street	D3-D4
Glenbeigh Terrace	A1-A2
Goldsmid Road	B2
Great Knollys Street	B3-C3
Greyfriars Road	C3
Gun Street	C2-D2
Henry Street	D1
Hill Street	D1
Inner Distribution Road	C3-C2-C1-D1-D2
Jesse Terrace	B2-C2
Katesgrove	C1-D1
Kendrick Road	E1
King's Road	D2-E2-F2
London Road	D1-E1-E2-F2
London Street	D1-D2
Lorne Street	B2
Loverock Road	A3-A4
Mansfield Road	B1-C1
Market Place	D2-D3
Mason Street	B3
Milford Road	B4
Mill Lane	D2
Minster Street	D2
Orts Road	E2-F2
Oxford Road	A3-A2-B2-C2
Pell Street	D1
Portman Road	A3-A4
Prospect Street	B2
Queen's Road	D2-E2
Redlands Road	E1
Richfield Avenue	A4-B4
Russell Street	B2
Salisbury Road	A3
Sidmouth Street	E1-E2
Silver Street	D1
Sherman Road	D1
Southampton Street	D1
Southcote Road	A1-A2
South Street	D2-E2
Station Hill	C3-D3
Swansea Road	C4
Tessa Road	B4
The Forbury	D3
Tilehurst Road	A2-B2-B1
Vachel Road	C3
Valpy Street	D3
Vastern Road	C4-D4
Watlington Street	E2
Waylen Street	B2
Weldale Street	B3-C3
Western Elms Avenue	A2
West Street	C2-C3
William Street	B3
Wolseley Street	C1
York Road	C4
Zinzan Street	C2
Radnor Close	B4-C4
Reading Road	B3-B2-C2-C1
Remenham Lane	C3-C4
Riverside	C3
River Terrace	C2-C3
Rupert Close	B4
St Andrew's Road	B1-C1
St Mark's Road	B1-C1
Simmons Road	A4
Station Road	C3
Thames Side	C3
The Close	A1
Upton Close	C1-C2
Vicarage Road	B1
Walton Avenue	C1
West Street	A3-B3
White Hill	C3
York Road	A3-B3

Henley

Albert Road	B2
Ancastle Green	A2-A3
Badgemore Lane	A4-B4
Bell Street	B3-B4
Crisp Road	A4
Deanfield Avenue	A2-B2
Deanfield Road	A1-A2
Duke Street	B3
Friday Street	B3-C3
Gainsborough Hill	A1
Grange Road	C1
Gravel Hill	A3-B3
Greys Hill	A1-A2-B2
Greys Road	A1-A2-B2-B3
Grove Road	C1
Hamilton Avenue	B1-B2-C2
Hart Street	B3-C3
Hop Gardens	A3-A4
King's Close	A3-B3
King's Road	B3-B4
Luker Avenue	A4
Market Place	B3
Meadow Road	C2
Milton Close	A3
Mount View	A4-B4
New Street	B4-C4-C3
Norman Avenue	B2
Queen Street	B3-B2-C2
Paradise Road	A2-A3
Park Road	C1

Wokingham

Arthur Drive	A2-A3
Ashridge Road	C3-C4
Barkham Road	A1-A2
Barrett Crescent	C2-C3
Bell Foundry Lane	B4
Benning Way	C4
Broad Street	B2
Budges Road	C3
Cantley Crescent	A4
Carey Road	B1
Clare Avenue	B3
Clifton Road	A3-A4
Copse Drive	A3
Crutchley Road	C3
Denmark Street	B2
Easthampstead Road	B2-C2-C1
Eastheath Avenue	A1
Elisabeth Road	C2-C3
Elms Road	B2
Finchampstead Road	A1-B1-B2
Fish Ponds Road	A1
Gipsy Lane	B2-B1-C1-C2
Glebelands Road	B3
Holmes Crescent	A1
Holt Lane	A3-B3
Howard Road	B2
Hughes Road	C3
Jubilee Avenue	A4-A3-B3
Keephatch Road	C3-C4
Langborough Road	B2
London Road	C2
Marks Road	A4
Martins Drive	A3-A4
Mathewsgreen Road	A4-B4
Meadow Road	A2
Milton Road	B2-B3-B4
Molly Millars Road	A2-A1-B1
Murdoch Road	B2-C2
Murray Road	A2
Norreys Avenue	C3
Oaklands Drive	A1
Oxford Road	A2-A3
Park Road	A2-B2
Peach Street	B2-C2
Reading Road	A3-B3
Rectory Road	B2-B3-C3
Rose Street	B2-C2
Sarum Crescent	C3
Sewell Avenue	A4
Shute End	B2-B3
South Drive	B2-B1-C1
Southlands Road	C1
Station Road	A2-B3
Sturges Road	B2-C2
Twyford Road	A4-B4
Warren House Road	B4-C4
Wellington Road	A2-B2
Westcott Road	C2
Wiltshire Road	B4-B3-C3

LEGEND

Town Plan
AA recommended route
Restricted roads
Other roads
Buildings of interest School
Car parks P
Parks and open spaces
One way streets

Area Plan
A roads
B roads
Locations
Urban area
Wilsden○

Reading

Shopping and light industry first spring to mind when thinking of Reading, but the town actually has a long and important history. Its rise to significance began in 1121 when Henry I founded an abbey here which became the third most important in England. However, after the Dissolution of the Monasteries, only a few ruins were left. Reading also used to be one of the major centres of the medieval cloth trade, but, already declining in the early 17th century, this source of income was reduced still further as a result of Civil War disturbances.

A fascinating collection of all types of farm implements and domestic equipment can be found in the extremely comprehensive Museum of English Rural Life, situated in the University Campus at Whiteknights Park. The town's own museum has major displays about nearby Silchester – the powerful Roman town of *Calleva*.

Henley-on-Thames, famous for its annual rowing regatta, is a lovely old town, well-provided with old coaching inns, Georgian façades and numerous listed buildings.

Wokingham has been a market town for centuries and over the years has been known for its silk industry and its bell-foundry. Half-timbered gabled houses can be seen in the town centre, although modern development surrounds it.

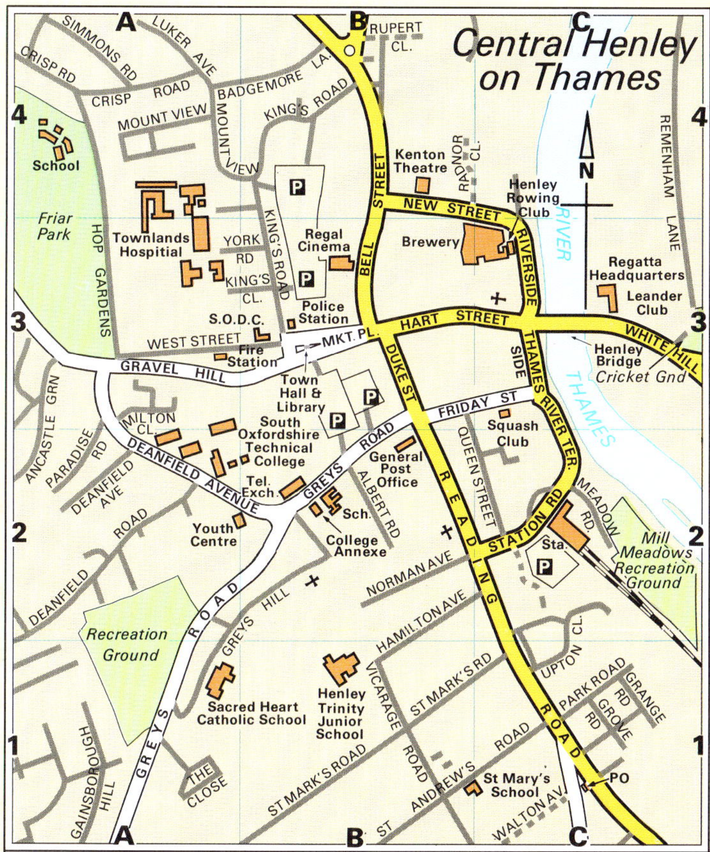

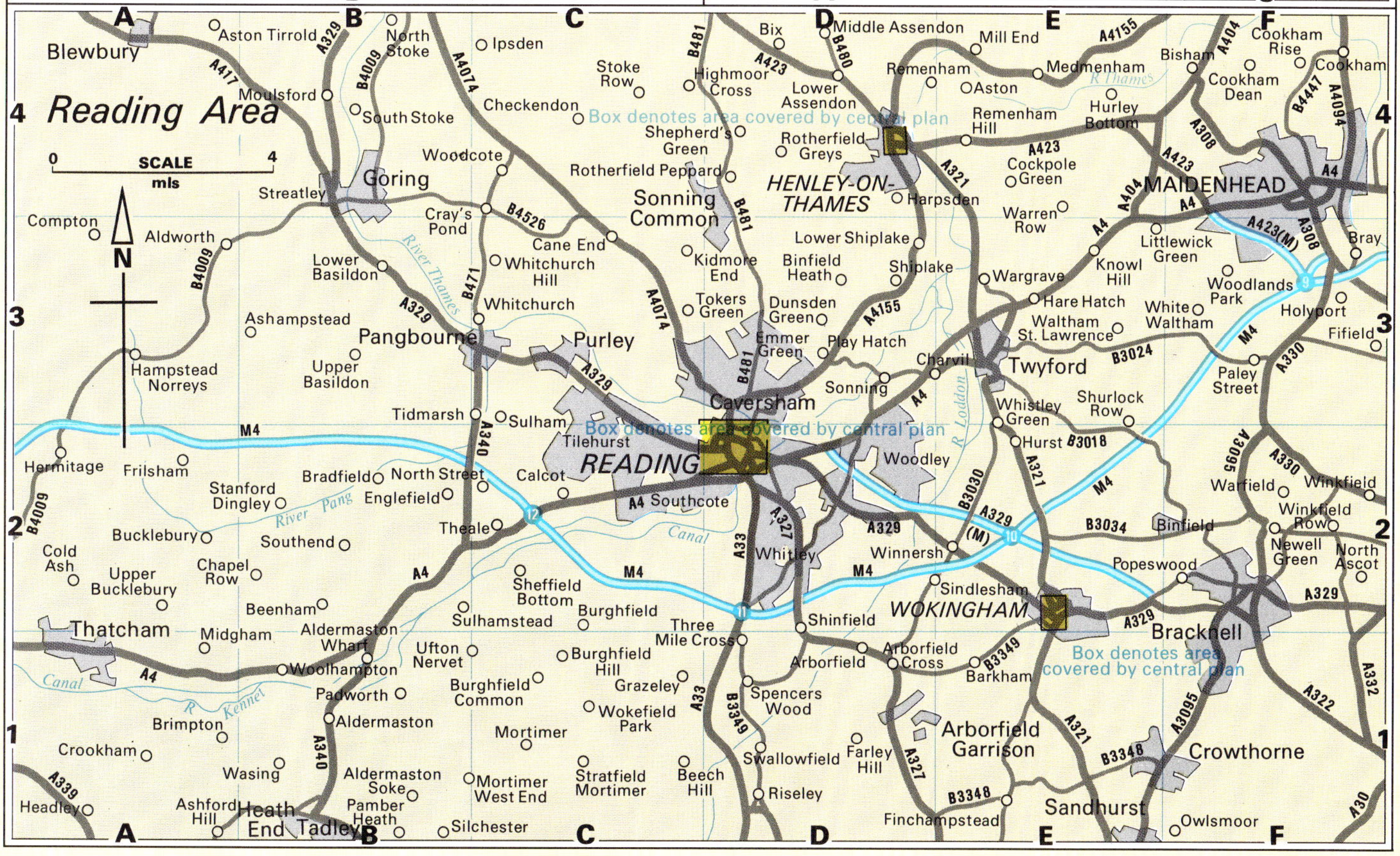

Central Henley on Thames

Central Wokingham

Reading Area

SCALE
mls
0   4

Box denotes area covered by central plan

READING
Whiteknights, which consists of 300 acres of landscaped parkland, provides Reading's modern university with an incomparable campus setting and includes a conservation area and a biological reserve for research purposes.

51

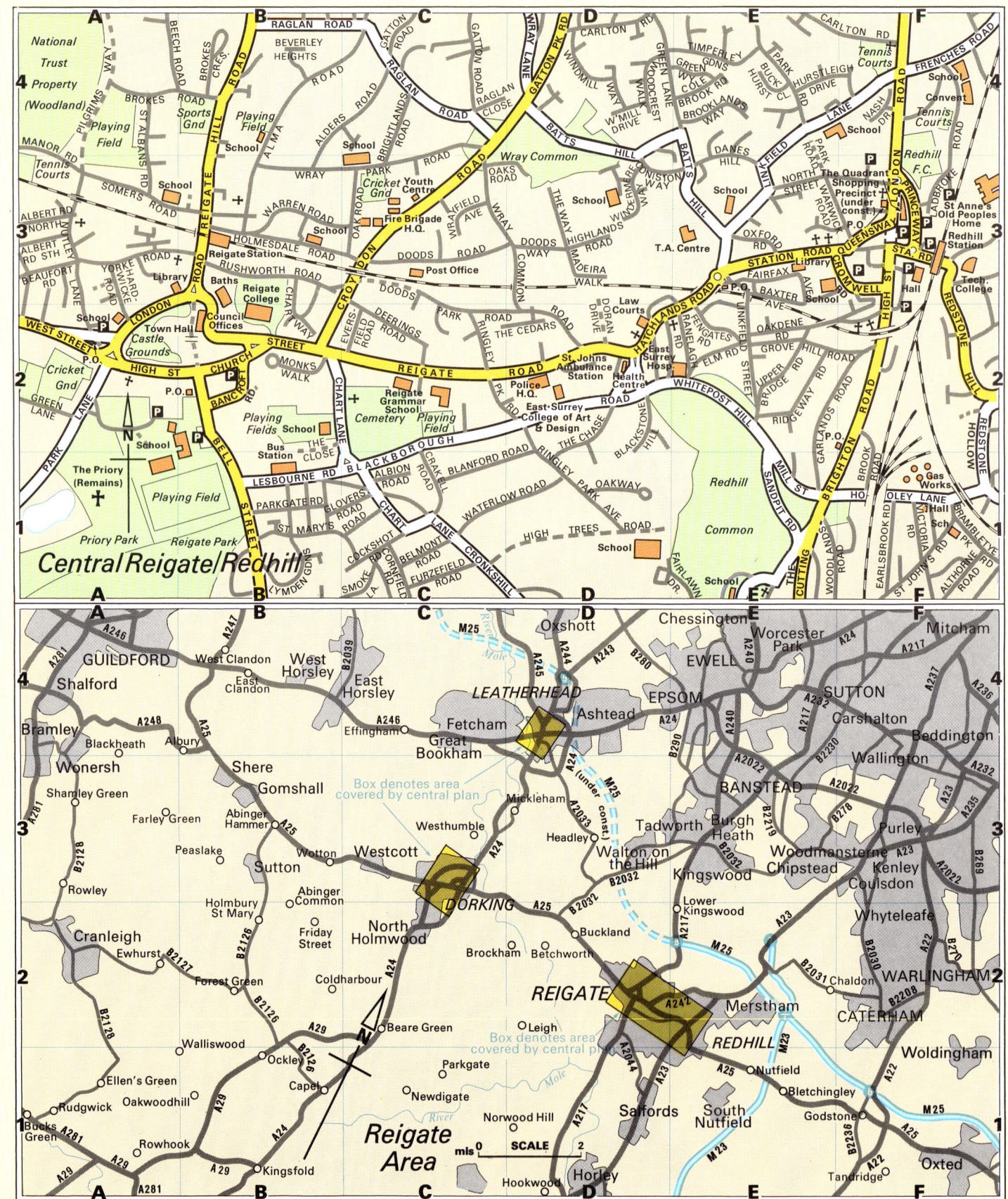

Central Reigate/Redhill

Reigate Area

Box denotes area covered by central plan

SCALE

Reigate/Redhill

One of the earliest public libraries in the country can be found in Reigate's parish church of St. Mary Magdalen. The library dates from 1701; the church goes back as far as the 12th century. Industry and commerce are changing the face of the area, but Reigate has kept a number of open spaces, such as Reigate Park (the site of a former priory), Reigate Heath (where an 18th-century windmill has been converted into a church) and Earlswood Common.

Dorking lies at the foot of Box Hill, a popular beauty spot today and at least as far back as the early 1800s, when Jane Austen featured it in her novel *Emma*.

Modernisation has done little to erode the charm of the town, where weeping willows surround the attractive Mill Pond. Overlooking the High Street is the gabled White Horse Inn, reminiscent of coaching days.

Leatherhead's Thorndyke Theatre has been entertaining the area since the 1960s, and the town is also known for its Royal School for the Blind, which was founded here in the late 18th century. With a museum that traces the history of the region, and a parish church which dates mainly from the 12th to the 15th centuries, Leatherhead today is the home of several industrial research establishments.

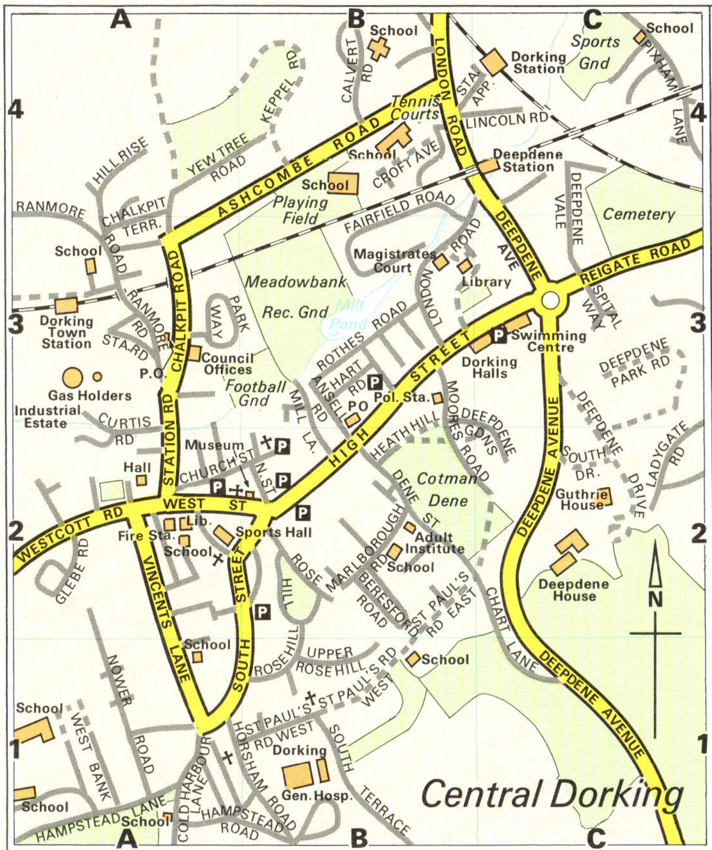

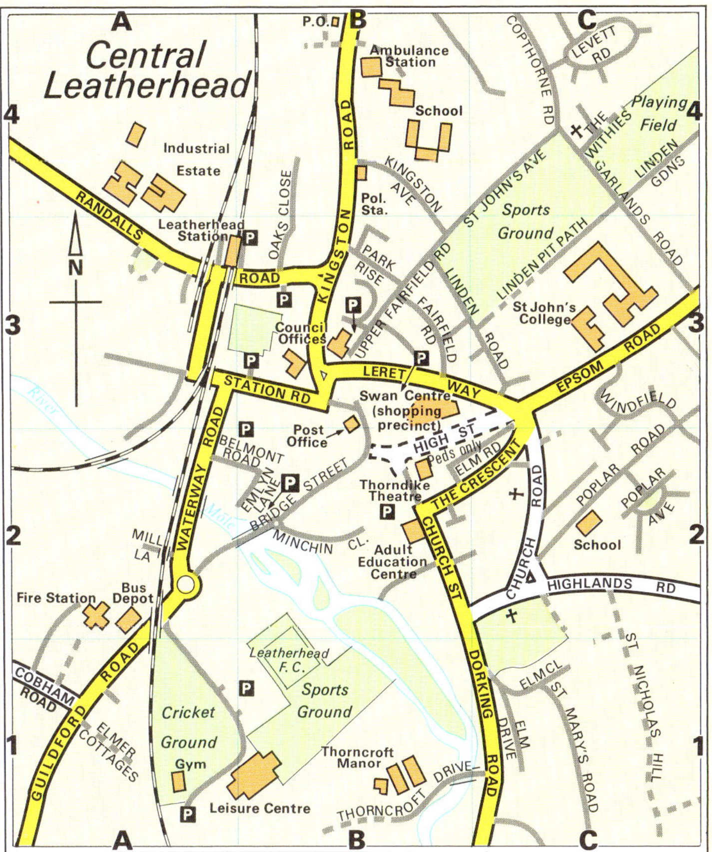

Central Dorking

Central Leatherhead

Key to Town Plan and Area Plan

Town Plan
A A Recommended roads
Other roads
Restricted roads
Buildings of interest — Theatre
Car Parks — P
Parks and open spaces
Churches

Area Plan
A roads
B roads
Locations — Leigh ○
Urban Area

Street Index with Grid Reference

Redhill/Reigate

Albert Road North	A3
Albert Road South	A3
Albion Road	C1
Alders Road	B3-B4-C4
Alma Road	B3-B4-C4
Althorne Road	F1
Bancroft Road	B2
Batts Hill	D4-E4-E3
Baxter Avenue	E3
Beaufort Road	A3
Beech Road	A4
Bell Street	B1-B2
Belmont Road	C1
Beverley Heights	B4
Blackborough Road	C1-C2-D2
Blackstone Hill	D2
Blanford Road	C1-D1-D2
Brambletye Park Road	F1
Brightlands Road	C3-C4
Brighton Road	E1-F1-F2
Brokes Crescent	B4
Brokes Road	A4-B4
Brook Road	F1-F2
Brooklands Way	E4
Buckhurst Close	E4
Carlton Road	D4, E4-F4
Chart Lane	B2-C2-C1
Chartway	B2-B3
Church Street	B2
Cockshot Road	C1
Colebrook Road	E4
Coniston Way	D3-E3
Cornfield Road	C1
Crakell Road	C1
Cromwell Road	E3-F3
Cronkshill	C1-D1
Croydon Road	B2-B3-C3-C4
Danes Hill	E3-E4
Deerings Road	C2-C3
Doods Road	C2-D3
Doods Way	D3
Doods Park Road	C3-C2-D2
Doran Drive	D2-D3
Earlsbrook Road	F1
Elm Road	E2
Eversfield Road	C2
Fairfax Avenue	E3
Fairlawn Drive	D1-E1
Fengates Road	E2
Frenches Road	F4
Furzefield Road	C1
Garlands Road	E1-E2-F2
Gatton Road	C4
Gatton Park Road	D4
Glovers Road	B1-C1
Green Lane	A2
Green Lane	D4-E4
Green Way	D4-E4
Grove Hill Road	E2-F2
Hardwicke Road	A2-A3
Hatchlands Road	D2-E2-E3
High Street	A2-B2
High Street	F2-F3
Highlands Road	D3
High Trees Road	C1-D1
Holmesdale Road	B3-C3
Hooley Lane	E1-F1
Hurstleigh Drive	E4-F4
Ladbroke Road	F3-F4
Lesbourne Road	B1
Linkfield Lane	E3-E4-F4
Linkfield Street	E2-E3
London Road	A2-A3-B3
London Road	F3-F4
Lymden Gardens	B1
Madeira Walk	D3
Manor Road	A3-A4
Mill Street	E1
Monks Walk	B2
Nash Drive	F4
North Street	E3
Nutley Lane	A2-A3
Oak Road	C3
Oakdene Road	E2
Oaks Road	C3-D3
Oakway	D1
Oxford Road	E3
Park Lane	A1-A2
Park Road	E3-E4
Parkgate Road	B1
Pilgrims Way	A3-A4
Prince Way	E3
Queensway	F3
Raglan Close	C4
Raglan Road	B4-C4
Ranelagh Road	E2
Redstone Hill	F2-F3
Redstone Hollow	F1-F2
Reigate Road	B2-C2-D2
Reigate Hill Road	B3-B4
Ridgeway Road	E2
Ringley Park Avenue	D1-D2
Ringley Park Road	C2-D2
Rushworth Road	B3
St Albans Road	A3-A4
St John's Road	F1
St Mary's Road	B1-C1
Sandpit Road	E1
Smoke Lane	C1
Somers Road	A3-B3
Station Road	E3-F3
The Cedars	C2-D2
The Chase	D1-D2
The Close	B2
The Cutting	E1
The Way	D3
Timperley Gardens	D4-E4
Upper Bridge Road	E2
Victoria Road	F1
Warren Road	B3-C3
Warwick Road	E3-F3
Waterlow Road	C1-D1
West Street	A2
Whitepost Hill	D2-E2
Windermere Way	D3
Windmill Drive	D4
Windmill Way	D4
Woodcrest Walk	D4
Woodlands Road	E1
Wray Lane	D4
Wray Common Road	C3-D3-D2
Wrayfield Avenue	C3
Wray Park Road	B3-C3-C4
Yorke Road	A3-B3

Dorking

Ansell Road	B2-B3
Ashcombe Road	A3-A4-B4
Beresford Road	B2
Calvert Road	B4
Chalkpit Road	A3
Chalkpit Terrace	A3-A4
Chart Lane	C1-C2
Church Street	A2-B2
Cold Harbour Lane	A1
Croft Avenue	B4
Curtis Road	A2-A3
Deepdene Avenue	C1-C2-C3-C4
Deepdene Drive	C2-C3
Deepdene Gardens	B3-C3-C2
Deepdene Park Road	C3
Deepdene Vale	C3-C4
Dene Street	B2
Fairfield Road	B3-B4
Glebe Road	A2
Hampstead Lane	A1
Hampstead Road	A1-B1
Hart Road	B3
Heath Hill	B2-B3
High Street	B2-B3-C3
Hill Rise	A4
Horsham Road	A1-B1
Keppel Road	A4-B4
Ladygate Road	C2-C3
Lincoln Road	B4-C4
London Road	B3-B4-C4-B4
Marlborough Road	B2
Mill Lane	B2-B3
Moores Road	B3-B2-C2
North Street	B2
Nower Road	A1-A2
Park Way	A3
Pixham Lane	C4

Leatherhead

Belmont Road	A2-B2
Bridge Street	A2-B2
Church Road	C2-C3
Church Street	B2
Cobham Road	A1
Copthorne Road	C4
Dorking Road	B2-B1-C1
Elm Close	C1
Elm Drive	C1
Elm Road	B2-C2
Elmer Cottages	A1
Emlyn Lane	B2
Epsom Road	C3
Fairfield Road	B3
Garlands Road	C3-C4
Guildford Road	A1-A2
High Street	B2-B3-C3
Highlands Road	C2
Kingston Avenue	B3-B4
Kingston Road	B3-B4
Leret Way	B3-C3
Levett Road	C4
Linden Gardens	C4
Linden Pit Path	C3-C4
Linden Road	B3-C3
Mill Lane	A2
Minchin Close	B2
Oaks Close	B3-B4
Park Rise	B3
Poplar Avenue	C2
Poplar Road	C2-C3
Randalls Road	A4-A3-B3
St John's Avenue	B3-B4-C4
St Mary's Road	C1
St Nicholas Hill	C1-C2
Station Road	A3-B3
The Crescent	B2-C2
The Withies	C4
Thorncroft Drive	B1-C1
Upper Fairfield Road	B3
Waterway Road	A2-A3
Windfield	C3

Ranmore Road etc.

Ranmore Road	A3-A4
Reigate Road	C3
Rose Hill	B1-B2
Rothes Road	B3
St Paul's Road East	B2
St Paul's Road West	A1-B1
South Drive	C2
South Street	A1-B1-B2-A2-B2
South Terrace	B1
Spital Way	C3
Station Approach	B4-C4
Station Road	A2-A3
Upper Rose Hill	B1
Vincents Lane	A1-A2
West Street	A2-B2
West Bank	A1
Westcott Road	A2
Yew Tree Road	A4-B4

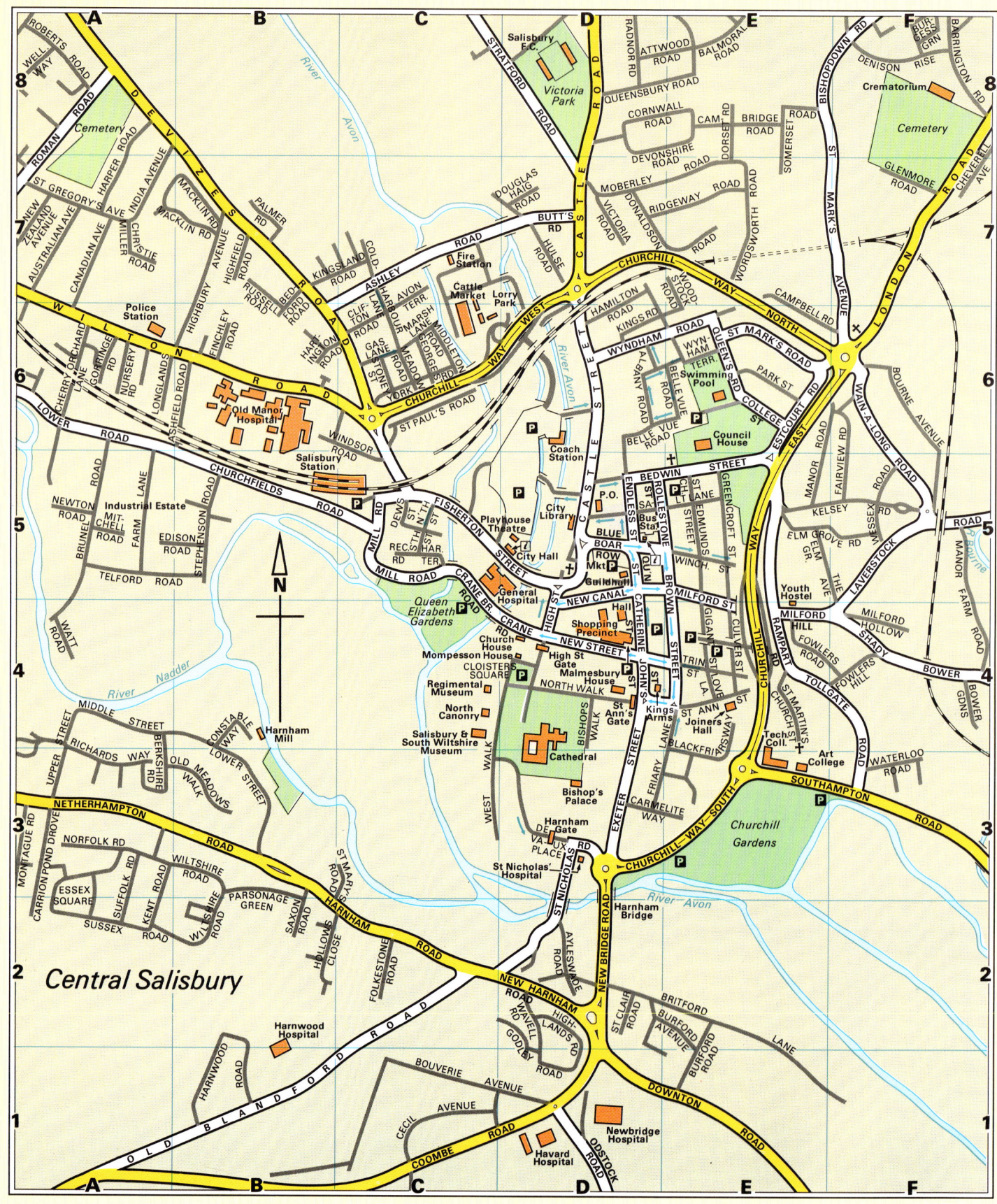

Salisbury

Its attractive site where the waters of the Avon and Nadder meet, its beautiful cathedral and its unspoilt centre put Salisbury among England's finest cities. In 1220 the people of the original settlement at Old Sarum, two miles to the north, moved down to the plain and laid the first stone of the cathedral. Within 38 years its was completed and the result is a superb example of Early English architecture.

The cloisters are the largest in England and the spire the tallest in Britain. All the houses within the Cathedral Close were built for cathedral functionaries, and although many have Georgian façades, most date back to the 13th century. Mompesson House is one of the handsome mansions here and as it belongs to the National Trust, its equally fine interior can be seen. Another building houses the Museum of the Duke of Edinburgh's Royal Regiment. At one time, relations between the clergy and the citizens of Salisbury were not always harmonious, so the former built a protective wall around the Close.

The streets of the modern city follow the medieval grid pattern of squares, or 'chequers', and the tightly-packed houses provide a very pleasing townscape. Salisbury was granted its first charter in 1227 and flourished as a market and wool centre; there is still a twice-weekly market in the spacious square.

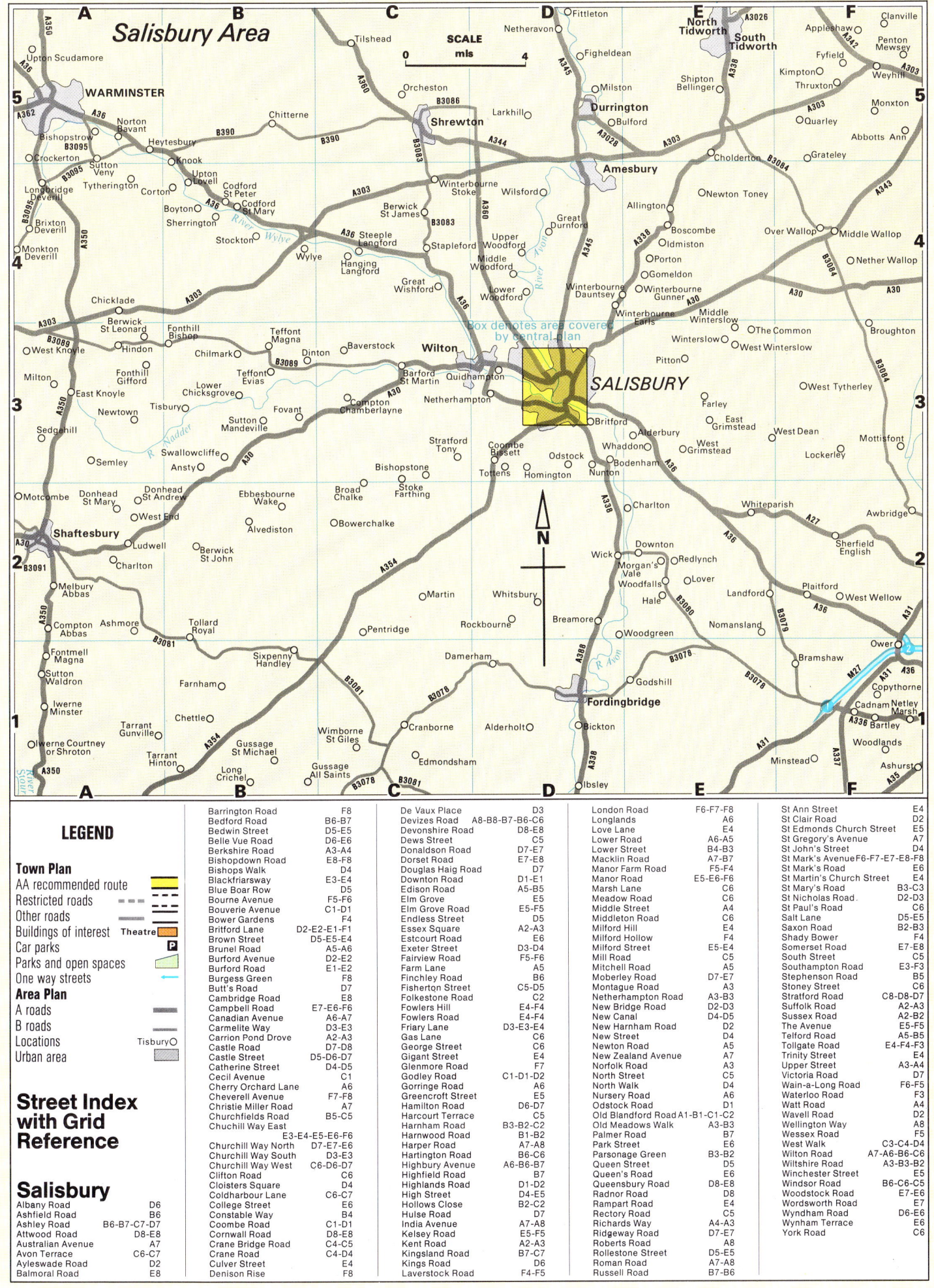

Salisbury Area

SCALE
0 mls 4

Box denotes area covered by central plan

SALISBURY

LEGEND

Town Plan
- AA recommended route
- Restricted roads
- Other roads
- Buildings of interest — Theatre
- Car parks — P
- Parks and open spaces
- One way streets

Area Plan
- A roads
- B roads
- Locations — Tisbury
- Urban area

Street Index with Grid Reference

Salisbury

Street	Grid
Albany Road	D6
Ashfield Road	B6
Ashley Road	B6-B7-C7-D7
Attwood Road	D8-E8
Australian Avenue	A7
Avon Terrace	C6-C7
Ayleswade Road	D2
Balmoral Road	E8
Barrington Road	F8
Bedford Road	B6-B7
Bedwin Street	D5-E5
Belle Vue Road	D6-E6
Berkshire Road	A3-A4
Bishopdown Road	E8-F8
Bishops Walk	D4
Blackfriarsway	E3-E4
Blue Boar Row	D5
Bourne Avenue	F5-F6
Bouverie Avenue	C1-D1
Bower Gardens	F4
Britford Lane	D2-E2-E1-F1
Brown Street	D5-E5-E4
Brunel Road	A5-A6
Burford Avenue	D2-E2
Burford Road	E1-E2
Burgess Green	F8
Butt's Road	D7
Cambridge Road	E8
Campbell Road	E7-E6-F6
Canadian Avenue	A6-A7
Carmelite Way	D3-E3
Carrion Pond Drove	A2-A3
Castle Road	D7-D8
Castle Street	D5-D6-D7
Catherine Street	D4-D5
Cecil Avenue	C1
Cherry Orchard Lane	A6
Cheverell Avenue	F7-F8
Christie Miller Road	A7
Churchfields Road	B5-C5
Chuchill Way East	E3-E4-E5-E6-F6
Churchill Way North	D7-E7-E6
Churchill Way South	D3-E3
Churchill Way West	C6-D6-D7
Clifton Road	C6
Cloisters Square	D4
Coldharbour Lane	C6-C7
College Street	E6
Constable Way	B4
Coombe Road	C1-D1
Cornwall Road	D8-E8
Crane Bridge Road	C4-C5
Crane Road	C4-D4
Culver Street	E4
Denison Rise	F8
De Vaux Place	D3
Devizes Road	A8-B8-B7-B6-C6
Devonshire Road	D8-E8
Dews Street	C5
Donaldson Road	D7-E7
Dorset Road	E7-E8
Douglas Haig Road	D7
Downton Road	D1-E1
Edison Road	A5-B5
Elm Grove	E5
Elm Grove Road	E5-F5
Endless Street	D5
Essex Square	A2-A3
Estcourt Road	E6
Exeter Street	D3-D4
Fairview Road	F5-F6
Farm Lane	A5
Finchley Road	B6
Fisherton Street	C5-D5
Folkestone Road	C2
Fowlers Hill	E4-F4
Fowlers Road	E4-F4
Friary Lane	D3-E3-E4
Gas Lane	C6
George Street	C6
Gigant Street	E4
Glenmore Road	F7
Godley Road	C1-D1-D2
Gorringe Road	A6
Greencroft Street	E5
Hamilton Road	D6-D7
Harcourt Terrace	C5
Harnham Road	B3-B2-C2
Harnwood Road	B1-B2
Harper Road	A7-A8
Hartington Road	B6-C6
Highbury Avenue	A6-B6-B7
Highfield Road	B7
Highlands Road	D1-D2
High Street	D4-E5
Hollows Close	B2-C2
Hulse Road	D7
India Avenue	A7-A8
Kelsey Road	E5-F5
Kent Road	A2-A3
Kingsland Road	B7-C7
Kings Road	D6
Laverstock Road	F4-F5
London Road	F6-F7-F8
Longlands	A6
Love Lane	E4
Lower Road	A6-A5
Lower Street	B4-B3
Macklin Road	A7-B7
Manor Farm Road	F5-F4
Manor Road	E5-E6-F6
Marsh Lane	C6
Meadow Road	C6
Middle Street	A4
Middleton Road	C6
Milford Hill	E4
Milford Hollow	F4
Milford Street	E5-E4
Mill Road	C5
Mitchell Road	A5
Moberley Road	D7-E7
Montague Road	A3
Netherhampton Road	A3-B3
New Bridge Road	D2-D3
New Canal	D4-D5
New Harnham Road	D2
New Street	D4
Newton Road	A5
New Zealand Avenue	A7
Norfolk Road	A3
North Street	C5
North Walk	D4
Nursery Road	A6
Odstock Road	D1
Old Blandford Road	A1-B1-C1-C2
Old Meadows Walk	A3-B3
Palmer Road	B7
Park Street	E6
Parsonage Green	B3-B2
Queen Street	D5
Queen's Road	E6
Queensbury Road	D8-E8
Radnor Road	D8
Rampart Road	E4
Rectory Road	C5
Richards Way	A4-A3
Ridgeway Road	D7-E7
Roberts Road	A8
Rollestone Street	D5-E5
Roman Road	A7-A8
Russell Road	B7-B6
St Ann Street	E4
St Clair Road	D2
St Edmonds Church Street	E5
St Gregory's Avenue	A7
St John's Street	D4
St Mark's Avenue	F6-F7-E7-E8-F8
St Mark's Road	E6
St Martin's Church Street	E4
St Mary's Road	B3-C3
St Nicholas Road	D2-D3
St Paul's Road	C6
Salt Lane	D5-E5
Saxon Road	B2-B3
Shady Bower	F4
Somerset Road	E7-E8
South Street	C5
Southampton Road	E3-F3
Stephenson Road	B5
Stoney Street	C6
Stratford Road	C8-D8-D7
Suffolk Road	A2-A3
Sussex Road	A2-B2
The Avenue	E5-F5
Telford Road	A5-B5
Tollgate Road	E4-F4-F3
Trinity Street	E4
Upper Street	A3-A4
Victoria Road	D7
Wain-a-Long Road	F6-F5
Waterloo Road	F3
Watt Road	A4
Wavell Road	D2
Wellington Way	A8
Wessex Road	F5
West Walk	C3-C4-D4
Wilton Road	A7-A6-B6-C6
Wiltshire Road	A3-B3-B2
Winchester Street	E4
Windsor Road	B6-C6-C5
Woodstock Road	E7-E6
Wordsworth Road	E7
Wyndham Road	D6-E6
Wynham Terrace	E6
York Road	C6

Slough

The town is something of a non-starter as far as architectural beauty or historical interest is concerned. However, it is a good shopping centre and has plenty of sports and leisure facilities.

Windsor The distinctive outline of the castle's towers and battlements above the Thames completely dominates the town. First built by the Normans to guard the approaches to London, it has been altered and added to at different times by various kings, but Henry III and Edward III contributed most to its present haphazard shape. The State Apartments are magnificent, as is St George's Chapel, with its superb fan-vaulted ceiling. Queen Mary's Dolls' House is an exquisite model house of the 1920s, complete down to the last detail. The town itself, squeezed between the castle walls and the river, has several attractive streets graced with fine buildings. One 17th-century colonnaded building by Sir Christopher Wren contains a small museum of local interest, and a recent new attraction is the Madame Tussaud's Royalty and Railways Exhibition.

Maidenhead used to be an important stage-post on the London to Bath road and is now a prosperous Thameside residential town. Oldfield House, near the ancient bridge designed by Brunel, contains the Henry Reitlinger Bequest Museum, specialising in glass and ceramics.

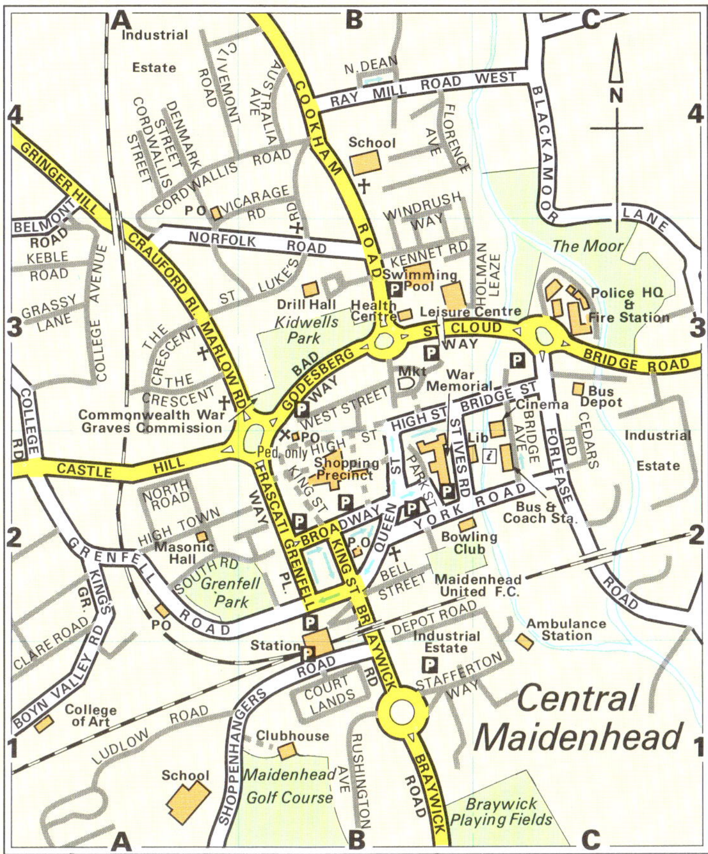

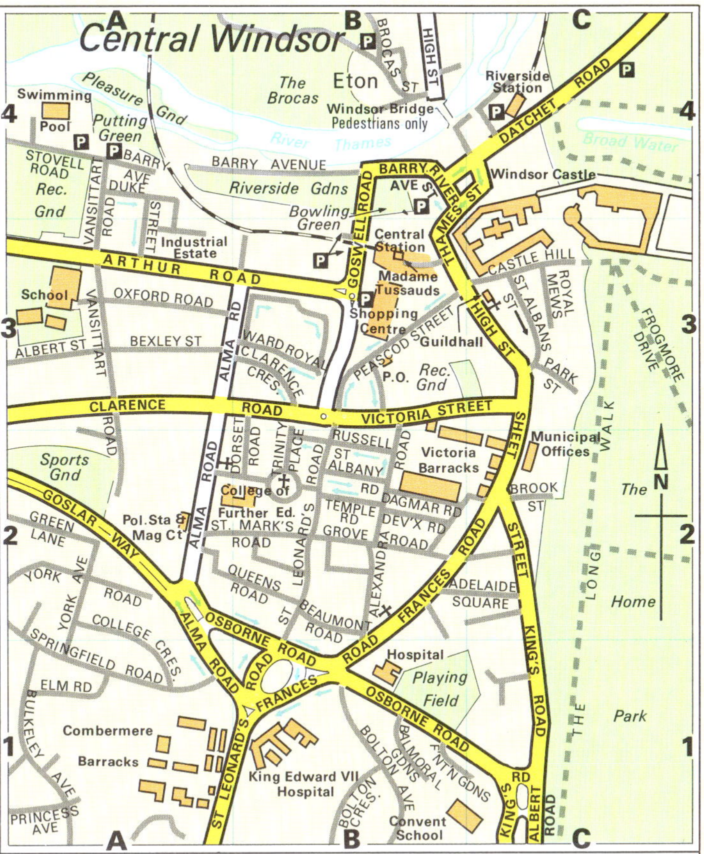

Maps

A | **B** | **C**

Central Maidenhead (map, left)

Industrial Estate · N. DEAN · RAY MILL ROAD WEST · BLACKAMOOR LANE · School · FLORENCE AVE · The Moor · Police HQ & Fire Station · Bus Depot · CEDARS · Industrial Estate · War Memorial · Cinema · Mkt · BRIDGE ST · Leisure Centre · Swimming Pool · HOLMAN LEAZE · KENNET RD · ST CLOUD WAY · BRIDGE ROAD · Drill Hall · Health Centre · Kidwells Park · ST LUKE'S · WINDRUSH WAY · BAD GODESBERG WAY · WEST STREET · HIGH ST · Shopping Precinct · PO · ST IVES RD · Lib · Commonwealth War Graves Commission · CASTLE HILL · NORTH ROAD · HIGH TOWN · BROADWAY · KING ST · QUEEN STREET · PARK ST · YORK ROAD · Bowling Club · BELL STREET · Maidenhead United F.C. · Masonic Hall · Grenfell Park · SOUTH RD · Station · COURT LANDS · STAFFERTON WAY · Industrial Estate · Ambulance Station · DEPOT ROAD · Clubhouse · Maidenhead Golf Course · School · RUSHINGTON AVE · BRAYWICK ROAD · Braywick Playing Fields · **Central Maidenhead** · College of Art · LUDLOW ROAD · SHOPPENHANGERS · BOYN VALLEY RD · CLARE ROAD · KINGS GR · GRENFELL ROAD · GRASSY LANE · COLLEGE AVENUE · GRINGER HILL · BELMONT ROAD · KEBLE ROAD · NORFOLK ROAD · CORDWALLIS ROAD · DENMARK STREET · AUSTRALIA AVE · CLIVEMONT · COOKHAM ROAD · MARLOW RD · CRAUFORD RD · THE CRESCENT · FRASCATI · VICARAGE RD

Central Windsor (map, right)

Central Windsor · Eton · The Brocas · Swimming Pool · Pleasure Grnd · Putting Green · Windsor Bridge Pedestrians only · Riverside Station · Riverside Road · BROCAS ST · HIGH ST · River Thames · BARRY AVENUE · Riverside Gdns · Windsor Castle · Bowling Green · Central Station · Madame Tussauds · Shopping Centre · Guildhall · Castle Hill · Royal Mews · ST ALBANS ST · Frogmore Drive · STOVELL ROAD · VANSITTART · BARRY AVE · DUKE ST · Industrial Estate · ARTHUR ROAD · School · OXFORD ROAD · ALBERT ST · BEXLEY ST · PEASCOD STREET · P.O. · Rec. Grnd · The Long Walk · CLARENCE ROAD · VICTORIA STREET · SHEET STREET · BROOK ST · Municipal Offices · The Home Park · Sports Grnd · GOSLAR WAY · GREEN LANE · YORK AVE · ALMA ROAD · DORSET RD · RUSSELL ST · TRINITY PLACE · ST ALBANY · Victoria Barracks · DAGMAR RD · College of Further Ed. · ST MARK'S · TEMPLE · DEV'X RD · GROVE · Pol. Sta. Mag Ct · QUEENS ROAD · ST LEONARD'S · BEAUMONT ROAD · ALEXANDRA ROAD · FRANCES · ADELAIDE SQUARE · COLLEGE CRES · SPRINGFIELD ROAD · ELM RD · OSBORNE ROAD · Hospital · Playing Field · BALMORAL GDNS · BOLTON AVE · KING'S ROAD · Combermere Barracks · BUKELEY AVE · King Edward VII Hospital · FNTN GDNS · BOLTON CRES · CONVENT · Convent School · PRINCESS AVE · ALBERT RD

LEGEND

Town Plan

AA recommended route	
Restricted roads	
Other roads	
Buildings of interest	
Car parks	P
Parks and open spaces	
One way streets	

Area Plan

A roads	
B roads	
Locations	Hightown○
Urban area	

Street Index with Grid Reference

Slough

Albert Street	C1-D1-E1
Aldin Avenue	E2-F2
Alexandra Road	B1-B2
Alpha Street	D1-E1-E2
Arthur Road	B2
Bath Road	A3-B3-C3
Baylis Road	B4-C4
Beechwood Gardens	C2
Belgrave Road	D4
Benson Close	E4
Bourne Road	A2
Bradley Road	B4-C4
Broadmark Road	F4
Brunel Way	D3
Burlington Avenue	C2-C3
Chalvey Park	C2
Chalvey Road East	B2-C2-C1
Chalvey Road West	B2
Church Street	A2-B2
Church Street	D1-D2
Cippenham Lane	A2-A3
Clifton Road	F2
Clive Court	A2-B2-B1
College Avenue	C1
Conegar Court	C3
Diamond Road	E3-F3-F2
Dolphin Road	F2
Ellis Avenue	B3-C3
Everard Avenue	B3-B2-C2
Farnham Road	A3-A4
Fleetwood Road	D4
Gilliat Road	C4
Glentworth Place	A3
Greys Road	D4
Harewood Place	E1
Hatfield Road	E1-E2
Hazlemere Road	F4
Hencroft Street	D1-D2
Henry Road	B2-B3
Herschel Street	D2-E2
High Street	D2-E2
High Street Chalvey	A2-A1-B1-B2
Hillside	B2
King Edward Street	B2
Kings Road	C1
Ladbroke Road	A1
Landsdowne Avenue	C3
Lascelles Road	F1
Ledgers Road	B1-B2-B3
Little Down Road	D4
London Road	F1-F2
Martin Road	B1
Mere Road	D1
Merton Road	E1
Mill Street	D4
Montem Lane	A3-B3-B2
Osborne Street	D1-D2
Park Street	D1-D2
Petersfield Avenue	E4-E3-F3
Pitts Road	A4
Princes Street	F2
Queens Road	D4
Ragstone Road	B1-C1
Richmond Crescent	E3
St John's Road	E4-F4
St Lawrence Way	E1
St Paul's Avenue	D4-E4-F4
Salt Hill Avenue	A3-A4
Salt Hill Drive	A4
Salt Hill Way	A4-B4
Shackleton Road	C4
Seymour Road	A2
Spackmans Way	A1
Stoke Gardens	C4-D4
Stoke Road	D3-D4
Stoke Poges Lane	B3-C3-C4
Stratford Road	E2-E3
Sussex Place	E2-F2-F1
The Crescent	B2-C2
The Green	A2-A1-B1
The Grove	E1-E2
Tuns Lane	A1-A2-A3
Upton Park	C1-D1
Upton Road	E1
Uxbridge Road	E2-F2-F3
Vale Grove	C1-D1
Wellesley Road	E3
Wellington Street	D3-E3-E2-F2
Wexham Road	E2-E3-F3-F4
White Hart Road	A1-B1
Windmill Road	A3-A4
Windsor Road	C1-C2-D2-D3
Woodland Avenue	B4
Yew Tree Road	E1-E2-F2

Maidenhead

Australia Avenue	B4
Bad Godesberg Way	B3
Bell Street	B2
Belmont Road	A3-A4
Blackamoor Lane	C3-C4
Boyn Valley Road	A1-A2
Braywick Road	B1-B2
Bridge Avenue	C2-C3
Bridge Road	C3
Bridge Street	B3-C3
Broadway	B2
Castle Hill	A2
Cedars Road	C2-C3
Clare Road	A1-A2
Clivemont Road	A4-B4
College Avenue	A3
College Road	A2-A3
Cookham Road	B3-B4
Cordwallis Road	A3-A4-B4
Cordwallis Street	A4
Court Lands	B1
Crauford Rise	A3
Denmark Street	A4
Depot Road	B1-B2-C2
Forlease Road	C2-C3
Frascati Way	B2
Grassy Lane	A3
Grenfell Place	B2
Grenfell Road	A2-B2
Gringer Hill	A4
High Street	B2-B3
High Town	A2-B2
Holman Leaze	B3-C3
Keble Road	A3
Kennet Road	B3
King's Grove	A2
King Street	B2
Ludlow Road	A1
Marlow Road	A3-B3
Norfolk Road	A3-B3
North Dean	B4
North Road	A2
Park Street	B2
Queen Street	B2-B3
Ray Mill Road West	B4-C4
Rushington Avenue	B1
St Cloud Way	B3-C3
St Ives Road	B2-B3
St Luke's Road	A3-B3-B4
Shoppenhangers Road	A1-B1
South Road	A2-B2
Stafferton Way	B1-C1
The Crescent	A3
Vicarage Road	A3-A4-B4
West Street	B3
Windrush Way	B3-B4
York Road	B2-C2

Windsor

Adelaide Square	B2-C2
Albany Road	B2
Albert Road	C1
Albert Street	A3
Alexandra Road	B2-B3
Alma Road	B3-A3-A2-A1-B1
Arthur Road	A3-B3
Balmoral Gardens	B1
Barry Avenue	A4-B4
Beaumont Road	B2
Bexley Street	A3
Bolton Avenue	B1
Bolton Crescent	B1
Brocas Street	B4
Brook Street	C2
Bulkeley Avenue	A1
Castle Hill	C3
Clarence Crescent	B3
Clarence Road	A3-B3
College Crescent	A1-A2
Dagmar Road	B2
Datchet Road	B4-C4
Devereux Road	B2
Dorset Road	B2-B3
Duke Street	A3-A4
Elm Road	A1
Fountain Gardens	B1-C1
Florence Avenue	B4
Frances Road	B1-B2-C2
Frogmore Drive	C3
Goslar Way	A2
Goswell Road	B3-B4
Green Lane	A2
Grove Road	B2
High Street	B4
High Street	B3-C3
King's Road	C1-C2
Osborne Road	A2-B2-B1-C1
Oxford Road	A3
Park Street	C3
Peascod Street	B3
Princess Avenue	A1
Queens Road	A2-B2
River Street	B4
Royal Mews	C3
Russell Street	B2
St Albans Street	C3
St Leonard's Road	A1-B1-B2
St Mark's Road	A2-B2
Sheet Street	C2-C3
Springfield Road	A1-A2
Stovell Road	A4
Temple Road	B2
Thames Street	B3-B4-C4
The Long Walk	C1-C2-C3
Trinity Place	B2-B3
Vansittart Road	A2-A3-A4
Victoria Street	B3-C3
Ward Royal	B3
York Avenue	A1-A2
York Road	A2

SLOUGH
Salt Hill Park in the centre of Slough features a bowling green, tennis courts and a children's play area, as well as pleasant walks through landscaped gardens. This is one of several recreational areas scattered throughout the town.

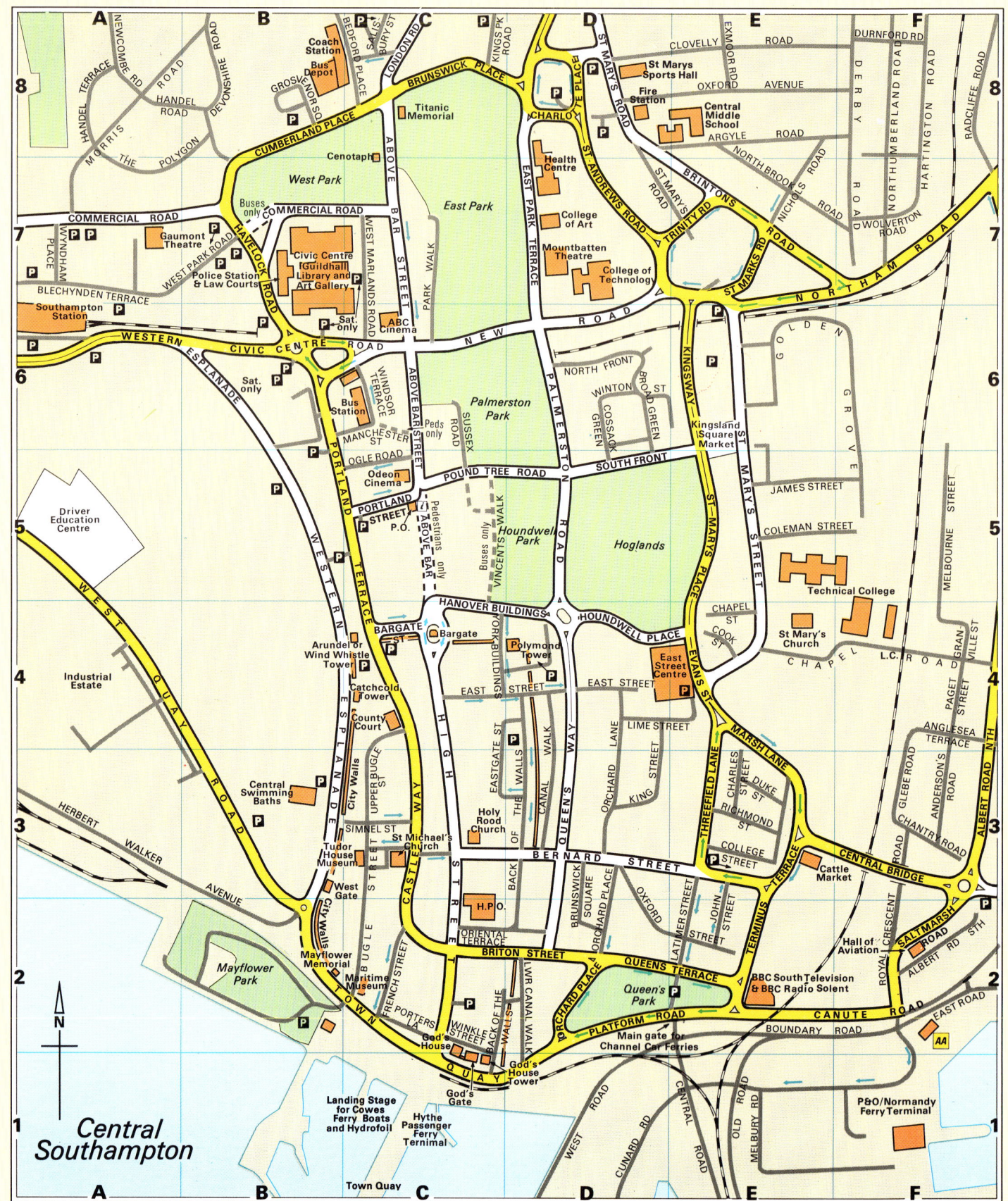

Southampton

In the days of the great ocean-going liners, Southampton was Britain's premier passenger port. Today container traffic is more important, but cruise liners still berth there. A unique double tide caused by the Solent waters, and protection from the open sea by the Isle of Wight, has meant that Southampton has always been a superb and important port. Like many great cities it was devastated by bombing raids during World War II. However, enough survives to make the city a fascinating place to explore. Outstanding are the town walls, which stand to their original height in some places, especially along Western Esplanade. The main landward entrance to the walled town was the Bargate – a superb medieval gateway with a Guildhall (now a museum) on its upper floor. The best place to appreciate old Southampton is in and around St Michael's Square. Here is St Michael's Church, oldest in the city and founded in 1070. Opposite is Tudor House Museum, a lovely gabled building housing much of interest. Down Bugle Street are old houses, with the town walls, pierced by the 13th-century West Gate, away to the right. At the corner of Bugle Street is the Wool House Maritime Museum, contained in a 14th-century warehouse. On the quayside is God's House Tower, part of the town's defences and now an archaeological museum.

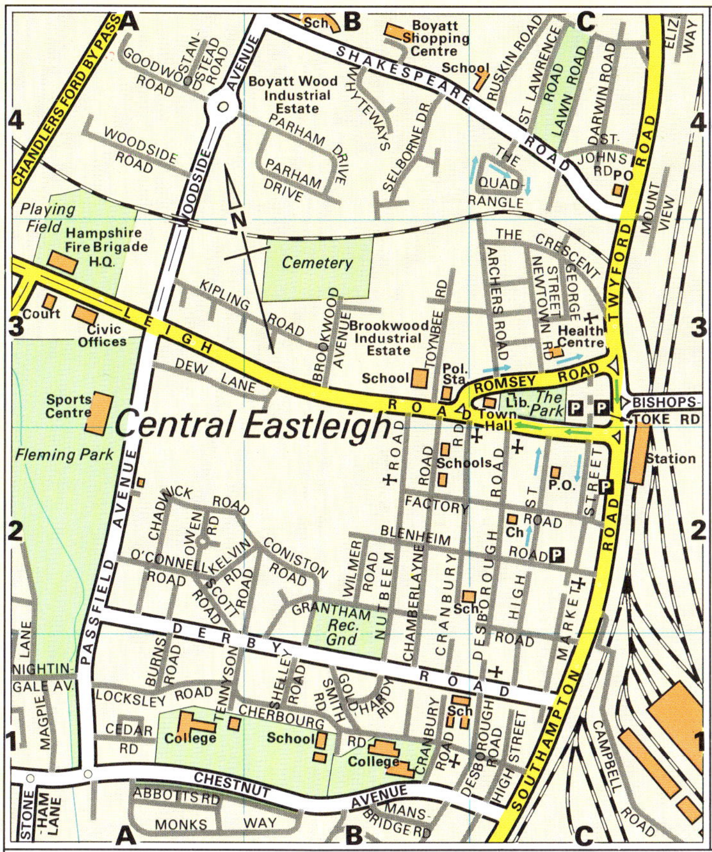

Map labels (Central Eastleigh — left map)

CHANDLERS FORD BY PASS · GOODWOOD ROAD · STANSTEAD ROAD · AVENUE · SHAKESPEARE ROAD · Sch · Boyatt Shopping Centre · School · RUSKIN ROAD · LAWN ROAD · DARWIN ROAD · ELIZ WAY
WOODSIDE ROAD · WOODSIDE AVENUE · WHYTEWAYS · SELBORNE DR · Boyatt Wood Industrial Estate · PARHAM DRIVE · PARHAM DRIVE · THE QUADRANGLE · ST JOHNS RD · PO · MOUNT VIEW · TWYFORD ROAD
Playing Field · Hampshire Fire Brigade H.Q. · KIPLING ROAD · Cemetery · N · ARCHERS ROAD · THE CRESCENT · GEORGE STREET · NEWTOWN · Health Centre
Court · Civic Offices · LEIGH ROAD · DEW LANE · BROOKWOOD AVENUE · Brookwood Industrial Estate · School · TOYNBEE RD · Pol. Sta · ROMSEY ROAD · Lib. · Town Hall · The Park · P P · BISHOPS STOKE RD
Sports Centre · CHADWICK ROAD · O'CONNELL ROAD · OWEN ROAD · KELVIN ROAD · CONISTON ROAD · Schools · FACTORY ROAD · Ch · ROAD · P · Station
Fleming Park · PASSFIELD AVENUE · SCOTT ROAD · NU BEEM · BLENHEIM ROAD · WILMER ROAD · CRANBURY ROAD · HIGH STREET · MARKET STREET · ROAD
NIGHTINGALE AV · MAGPIE LANE · BURNS ROAD · DERBY ROAD · FENNYSON ROAD · SHELLEY ROAD · GRANTHAM Rec. Gnd · CHAMBERLAYNE ROAD · CRANBURY ROAD · DESBOROUGH ROAD · CAMPBELL ROAD
STONEHAM LANE · CEDAR RD · LOCKSLEY ROAD · College · CHERBOURG ROAD · School · SMITH · GOODHARDY · RD · Sch · College
ABBOTS RD · CHESTNUT AVENUE · MONKS WAY · MANS-BRIDGE RD · HIGH STREET · SOUTHAMPTON ROAD

Map labels (Southampton Area — right map)

WINCHESTER · A31 · A31 · A272 · M3 (under construction) · A3090 · Olivers Battery · Lockerley · Mottisfont · Michelmersh · Braishfield · Hursley · Compton · Shawford · A333 · Twyford · Owslebury
Awbridge · Timsbury · A31 · Ampfield · Hiltingbury · Chandler's Ford · Colden Common · Upham · Lower Upham
Sherfield English · A27 · ROMSEY · North Baddesley · Chilworth · EASTLEIGH · Bishopstoke · B3037 · Fair Oak · Horton Heath · Durley · Curdridge
Canada · Ower · M27 · Upton · Rownhams · Nursling · Swaythling · West End · Botley
Bramshaw · Copythorne · Testwood · Netley Marsh · Shirley · Portswood · Bitterne · A3051 · Hedge End · Burridge
Cadnam · TOTTON · SOUTHAMPTON · Millbrook · Sholing · Woolston · Bursledon · Swanwick · M27
Minstead · Bartley · Woodlands · Ashurst · Marchwood · Lower Swanwick · Sarisbury · Park Gate
Lyndhurst · Netley · Hythe · Hamble · Locks Heath · Warsash · Titchfield
Southampton Area · Holbury · Fawley · A27
Brockenhurst · Beaulieu · Blackfield · Langley · Calshot · The Solent
Sway · East Boldre · Bucklers Hard · Exbury · SCALE · mls 0 · 4

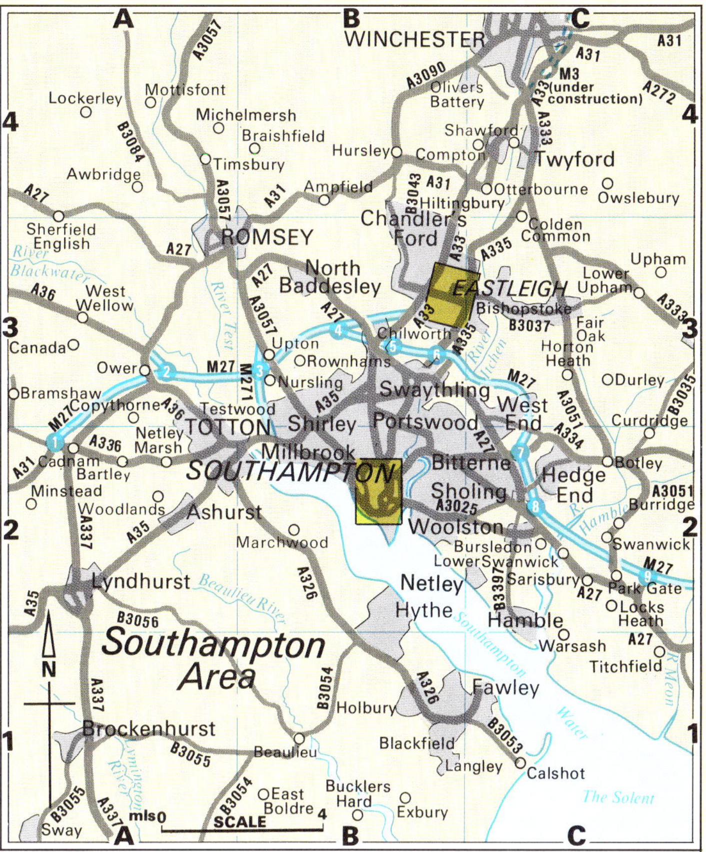

Key to Town Plan and Area Plan

Town Plan
A.A. Recommended roads
Other roads
Restricted roads
Buildings of interest — Cinema
A A Service Centre — AA
Car Parks — P
Parks and open spaces
One way streets

Area Plan
A roads
B roads
Locations — Ower O
Urban Area

SOUTHAMPTON

Above Bar	C5
Above Bar Street	C5-C6-C7-C8
Albert Road North	F3-F4
Albert Road South	F2
Anderson's Road	F3-F4
Anglesea Terrace	F4
Argyle Road	E8-F8
Back of the Walls	C1-C2-D2-D3-D4
Bargate Street	C4
Bedford Place	B8-C8
Bernard Street	C3-D3-E3
Blechynden Terrace	A7
Boundary Road	E2-F2
Briton Street	C2-D2
Britons Road	D8-E8-E7
Broad Green	D6
Brunswick Place	C8-D8
Brunswick Square	D2-D3
Bugle Street	C2-C3
Canal Walk	D3-D4
Canute Road	E2-F2
Castle Way	C2-C3-C4
Central Bridge	E3-F3
Central Road	E1-E2
Chantry Road	F3
Chapel Road	E4-F4
Chapel Street	E4
Charles Street	E3
Charlotte Place	D8
Civic Centre Road	B6-C6
Clovelly Road	D8-E8-F8
Coleman Street	E5-F5
College Street	E3
Commercial Road	A7-B7-C7
Cook Street	E4
Cossack Green	D5-D6
Cumberland Place	B7-B8-C8
Cunard Road	D1-E1
Derby Road	F7-F8
Devonshire Road	B8
Duke Street	E3
Durnford Road	F8
East Road	F2
East Street	C4-D4
East Park Terrace	D6-D7-D8
Eastgate Street	D3-C3-C4-D4
Evans Street	E4
Exmoor Road	E8
French Street	C2
Glebe Road	F3-F4
Golden Grove	E6-F6-F5
Granville Street	F4
Grosvenor Square	B8
Handel Road	A8-B8
Handel Terrace	A8
Hanover Buildings	C5-C4-D4
Hartington Road	F7-F8
Havelock Road	B6-B7
Herbert Walker Avenue	A3-B3-B2
High Street	C1-C2-C3-C4
Houndwell Place	D4-E4
James Street	E5-F5
John Street	E2-E3
Kingsway	E6-E7
King Street	D3-D4
Kings Park Road	C8
Latimer Street	E2-E3
Lime Street	D4-E4
London Road	C8
Lower Canal Walk	D1-D2
Manchester Street	B6-C6
Marsh Lane	E3-E4
Melbourne Street	F4-F5-F6
Melbury Road	E1
Morris Road	A7-A8-B8
New Road	E6-D6-D7
Newcombe Road	A8
Nichols Road	E7-E8
North Brook Road	E8-E7-F7
North Front	D6
Northam Road	E6-E7-F7
Northumberland Road	F7-F8
Ogle Road	C5
Old Road	E1-E2
Orchard Lane	D3-D4
Orchard Place	D2-D3
Oriental Terrace	C2-D2
Oxford Avenue	D8-E8-F8
Oxford Street	D3-D2-E2
Paget Street	F4
Palmerston Road	D5-D6
Park Walk	C6-C7
Platform Road	D2-E2
Porters Lane	C2
Portland Street	C5
Portland Terrace	B6-B5-C5-C4
Pound Tree Road	C5-D5
Queens Terrace	D2-E2
Queen's Way	D2-D3-D4
Radcliffe Road	F7-F8
Richmond Street	E3
Royal Crescent Road	F2-F3
St Andrews Road	D7-D8
St Marks Road	E7
St Mary's Place	E4-E5
St Mary's Road	D8-D7-E7
St Mary's Street	E4-E5-E6
Salisbury Street	C8
Saltmarsh Road	F2-F3
Simnel Street	C3
South Front	D5-E5-E6-D6
Sussex Road	C5-C6
The Polygon	A8-A7-B7-B8
Terminus Terrace	E2-E3
Threefield Lane	E3-E4
Town Quay	B2-C2-C1-D1
Trinity Road	D7-E7
Upper Bugle Street	C3-C4
Vincents Walk	C5
West Marlands Road	C6-C7
West Road	D1-D2-E2
West Park Road	A7-B7
West Quay Road	A5-A4-B4-B3
Western Esplanade	B2-B3-B4-B5-B6-A6
Windsor Terrace	C6
Winkle Street	C1-C2
Winton Street	D6-E6
Wolverton Road	F7
Wyndham Place	A7
York Buildings	C4-D4

EASTLEIGH

Abbots Road	A1
Archers Road	C3
Blenheim Road	B2-C2
Brookwood Avenue	B3
Burns Road	A1
Campbell Road	C1
Cedar Road	A1
Chadwick Road	A2-B2
Chamberlayne Road	B1-B2-B3
Chandlers Ford By-pass	A4
Cherbourg Road	A1-B1-C1
Chestnut Avenue	A1-B1-C1
Coniston Road	B2
Cranbury Road	C1-C2-C3
Darwin Road	C4
Cranbury Road	C1-C2-C3
Darwin Road	C4
Derby Road	A2-A1-B1-C1
Desborough Road	B1-C1-C2
Dew Lane	A3-B3
Elizabeth Way	C4
Factory Road	B2-C2
George Street	C3
Goldsmith Road	B1
Goodwood Road	A4
Grantham Road	B1-B2-C2-C1
High Street	C1-C2
Kelvin Road	A2-B2
Kipling Road	A3-B3
Lawn Road	C4
Leigh Road	A3-B3-C3-C2
Locksley Road	A1
Magpie Lane	A1-A2
Mansbridge Road	B1
Market Street	C1-C2-C3
Monks Way	A1-B1
Mount View	C3-C4
Newtown Road	C3
Nightingale Avenue	C3
Nutbeem Road	B1-B2-B3
O'Connell Road	A2
Owen Road	A2
Parnham Drive	A4-B4
Passfield Avenue	A1-A2-A3
Romsey Road	B3-C3
Ruskin Road	C4
Stanstead Road	A4
Stoneham Lane	A1
St John's Road	C4
St Lawrence Road	C4
Scott Road	A2
Selborne Drive	B4
Shakespeare Road	B4-C4
Shelley Road	B1
Southampton Road	C1-C2
The Crescent	C3
The Quadrangle	C4
Tennyson Road	A1-A2-B2
Toynbee Road	B3
Twyford Road	C3-C4
Whyteways	B4
Wilmer Road	B2
Woodside Avenue	A3-A4
Woodside Road	A4

SOUTHAMPTON
Although liners still use Southampton's docks which handled all the great ocean-going passenger ships before the age of air travel replaced sea travel, the port is chiefly used by commercial traffic today.

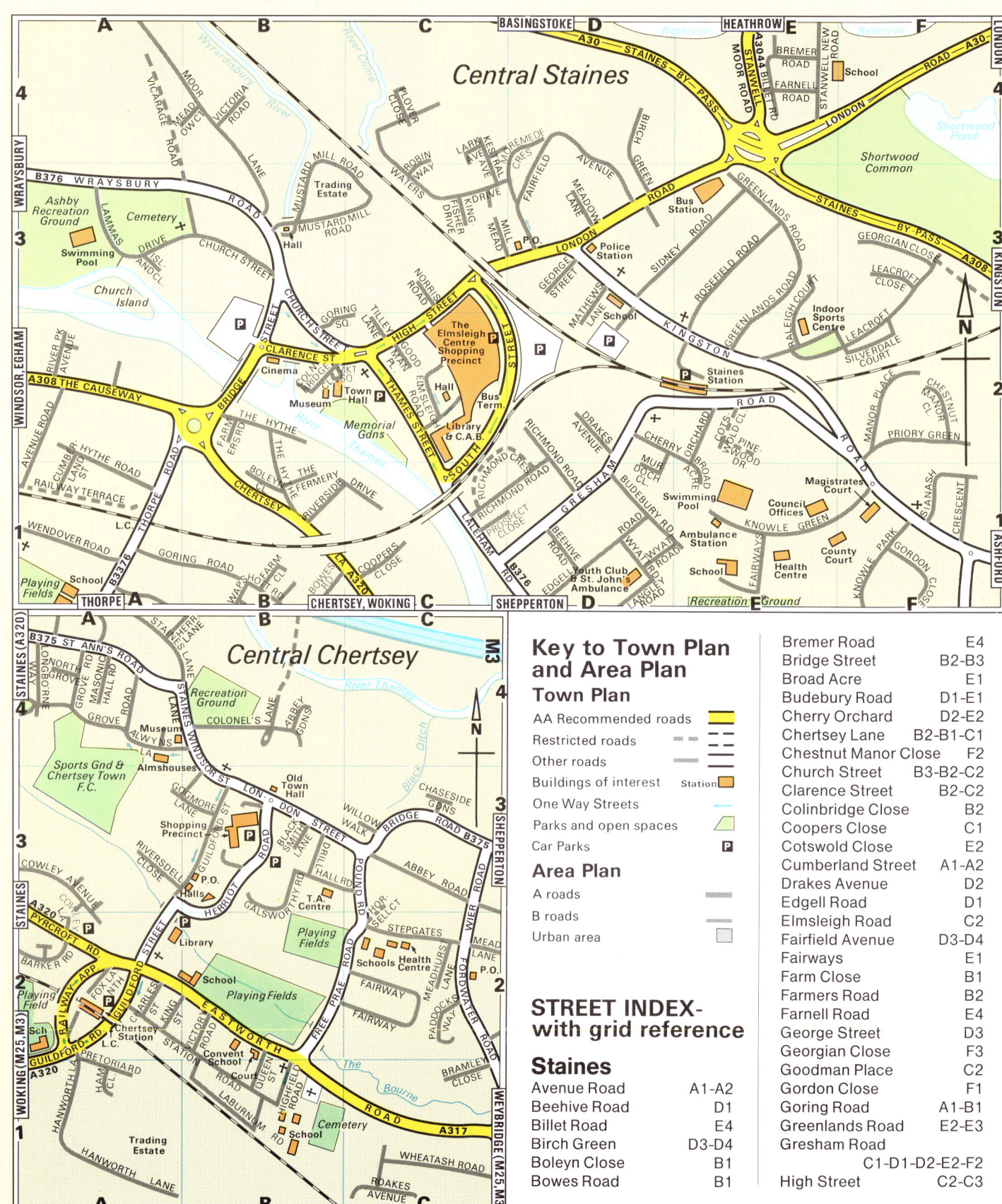

Key to Town Plan and Area Plan

Town Plan

AA Recommended roads	
Restricted roads	
Other roads	
Buildings of interest	Station
One Way Streets	
Parks and open spaces	
Car Parks	P

Area Plan

A roads	
B roads	
Urban area	

STREET INDEX- with grid reference

Staines

Staines

The old and the new exist surprisingly happily together in Staines, a flourishing township which pre-dates the Domesday Survey of 1086.

Set in the Surrey countryside, Staines has attracted many new industries. But as well as signs of prosperity like the popular modern shopping centre, the town has a good number of churches and other features to mark its long history, including graceful Staines Bridge, opened in 1832. The London Stone nearby was put in place in 1285 and now marks the Surrey-Berkshire border.

Chertsey has been a boatbuilding centre for many years, and its attractive position on the River Thames appeals both to boating enthusiasts and to commuters working in London and nearby towns. Central to all river activity is handsome Chertsey Bridge. Alongside the water lies the 150-acre open space of Chertsey Meads and Orchard Gardens (site of the ancient Abbey fishponds), while just upstream, Salter river steamers ply their trade.

The local museum has good collections of costumes and porcelain, along with interesting examples of tiles uncovered during the excavation of the original Abbey site. Various sports and recreation facilities are to be found in the town, and visitors can survey a fine view of the surrounding countryside from the top of St Anne's Hill. Lying to the north, it rises to 240ft (73m).

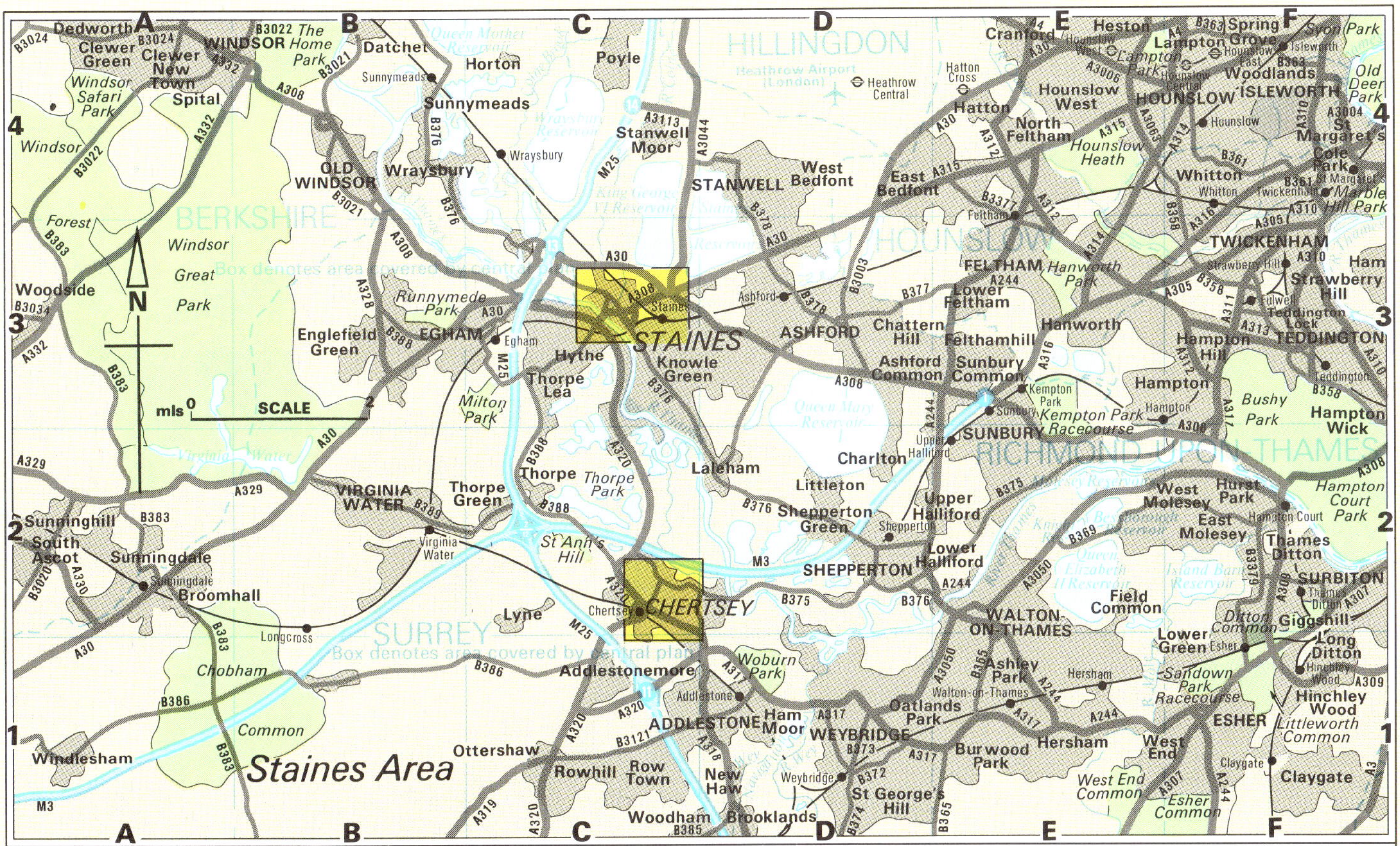

Staines Area

Hythe Road	A1-A2
Island Close	A3
Kestral Avenue	C3-C4
Kingfisher Drive	C3
Kingston Road	D3-D2-E2-F2-F1
Knowle Green	E1-F1
Knowle Park	F1
Laleham Road	C1-D1
Lammas Drive	A3-B3
Langley Road	D1
Lark Avenue	C4
Leacroft	E2-F2-F3
Leacroft Close	F3
London Road	C3-D3-E3-E4-F4
Manor Place	F2
Market Square	B2
Mathews Lane	D2-D3
Meadow Court	A4-B4
Meadow Lane	D3
Mill Mead	C3
Moor Lane	A4-B4-B3
Moremede Crescent	C3-C4-D4-D3
Murdoch Close	D1
Mustard Mill Road	B4-B3-C3
Norris Road	C3
Pinewood Drive	E2
Plover Close	C4
Priory Green	F2
Prospect Close	C1-D1
Railway Terrace	A1
Raleigh Court	E2-E3
Richmond Crescent	C1-C2-D2-D1
Richmond Road	C1-D1-D2
River Park Avenue	A2
Riverside Drive	B1-C1
Robin Way	C3-C4
Rosefield Road	E2-E3
Sianash Crescent	F1
Sidney Road	D3-E3
Silverdale Court	F2
South Street	C1-C2-D2-C3
Staines By-Pass	C4-D4-E4-E3-F3
Stanwell Moor Road	E4
Stanwell New Road	E4
Thames Street	C1-C2
The Causeway	A2
The Fernery	B1
The Hythe	B1-B2
Thorpe Road	A1-A2
Tilley Lane	C2
Vicarage Road	A4-A3-B3
Victoria Road	B4
Wapshott Road	B1
Waters Drive	C4-C3-D3
Wendover Road	A1
Wraysbury Road	A3-B3
Wyatt Road	D1-E1

Chertsey

Abbey Gardens	B4
Abbey Road	C2-C3
Alwyns Lane	A4-B4
Barker Road	A2
Black Smith Lane	B3
Bramley Close	C1
Bridge Road	C3
Chaeside Gardens	C3
Charles Street	A2
Colonel's Lane	B4
Cowley Avenue	A2-A3
Cowley Lane	A2-A3
Drill Hall Road	B3-C3
Eastworth Road	A2-B2-B1-C1
Fairway	B2-C2
Fordwater Road	C1-C2
Fox Lane North	A2
Free Prae Road	B2-C2
Galsworthy Road	B3
Gogmore Lane	A3-B3
Grove Road	A4
Guildford Road	A1-A2
Guildford Street	A2-A3-B3
Hamilton Close	A1
Hanworth Lane	A1-A2
Herrings Lane	A4-B4
Herriot Road	A3-A2-B2-B3
Highfield Road	B1
Horsell Court	C2-C3
King Street	A2-B2
Laburnum Road	B1
London Street	B3-C3
Longbourne Way	A4
Masonic Hall Road	A4
Meadhurst Lane	C2
Mead Lane	C2
North Grove	A4
Paddocks Way	C2
Pound Road	C2-C3
Pretoria Road	A1-A2
Pyrcroft Road	A2-A3
Queen Street	B1-B2
Railway Approach	A2
Riversdell Close	A3
Roakes Avenue	C1
St Ann's Road	A4
Staines Lane	A4-B4
Station Road	A2-B2-B1
Stepgates	C2
Victory Road	B2
Wheatash Road	C1
Wier Road	C2-C3
Willow Walk	C3
Windsor Street	B3-B4

CHERTSEY
Designed by James Paine and completed in 1785, the graceful arches and ashlar stonework of the Bridge overlook the serenity of Chertsey meads and a bustle of activity from boatyards, riverside pubs and river traffic.

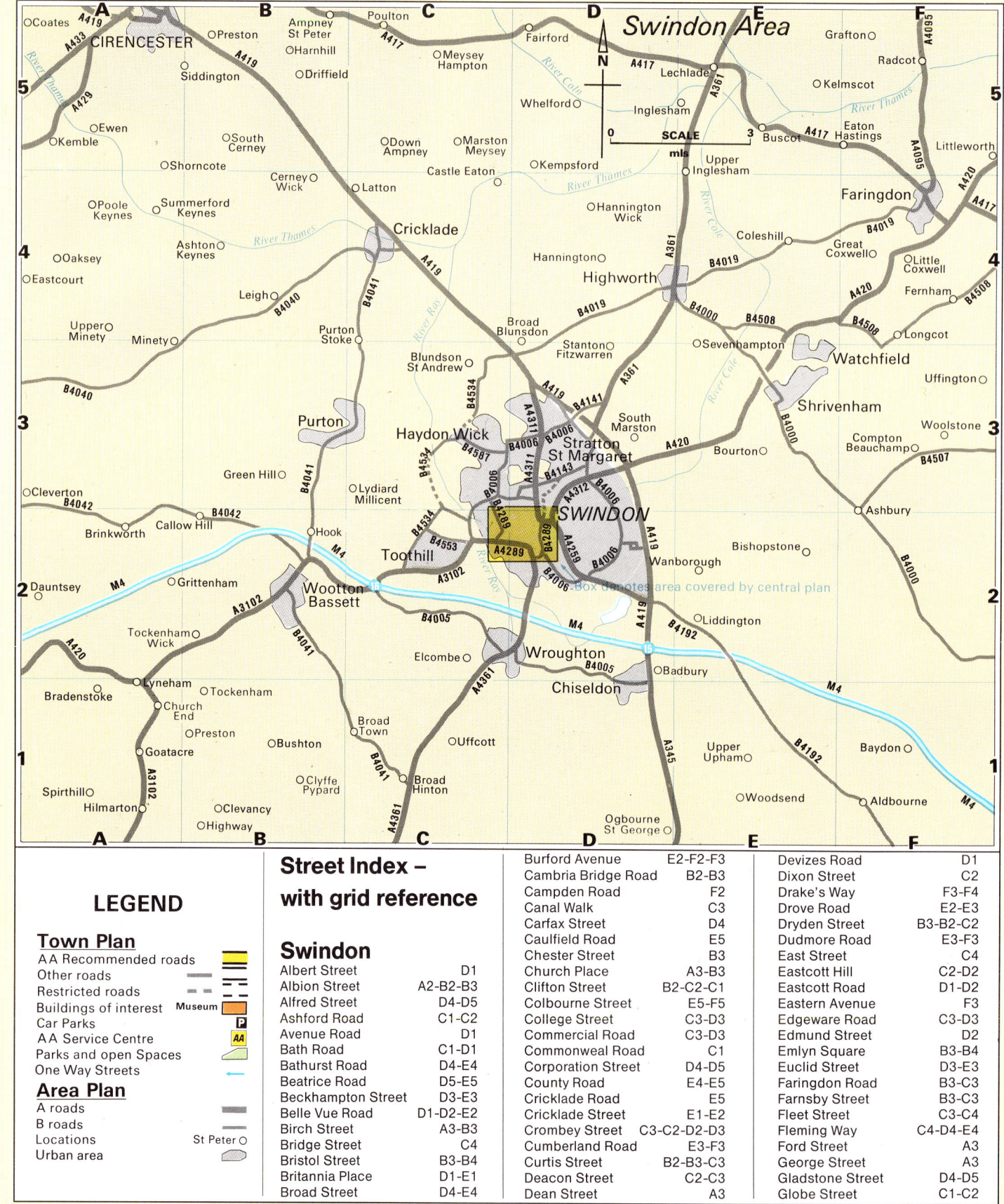

Swindon Area

Swindon

Brunel's decision in 1841 to build the Great Western Railway's workshops here transformed Swindon from an agricultural village into a major industrial centre. The surviving buildings of the original railway village have been restored.

Regrettably the fortunes of the BR Engineering Ltd locomotive and other workshops (the heart of the Great Western system and renowned for locomotives such as the King George V) have declined considerably and even face complete closure — but modern Swindon has seen a remarkable revival. Plans were made in the 1950s to reduce the town's dependence on one industry, and with the combination of development aid and improved road access via the M4, Swindon has seen the arrival of a wide range of manufacturing industries and a near doubling of its population, to 150,000. Aptly chosen for the relocation of the British Rail's Western Region Headquarters from Paddington, the town now boasts a modern shopping complex, a regional theatre and the impressive Oasis Leisure Centre, while an illustrious past is recalled in the Great Western Railway Museum.

Outside Swindon are 19th-century Lydiard Mansion, standing in 150 acres of parkland, the leisure facilities of Coate Water, and a museum on naturalist and writer Richard Jeffries.

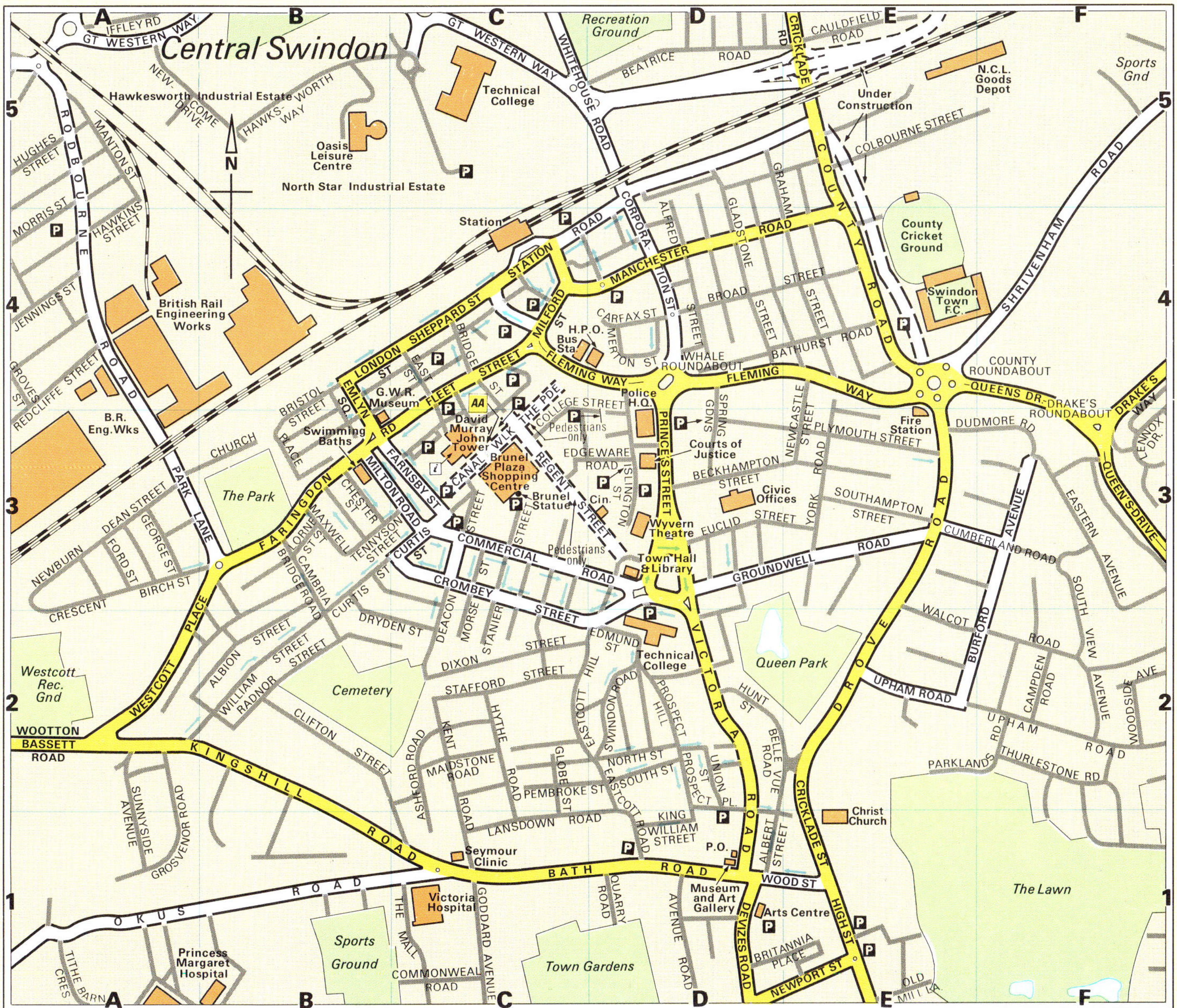

Central Swindon

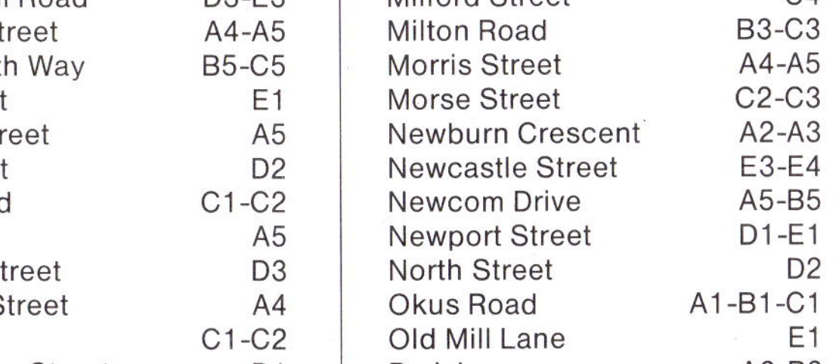

SWINDON
Making waves at the Oasis Leisure Centre 'free-shaped' pool — under the biggest glazed dome in Britain, the water drops away gradually from inches-deep for paddling to a portholed diving area, and is fringed with tropical shrubs.

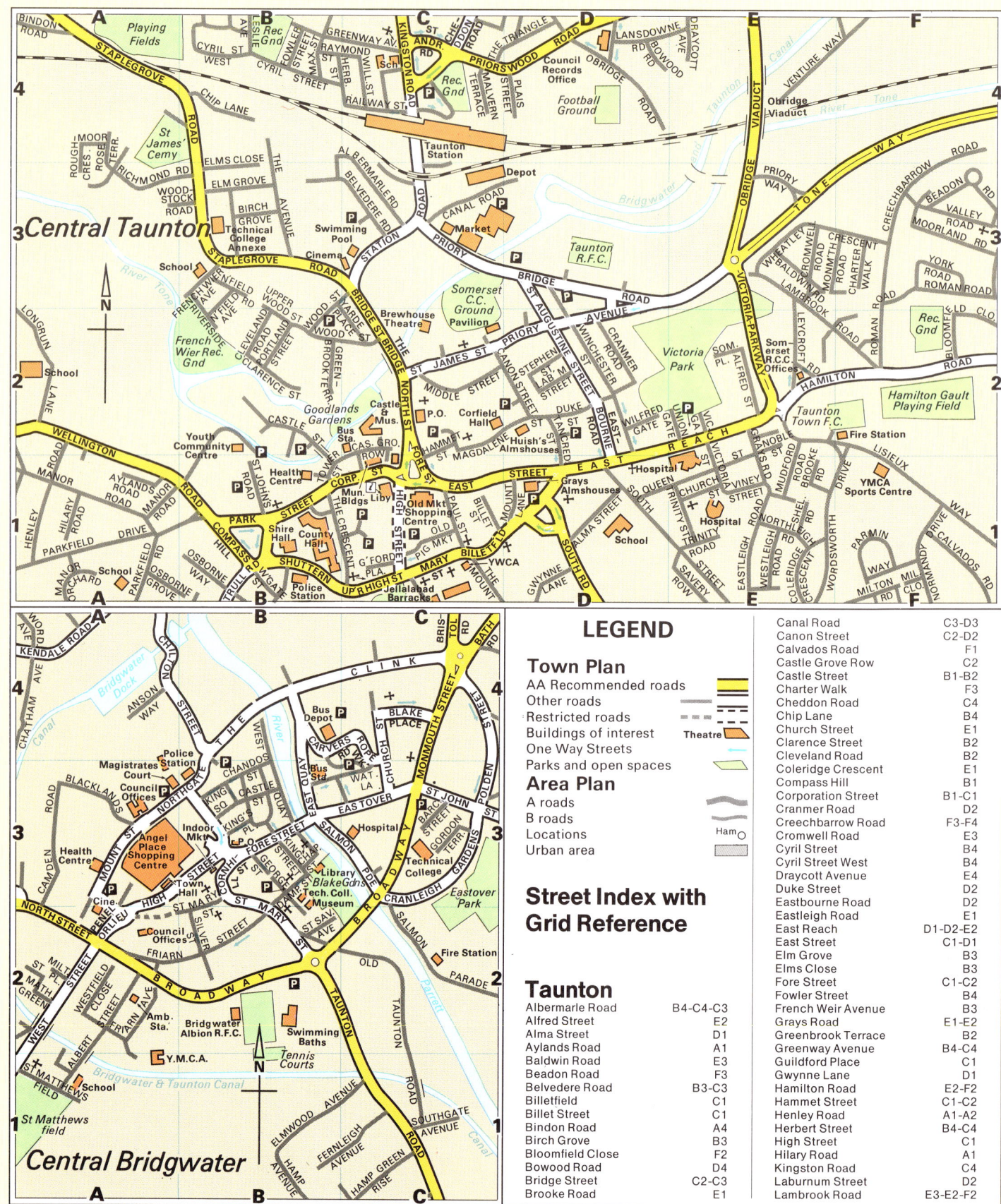

LEGEND

Town Plan
AA Recommended roads	
Other roads	
Restricted roads	
Buildings of interest	Theatre
One Way Streets	
Parks and open spaces	

Area Plan
A roads	
B roads	
Locations	Ham ○
Urban area	

Street Index with Grid Reference

Taunton

Albermarle Road	B4-C4-C3
Alfred Street	E2
Alma Street	D1
Aylands Road	A1
Baldwin Road	E3
Beadon Road	F3
Belvedere Road	B3-C3
Billetfield	C1
Billet Street	C1
Bindon Road	A4
Birch Grove	B3
Bloomfield Close	F2
Bowood Road	D4
Bridge Street	C2-C3
Brooke Road	E1
Canal Road	C3-D3
Canon Street	C2-D2
Calvados Road	F1
Castle Grove Row	C2
Castle Street	B1-B2
Charter Walk	F3
Cheddon Road	C4
Chip Lane	B4
Church Street	E1
Clarence Street	B2
Cleveland Road	B2
Coleridge Crescent	E1
Compass Hill	B1
Corporation Street	B1-C1
Cranmer Road	D2
Creechbarrow Road	F3-F4
Cromwell Road	E3
Cyril Street	B4
Cyril Street West	B4
Draycott Avenue	E4
Duke Street	D2
Eastbourne Road	D2
Eastleigh Road	E1
East Reach	D1-D2-E2
East Street	C1-D1
Elm Grove	B3
Elms Close	B3
Fore Street	C1-C2
Fowler Street	B4
French Weir Avenue	B3
Grays Road	E1-E2
Greenbrook Terrace	B2
Greenway Avenue	B4-C4
Guildford Place	C1
Gwynne Lane	D1
Hamilton Road	E2-F2
Hammet Street	C1-C2
Henley Road	A1-A2
Herbert Street	B4-C4
High Street	C1
Hilary Road	A1
Kingston Road	C4
Laburnum Street	D2
Lambrook Road	E3-E2-F2

Taunton

The hub of Somerset, surrounded by the rolling, wooded Quantocks and the Blackdown Hills, Taunton lies on the River Tone in the fertile Vale of Taunton Dene. Famous for its thriving local cider industry, the town is also a lively commercial and agricultural centre whose livestock market rivals Exeter's as the most important in the West Country. In the past it was a major centre of the wool trade.

As befits a county town, Taunton is the headquarters of Somerset's entertaining and successful cricket team. It also offers National Hunt racing, has no fewer than three public schools and, somewhat improbably, the British Telecom Museum where antique telephone equipment is kept. There has been a castle in the town since Norman times: now it is home for the Somerset County and Military Museums.

Bridgwater, an industrial centre, was a busy port until Bristol overshadowed it. Twice a day a bore – a great tidal wave – surges up the River Parrett from Bridgwater Bay; the times are posted on the bridge in the town centre for those who want to see it.

In 1695 the rebel Duke of Monmouth is reputed to have surveyed the field before the Battle of Sedgemoor from the town's church tower. Dating from the 14th century, the Church of St Mary has some particularly fine Jacobean screenwork.

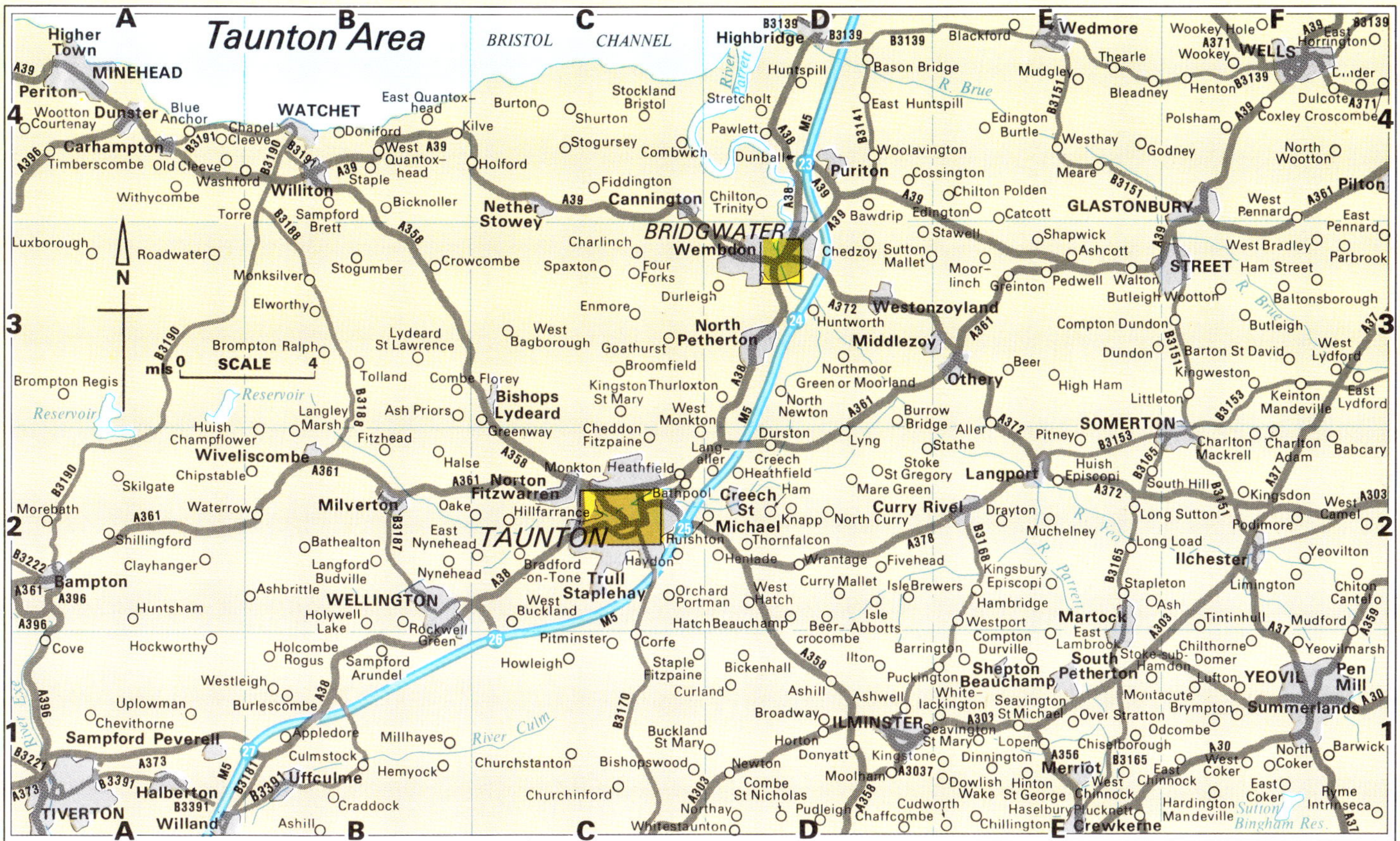

Lansdowne Road	D4-E4
Leslie Avenue	B4
Leycroft Road	E2-E3
Lisieux Way	E2-F2-F1
Longrun Lane	A2
Magdalene Street	C2-D2
Malvern Terrace	C4
Manor Orchard	A1
Manor Road	A1
Mary Street	C1
Maxwell Street	B4
Middle Street	C2
Milton Close	F1
Milton Road	F1
Monmouth Road	E3-F3
Moorland Road	F3
Mount Lane	D1
Mudford Road	E1-E2
Noble Street	E2
Normandy Drive	F1
Northfield Avenue	B2-B3
Northfield Road	B3
Northleigh Road	E1
North Street	C2
Obridge Road	D4
Obridge Viaduct	E3-E4
Old Pig Market	C1
Osborne Grove	A1-B1
Osborne Way	B1
Parmin Way	F1
Parkfield Drive	A1
Parkfield Road	A1
Park Street	B1
Paul Street	C1
Plais Street	D4
Portland Street	B2
Priorswood Road	C4-D4
Priory Avenue	C2-D2-D3
Priory Bridge Road	C3-D3-E3
Priory Way	E3
Queen Street	D1-E1-E2
Railway Street	C4
Raymond Street	B4-C4
Richmond Road	A3-B3

Riverside	B2-B3
Roman Road	F2-F3
Roseberry Terrace	A3-A4
Roughmoor Crescent	A3-A4
St Andrews Road	C4
St Augustine Street	D2-D3
St James Street	C2
St John's Road	B1
Savery Row	E1
Shelley Road	E1
Shuttern	B1
Somerset Place	E2
South Road	D1
South Street	D1-E1
Staplegrove Road	A4-B4-B3-C3
Station Road	C3-C4
Stephen Street	D2
Tancred Street	D1-D2
The Avenue	B3-B4
The Bridge	C2
The Crescent	B1-C1
The Mount	C1
The Triangle	C4-D4
Toneway	E3-F3-F4
Tower Street	B1-C1-C2
Trinity Road	E1
Trinity Street	E1
Trull Road	B1
Union Gate	E2
Upper High Street	C1
Upper Wood Street	B2-B3
Valley Road	F3
Venture Way	E4-F4
Victoria Gate	E2
Victoria Parkway	E2-E3
Victoria Street	E1-E2
Viney Street	E1
Wellington Road	A2-A1-B1
Westgate Street	B1
Westleigh Road	E1
Wheatley Crescent	E3-F3
Wilfred Gate	D2
William Street	C4
Winchester Street	D2-D3

Woodstock Road	A3-B3
Wood Street	C2-B2-B3-C3
Wordsworth Drive	E1-F1-F2
Yarde Place	B3-B2-C2
York Road	F3

Bridgewater

Albert Street	A1-A2
Angel Crescent	A3-B3
Anson Way	A4
Barclay Street	C3
Bath Road	C4
Blacklands	A3
Blake Place	C4
Bristol Road	C4
Broadway	A2-B2-C2-C3
Camden Road	A3
Carvers Road	B3-B4-C4
Castle Street	B3
Chandos Street	B3
Chapel Street	B3
Chatham Avenue	A4
Chilton Street	A4-B4
Church Street	C3-C4
Cornhill Street	B3
Cranleigh Gardens	C3
Dampiet Street	B3
Eastover	B3-C3
East Quay	B3-B4
Elmwood Avenue	B1-C1
Fernleigh Avenue	B1-C1
Fore Street	B3
Friarn Avenue	A2
Friarn Street	A2-B2
George Street	B3
Gordon Terrace	C3
Hamp Avenue	B1
Hamp Green Rise	B1-C1
High Street	A2-A3-B3
Kendale Road	A4
King's Place	B3
King Square	B3
King Street	B3
Mary Street	B2-B3-B2
Milton Place	A2
Monmouth Street	C3-C4
Mount Street	A2-A3
New Road	B3-C3
Northgate	A3-B3-B4
North Street	A2-A3
Old Taunton Road	B2-C2-C1
Penel Orlieu	A2
Polden Street	C3-C4
Rope Walk	C4
Taunton Road	B2-C2-C1
St John Street	C3
St Matthews Field	A1
St Matthews Green	A2
St Saviors Avenue	B2
Salmon Parade	B3-C3-C2
Silver Street	B2
Southgate Avenue	C1
Taunton Road	B2-C2-C1
The Clink	B4-C4
Watson Lane	B3-C3
Westfield Close	A2
West Quay	B3-B4
West Street	A1-A2
Wordsworth Avenue	A4

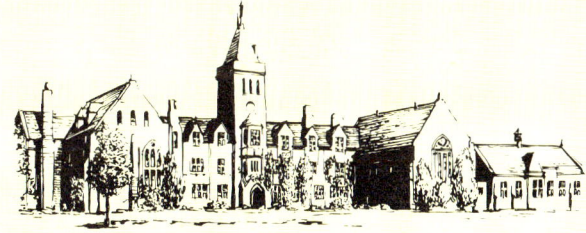

TAUNTON
Taunton School, an attractive rambling building in Staplegrove Road, is one of the town's three public schools for boys. This is the largest of the three in terms of numbers of pupils and is inter-denominational.

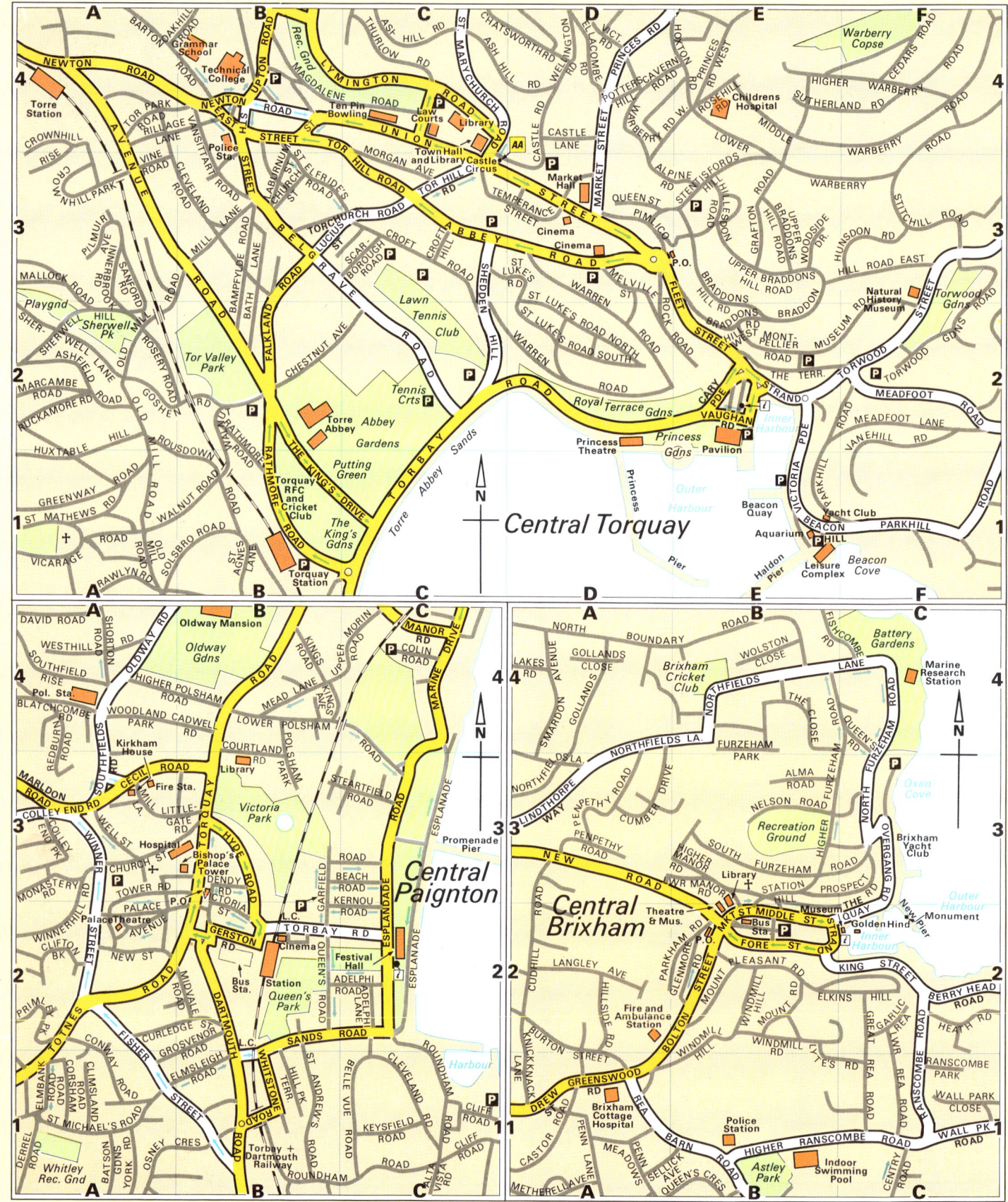

Central Torquay

Central Paignton

Central Brixham

Torquay

With its sparkling houses, colourful gardens and sub-tropical plants set among the limestone crags of the steep hillside, Torquay has the air of a resort on the French Riviera – an impression strengthened by the superb views of sea and coast from Marine Drive, the 'corniche' road that sweeps around the rocky headland. Torquay is undoubtedly the Queen of the Devon coast, a resort carefully planned in

the early 19th century to cater for the wealthy and discriminating visitor. It had begun to be popular with naval officers' families during the Napoleonic wars when no one could travel to the continent, and this burgeoning popularity was exploited by the Palk family through two generations. Sir Robert Palk, who had made his fortune in India, inherited from a friend an estate which included Torquay, and he and his descendants set about transforming it into the spacious, well-planned

town we see today. Among the numerous amenities, Aqualand is particularly interesting.

Paignton, set on the huge sweep of Tor Bay south of Torquay, continues the range of holiday amenities and has good, sandy beaches.

Brixham, which lies a little further down the coast, falls into two parts – the old village on the hill slopes – and the fishing village half a mile below. Less commercialised than its neighbours, it is popular with holidaymakers.

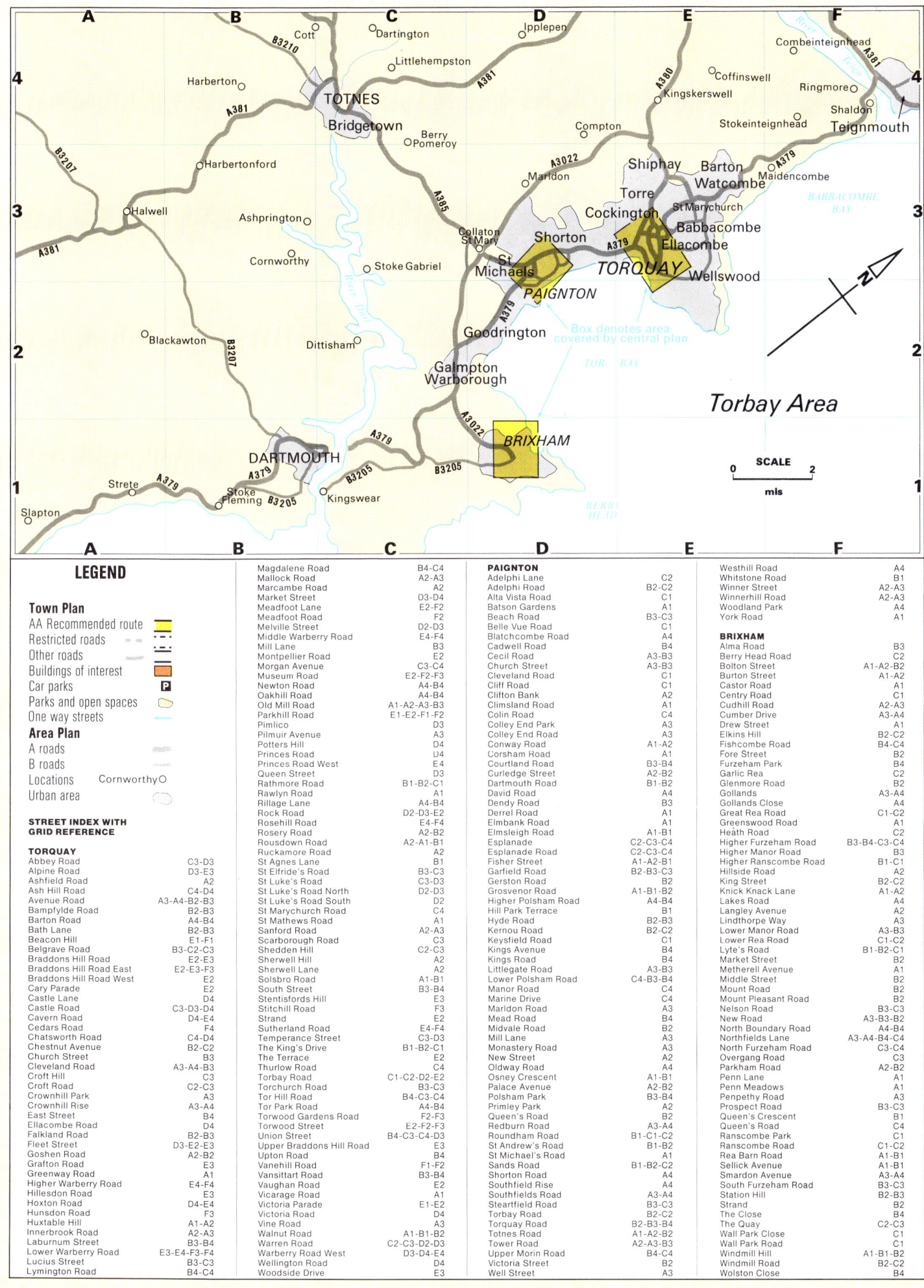

LEGEND

Town Plan

AA Recommended route
Restricted roads
Other roads
Buildings of interest
Car parks
Parks and open spaces
One way streets

Area Plan

A roads
B roads
Locations — Cornworthy ○
Urban area

STREET INDEX WITH GRID REFERENCE

TORQUAY

Abbey Road	C3-D3
Alpine Road	D3-E3
Ashfield Road	A2
Ash Hill Road	C4-D4
Avenue Road	A3-A4-B2-B3
Bampfylde Road	B2-B3
Barton Road	A4-B4
Bath Lane	B2-B3
Beacon Hill	E1-F1
Belgrave Road	B3-C2-C3
Braddons Hill Road	E2-E3
Braddons Hill Road East	E2-E3-F3
Braddons Hill Road West	E2
Cary Parade	E2
Castle Lane	D4
Castle Road	C3-D3-D4
Cavern Road	D4-E4
Cedars Road	F4
Chatsworth Road	C4-D4
Chestnut Avenue	B2-C2
Church Street	B3
Cleveland Road	A3-A4-B3
Croft Hill	C3
Croft Road	C2-C3
Crownhill Park	A3
Crownhill Rise	A3-A4
East Street	B4
Ellacombe Road	D4
Falkland Road	B2-B3
Fleet Street	D3-E2-E3
Goshen Road	A2-B2
Grafton Road	E3
Greenway Road	A1
Higher Warberry Road	E4-F4
Hillesdon Road	E3
Hoxton Road	D4-E4
Hunsdon Road	F3
Huxtable Hill	A1-A2
Innerbrook Road	A2-A3
Laburnum Street	B3-B4
Lower Warberry Road	E3-E4-F3-F4
Lucius Street	B3-C3
Lymington Road	B4-C4
Magdalene Road	B4-C4
Mallock Road	A2-A3
Marcombe Road	A2
Market Street	D3-D4
Meadfoot Lane	E2-F2
Meadfoot Road	F2
Melville Street	D2-D3
Middle Warberry Road	E4-F4
Mill Lane	B3
Montpellier Road	E2
Morgan Avenue	C3-C4
Museum Road	E2-F2-F3
Newton Road	A4-B4
Oakhill Road	A4-B4
Old Mill Road	A1-A2-A3-B3
Parkhill Road	E1-E2-F1-F2
Pimlico	D3
Pilmuir Avenue	A3
Potters Hill	D4
Princes Road	D4
Princes Road West	E4
Queen Street	D3
Rathmore Road	B1-B2-C1
Rawlyn Road	A1
Rillage Lane	A4-B4
Rock Road	D2-D3-E2
Rosehill Road	E4-F4
Rosery Road	A2-B2
Rousdown Road	A2-A1-B1
Ruckamore Road	A2
St Agnes Lane	B1
St Elfride's Road	B3-C3
St Luke's Road	C3-D3
St Luke's Road North	D2-D3
St Luke's Road South	D2
St Marychurch Road	C4
St Mathews Road	A1
Sanford Road	A2-A3
Scarborough Road	C3
Shedden Hill	C2-C3
Sherwell Hill	A2
Sherwell Lane	A2
Solsbro Road	A1-B1
South Street	B3-B4
Stentisfords Hill	E3
Stitchill Road	F3
Strand	E2
Sutherland Road	E4-F4
Temperance Street	C3-D3
The King's Drive	B1-B2-C1
The Terrace	E2
Thurlow Road	C4
Torbay Road	C1-C2-D2-E2
Torchurch Road	B3-C3
Tor Hill Road	B4-C3-C4
Tor Park Road	A4-B4
Torwood Gardens Road	F2-F3
Torwood Street	E2-F2-F3
Union Street	B4-C3-C4-D3
Upper Braddons Hill Road	E3
Upton Road	B4
Vanehill Road	F1-F2
Vansittart Road	B3-B4
Vaughan Road	E2
Vicarage Road	A1
Victoria Parade	E1-E2
Victoria Road	D4
Vine Road	A3
Walnut Road	A1-B1-B2
Warren Road	C2-C3-D2-D3
Warberry Road West	D3-D4-E4
Wellington Road	D4
Woodside Drive	E3

PAIGNTON

Adelphi Lane	C2
Adelphi Road	B2-C2
Alta Vista Road	C1
Batson Gardens	A1
Beach Road	B3-C3
Belle Vue Road	C1
Blatchcombe Road	A4
Cadwell Road	B4
Cecil Road	A3-B3
Church Street	A3-B3
Cleveland Road	C1
Cliff Road	C1
Clifton Bank	A2
Climsland Road	A1
Colin Road	C4
Colley End Park	A3
Colley End Road	A3
Conway Road	A1-A2
Corsham Road	A1
Courtland Road	B3-B4
Curledge Street	A2-B2
Dartmouth Road	B1-B2
David Road	A4
Dendy Road	B3
Derrel Road	A1
Elmbank Road	A1
Elmsleigh Road	A1-B1
Esplanade	C2-C3-C4
Esplanade Road	C2-C3-C4
Fisher Street	A1-A2-B1
Garfield Road	B2-B3-C3
Gerston Road	B2
Grosvenor Road	A1-B1-B2
Higher Polsham Road	A4-B4
Hill Park Terrace	B1
Hyde Road	B2-B3
Kernou Road	B2-C2
Keysfield Road	C1
Kings Avenue	B4
Kings Road	B4
Littlegate Road	A3-B3
Lower Polsham Road	C4-B3-B4
Manor Road	C4
Marine Drive	C4
Marldon Road	A3
Mead Road	B4
Midvale Road	B2
Mill Lane	A3
Monastery Road	A3
New Street	A2
Oldway Road	A4
Osney Crescent	A1-B1
Palace Avenue	A2-B2
Polsham Park	B3-B4
Primley Park	A2
Queen's Road	B2
Redburn Road	A3-A4
Roundham Road	B1-C1-C2
St Andrew's Road	B1-B2
St Michael's Road	A1
Sands Road	B1-B2-C2
Shorton Road	A4
Southfield Rise	A4
Southfields Road	A3-A4
Steartfield Road	B3-C3
Torbay Road	B2-C2
Torquay Road	B2-B3-B4
Totnes Road	A1-A2-B2
Tower Road	A2-A3-B3
Upper Morin Road	B4-C4
Victoria Street	B2
Well Street	A3
Westhill Road	A4
Whitstone Road	B1
Winner Street	A2-A3
Winnerhill Road	A2-A3
Woodland Park	A4
York Road	A1

BRIXHAM

Alma Road	B3
Berry Head Road	C2
Bolton Street	A1-A2-B2
Burton Street	A1-A2
Castor Road	A1
Centry Road	C1
Cudhill Road	A2-A3
Cumber Drive	A3-A4
Drew Street	A1
Elkins Hill	B2-C2
Fishcombe Road	B4-C4
Fore Street	B2
Furzeham Park	B4
Garlic Rea	C2
Glenmore Road	B2
Gollands	A3-A4
Gollands Close	A4
Great Rea Road	C1-C2
Greenswood Road	A1
Heath Road	C2
Higher Furzeham Road	B3-B4-C3-C4
Higher Manor Road	B3
Higher Ranscombe Road	B1-C1
Hillside Road	A2
King Street	B2-C2
Knick Knack Lane	A1-A2
Lakes Road	A4
Langley Avenue	A2
Lindthorpe Way	A3
Lower Manor Road	A3-B3
Lower Rea Road	C1-C2
Lyte's Road	B1-B2-C1
Market Street	B2
Metherell Avenue	A1
Middle Street	B2
Mount Road	B2
Mount Pleasant Road	B2
Nelson Road	B3-C3
New Road	A3-B3-B2
North Boundary Road	A4-B4
Northfields Lane	A3-A4-B4-C4
North Furzeham Road	C3-C4
Overgang Road	C3
Parkham Road	A2-B2
Penn Lane	A1
Penn Meadows	A1
Penpethy Road	A3
Prospect Road	B3-C3
Queen's Crescent	B1
Queen's Road	C4
Ranscombe Park	C1
Ranscombe Road	C1-C2
Rea Barn Road	A1-B1
Sellick Avenue	A1-B1
Smardon Avenue	A3-A4
South Furzeham Road	B3-C3
Station Hill	B2-B3
Strand	B2
The Close	B4
The Quay	C2-C3
Wall Park Close	C1
Wall Park Road	C1
Windmill Hill	A1-B1-B2
Windmill Road	B2-C2
Wolston Close	B4

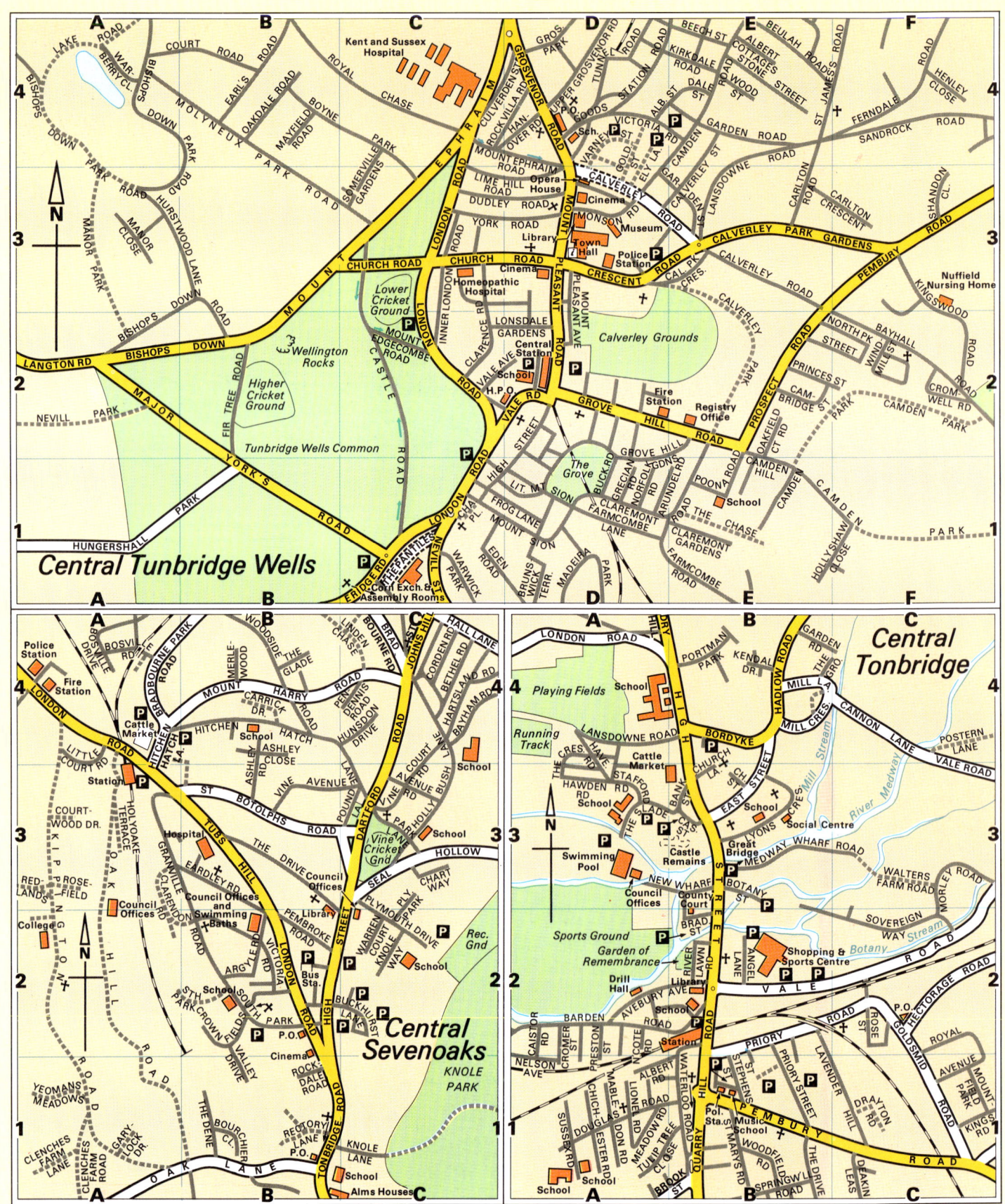

Tunbridge Wells

Dudley, Lord North, set this spa town on the road to fame in the 17th century, when he pronounced on the restorative properties of its Chalybeate Spring. Tunbridge Wells became a fashionable resort under the patronage of Queen Henrietta Maria, wife of Charles I, and later under that of Queen Victoria. It was awarded the title of 'Royal' Tunbridge Wells in 1909.

Today the Chalybeate Spring can still be sampled in the delightful setting of the Pantiles, an elegant precinct started in 1700 and lined with picturesque shops and inns. Fine examples of 19th-century architecture can also be seen in the Mount Pleasant and Mount Ephraim areas, where exclusive Victorian housing estates were built. The Museum and Art Gallery features examples of the wooden souvenir ware which has been produced by the town for over 200 years.

Sevenoaks is a residential town with an old-established Grammar School. Nearby Knole, a fine manor house set in an extensive deer park, was the birthplace of Vita Sackville-West.

Tonbridge has the remains of the Norman castle built here to guard the crossing of the River Medway. Part of the 11th-century wall and the gatehouse, added in the 13th century, are still intact, and stand in attractive gardens. The Angel Centre offers sports, music and drama.

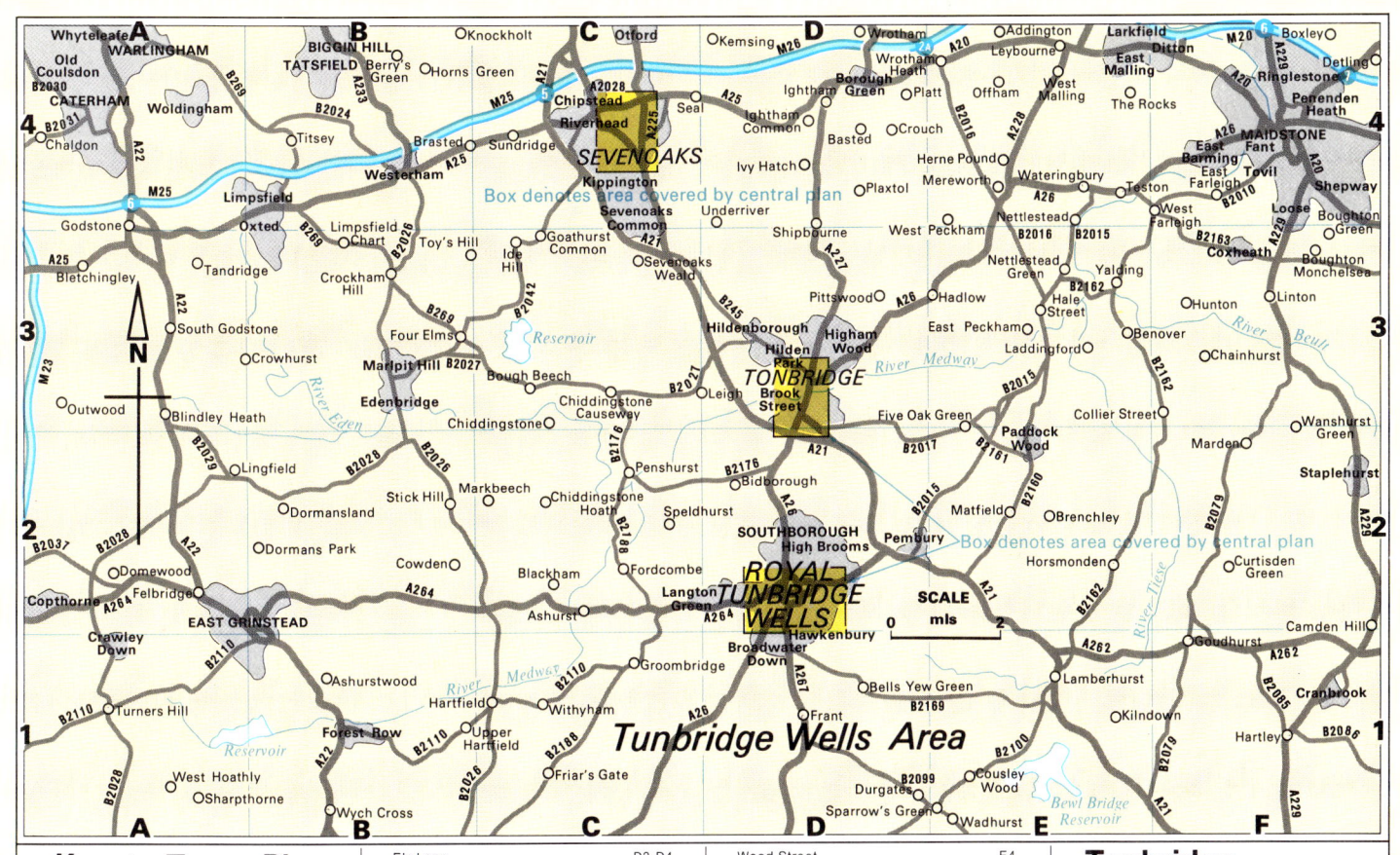

Key to Town Plan and Area Plan

Town Plan
- AA Recommended roads
- Restricted roads
- Other roads
- Buildings of interest — Museum
- Car Parks — P
- Parks and open spaces
- One way streets

Area Plan
- A roads
- B roads
- Locations — Godstone
- Urban area

Street Index with Grid Reference

Tunbridge Wells

Albert Cottages	E4
Albert Street	D4-E4
Arundel Road	D1-E1
Bayhall Road	F2
Beech Street	E4
Beulah Road	E4
Bishops Down	A2-B2
Bishops Down Park Road	A4-A3-B3-B4-A4
Bishops Down Road	A2-A3-B3-B2
Boyne Park	B4-C4-C3
Brunswick Terrace	D1
Buckingham Road	D1-D2
Calverley Park	D3-E3-E2
Calverley Park Crescent	D3-E3
Calverley Park Gardens	E3-F3
Calverley Road	D3-E3
Calverley Street	D3-E3-E4
Cambridge Street	E2
Camden Hill	E1-E2
Camden Park	F1-E1-E2-F2
Camden Road	D3-D4-E4
Carlton Crescent	E3-F3
Carlton Road	E3-E4
Castle Road	C1-C2-C3
Chapel Place	C1
Church Road	C3-D3
Claremont Gardens	E1
Claremont Road	D1-E1-E2
Clarence Road	C2-C3
Court Road	A4-B4
Crescent Road	D3-E3
Cromwell Road	F2
Culverden Street	C4-D4
Dale Street	E4
Dudley Road	C3-D3
Earl's Road	B4
Eden Road	C1-D1
Ely Lane	D3-D4
Eridge Road	B1-C1
Farmcombe Lane	D1
Farmcombe Road	D1-E1
Ferndale Road	E4-F4
Fir Tree Road	B2
Frog Lane	C1-D1
Garden Road	E4
Garden Street	D3-E3
Golding Street	D3-D4
Goods Station Road	D4-E4
Grecian Road	D1
Grosvenor Park	D4
Grosvenor Road	D3-D4
Grove Hill Gardens	D1-D2-E2
Grove Hill Road	D2-E2
Hanover Road	C4-D4
Henley Close	F4
High Street	C1-D1-D2
Hollyshaw Close	E1-F1
Hungershall Park	A1-B1
Hurstwood Lane	A3-B3
Inner London Road	C2-C3
Kingswood Road	F2-F3
Kirkdale Road	D4-E4
Lake Road	A4
Langton Road	A2
Lansdowne Road	E3-E4
Lime Hill Road	C3-D3
Little Mount Sion	C1-D1
London Road	C1-C2-C3-C4
Lonsdale Gardens	C2-D2
Madeira Park	D1
Major York's Road	A2-B2-B1-C1
Manor Close	A3
Manor Park	A2-A3
Mayfield Road	B4
Molyneux Park Road	A4-B4-B3-C3
Monson Road	D3
Mount Edgecombe Road	C2
Mount Ephraim	B2-B3-C3-C4
Mount Ephraim Road	C4-D4-D3
Mount Pleasant Avenue	D2-D3
Mount Pleasant Road	D2-D3
Mount Sion	C1-D1
Nevill Park	A2
Nevill Street	C1
Norfolk Road	D1
North Park Street	E2-F2
Oakdale Road	E2
Oakfield Court Road	E2
Pembury Road	E3-F3
Poona Road	E1-E2
Princes Street	E2-F2
Prospect Road	E2-E3
Rock Villa Road	C4-D4
Royal Chase	B4-C4
St James's Road	E4-F4
Sandrock Road	E4-F4
Shandon Close	F3
Somerville Gardens	C3-C4
Stone Street	E4
The Chase	E1
The Pantiles	C1
Tunnel Road	D4
Upper Grosvenor Road	D4
Vale Avenue	C2-D2
Vale Road	C2-D2
Varney Street	D3-D4
Victoria Road	D4-E4
Warberry Close	A4
Warwick Park	C1
Windmill Street	F2
Wood Street	E4
York Road	C3-D3

Sevenoaks

Argyle Road	B2
Ashley Close	B4
Ashley Road	B3-B4
Avenue Road	C3
Bayham Road	C4
Bethel Road	C4
Bosville Drive	A4
Bosville Road	A4
Bourchier Close	B1
Bradbourne Park Road	A4-B4
Bradbourne Road	C4
Buckhurst Lane	B2-C2
Carrick Drive	B4
Chart Way	C3
Clarendon Road	A3-A2-B2
Clenches Farm Lane	A1
Clenches Farm Road	A1
Corden Road	C4
Courtwood Drive	A3
Crownfields	B2
Dartford Road	C3-C4
Eardley Road	A3-B3-B2
Garylock Drive	A1
Granville Road	A3-B3-B2
Hartsland Road	C4
Hall Lane	C4
High Street	B2-C2-C3
Hitchen Hatch Lane	A3-A4-B4-C4-C3
Holly Bush Lane	C3-C4
Holyoake Terrace	A3
Hunsdon Drive	C4
Kippington Road	A1-A2-A3-A4
Knole Lane	B1-C1
Knole Way	C2
Linden Chase	B4-C4
Little Court Road	A3-A4
London Road	A3-A4, B1-B2
Merlewood	B4
Mount Harry Road	A4-B4-C4
Oak Hill Road	A4-A3-A2-A1-B1
Oak Lane	A1-B1
Park Lane	C3
Pembroke Road	B2
Pendennis Road	C4
Plymouth Drive	C2-C3
Plymouth Park	C2-C3
Pound Lane	C3
Rectory Lane	B1
Redlands	A3
Rockdale Road	B1
Rosefields	B1
St Botolphs Road	A3-B3-C3
St Johns Hill	C4
Seal Hollow	C3
South Park	A2-B2
The Dene	B1
The Drive	B2-B3
The Glade	B4
Tonbridge Road	B1-C1-B1-B2
Tubs Hill	B2-B3
Valley Drive	B1-B2
Victoria Road	B2
Vine Avenue	B3-C3
Vine Court Road	C3-C4
Warren Court	C2
Woodside Road	B4
Yeomans Meadow	A1

Tonbridge

Albert Road	A1-B1
Angel Lane	B2
Avebury Avenue	A2-B2
Bank Street	B3
Barden Road	A2-B2
Bordyke	B4
Botany Street	B3
Bradford Street	B2
Brook Street	A1-B1
Caistor Road	A1-A2
Cannon Lane	C4
Castle Street	B3
Chichester Road	A1
Church Lane	B3
Church Street	B3
Cromer Street	A1-A2
Deakin Leas	C1
Douglas Road	A1-B1
Drayton Road	C1
Dry Hill	A4-B4
East Street	B3-B4
Garden Road	B4-C4
Goldsmid Road	C1-C2
Hadlow Road	B4
Havelock Road	A3-A4
Hawden Road	A3
Hectorage Road	C2
High Street	B2-B3-B4
Kendall Drive	B4
Kings Road	C1
Lansdowne Road	A4-B4
Lavender Hill	B2-B1-C1
Lionel Road	A1
London Road	A4-B4
Lyons Crescent	B3
Mabledon Road	A1
Meadow Road	A1
Medway Wharf Road	B3-C3
Mill Crescent	B4
Mill Lane	B4-C4
Morley Road	C2-C3
Mountfield Park	C1
Nelson Avenue	A1-A2
New Wharf	A3-B3
Northcote Road	A2
Pembury Road	B1-C1
Portman Park	B4
Postern Lane	C4
Preston Street	A1-A2
Priory Road	B1-B2-C2
Priory Street	B1-B2
Quarry Hill Road	B1-B2
River Lawn Road	B2
Rose Street	C2
Royal Avenue	C1-C2
St Marys Road	B1
St Stephens Street	B1
Sovereign Way	C2
Springwell Road	B1
Stafford Road	A3
Sussex Road	A1
The Crescent	A3-A4
The Drive	B4-C4
The Grove	A3-B3
The Slade	A3-B3
Tulip Tree Close	A1-B1
Vale Road	B2-C2-C3, C3-C4
Walters Farm Road	C3
Waterloo Road	B1-B2
Woodfield Road	B1

69

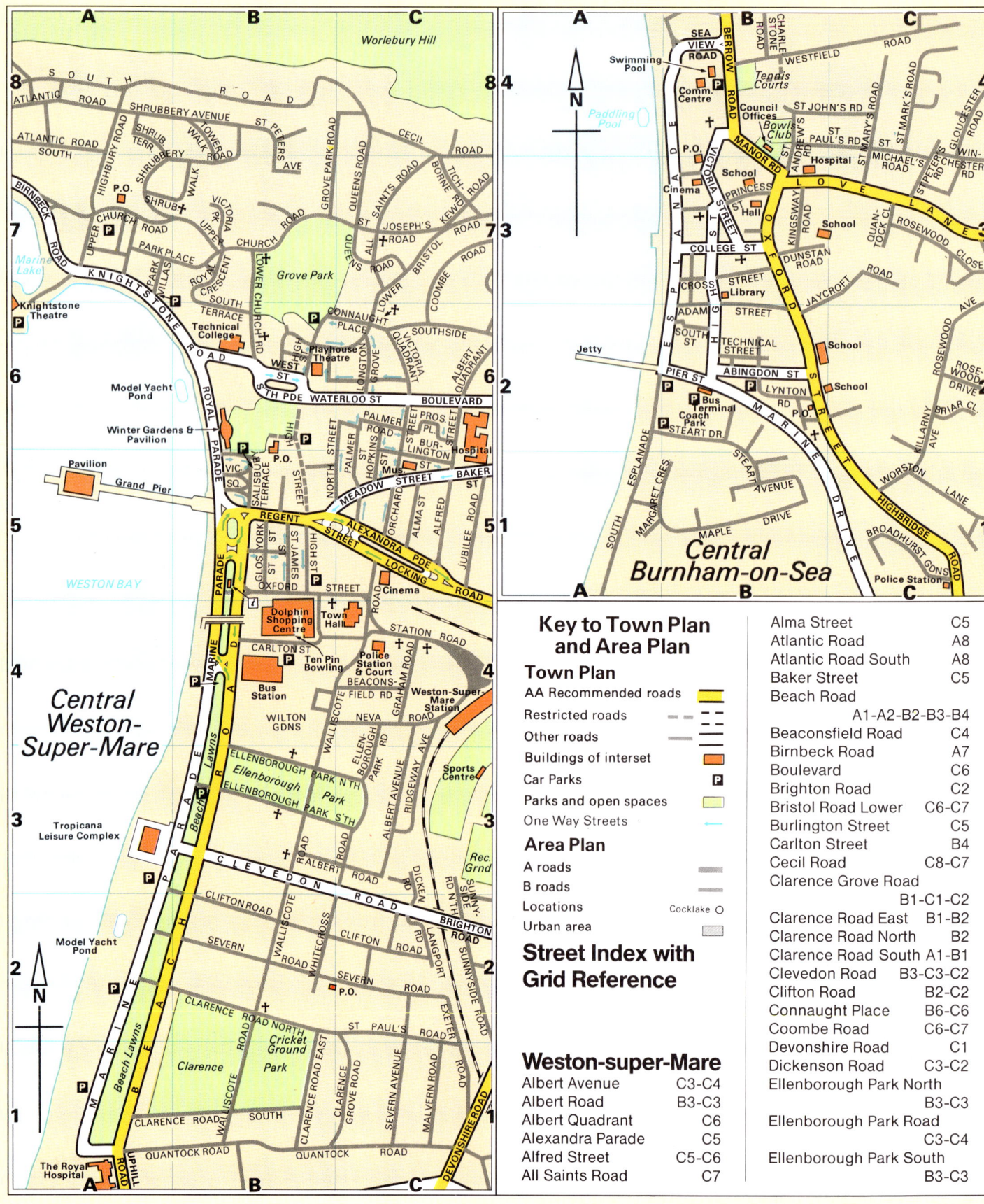

Key to Town Plan and Area Plan

Town Plan

AA Recommended roads	
Restricted roads	
Other roads	
Buildings of interset	
Car Parks	P
Parks and open spaces	
One Way Streets	

Area Plan

A roads	
B roads	
Locations	Cocklake O
Urban area	

Street Index with Grid Reference

Weston-super-Mare

Albert Avenue	C3-C4
Albert Road	B3-C3
Albert Quadrant	C6
Alexandra Parade	C5
Alfred Street	C5-C6
All Saints Road	C7
Alma Street	C5
Atlantic Road	A8
Atlantic Road South	A8
Baker Street	C5
Beach Road	
	A1-A2-B2-B3-B4
Beaconsfield Road	C4
Birnbeck Road	A7
Boulevard	C6
Brighton Road	C2
Bristol Road Lower	C6-C7
Burlington Street	C5
Carlton Street	B4
Cecil Road	C8-C7
Clarence Grove Road	
	B1-C1-C2
Clarence Road East	B1-B2
Clarence Road North	B2
Clarence Road South	A1-B1
Clevedon Road	B3-C3-C2
Clifton Road	B2-C2
Connaught Place	B6-C6
Coombe Road	C6-C7
Devonshire Road	C1
Dickenson Road	C3-C2
Ellenborough Park North	
	B3-C3
Ellenborough Park Road	
	C3-C4
Ellenborough Park South	
	B3-C3

Weston-Super-Mare

Elegant piers, promenades and hotels mark Weston-Super-Mare's 19th-century transformation into a flourishing seaside resort. At one time nothing more than a small fishing village, the town now boasts several attractive parks and gardens, and near the beach are numerous entertainment and leisure centres.

Havens for children are the Winter Garden Complex and Tropicana, both equipped with water slides, swimming pools and solaria. Madeira Cove attracts visitors to its Marine Lake, aquarium and model village, and Knightstone Island nearby provides further entertainments.

The High Street has been turned into a pedestrian area for easy shopping, and tucked away down a cobbled street is the Woodspring Museum full of nostalgic memories of a town which still retains its character and charm.

Burnham-on-Sea enjoys two local breweries, responsible for supplying the real ales which are exclusive to the pubs in this area. Developed into a resort as early as the 18th century, Burnham-on-Sea also offers many other amenities, including a mild Somerset climate, acres of sandy beaches, a Leisure Park and a pier which was built in 1856 as a terminal for passing steamers and the railway. Live entertainment can be seen at Princess Hall.

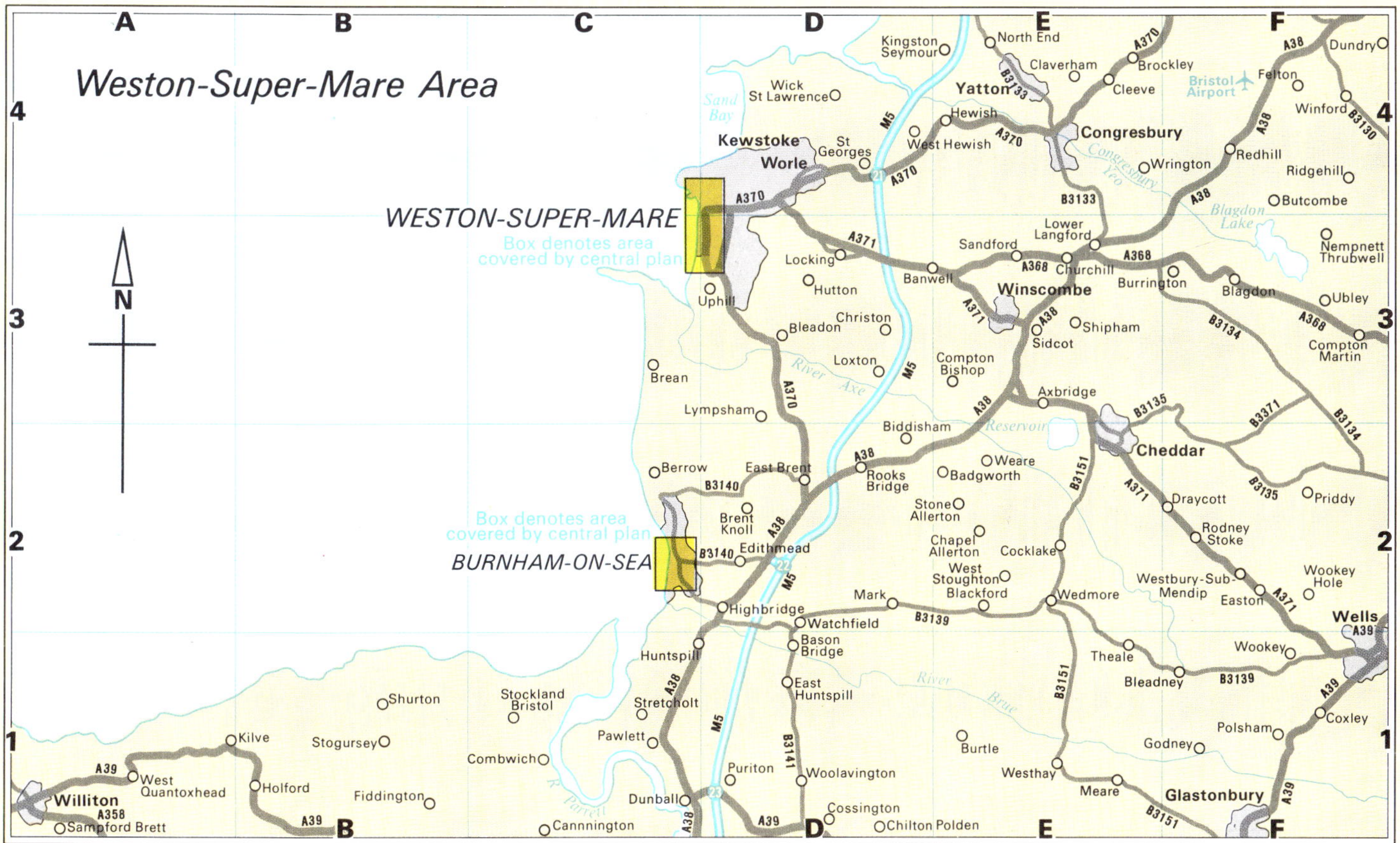

Weston-Super-Mare Area

N

Map labels (regional):

Kingston Seymour, North End, Claverham, Brockley, Dundry, A38, A370, Felten, Bristol Airport, Winford, B3130, Wick St Lawrence, Yatton, B3133, Hewish, Cleeve, Redhill, Ridgehill, Sand Bay, Kewstoke, St Georges, West Hewish, A370, Congresbury, Wrington, Worle, A371, A370, Congresbury Yeo, Butcombe, WESTON-SUPER-MARE, *Box denotes area covered by central plan*, Locking, Banwell, Sandford, A368, Churchill, A368, Burrington, Blagdon, Blagdon Lake, Uphill, Hutton, Lower Langford, Winscombe, Nempnett Thrubwell, Christon, Shipham, Sidcot, A38, A368, Ubley, Bleadon, Loxton, Compton Bishop, Axbridge, Compton Martin, Brean, M5, River Axe, B3135, B3371, B3134, Cheddar, Lympsham, Biddisham, Reservoir, A38, Draycott, B3135, Priddy, Berrow, East Brent, A38, Rooks Bridge, Weare, Badgworth, B3151, A371, Rodney Stoke, Wookey Hole, B3140, Brent Knoll, Stone Allerton, Chapel Allerton, Cocklake, Wedmore, Westbury-Sub-Mendip, Easton, A371, Wells, A39, Edithmead, West Stoughton, Blackford, Mark, B3139, Theale, Bleadney, B3139, Wookey, Highbridge, Watchfield, Bason Bridge, River Brue, B3151, A39, Huntspill, A38, East Huntspill, Shurton, Stockland Bristol, Stretcholt, M5, B3141, Burtle, Godney, Polsham, Coxley, Kilve, Stogursey, Pawlett, Woolavington, Westhay, Meare, Glastonbury, Combwich, Puriton, A39, Cossington, A39, B3151, West Quantoxhead, Holford, Fiddington, Dunball, Cannington, Chilton Polden, Williton, A358, Sampford Brett, A39, BURNHAM-ON-SEA, *Box denotes area covered by central plan*

Street Index (Weston-Super-Mare)

Exeter Road	C2-C1
Gloucester Street	B5
Graham Road	C4
Grove Park Road	B7-B8-C8
Highbury Road	A7-A8
High Street	B6-B5
Hopkin Street	C5-C6
Jubilee Road	C5
Kew Road	C7
Knightstone Road	A7-A6-B6
Langport Road	C2
Locking Road	C5-C4
Longton Grove	C6
Lower Church Road	B7-B6
Malvern Road	C1
Marine Parade	A1-A2-A3-B3-B4-B5
Meadow Street	B5-C5
Neva Road	B4-C4
North Street	B5-C5-C6
Orchard Street	C5-C6
Oxford Street	B5-C5
Palmer Road	C6
Palmer Street	C5-C6
Park Place	A7-B7
Park Villas	A7
Prospect Place	C6
Quantock Road	A1-B1-C1
Queens Road	C7-C8
Regent Street	B5-C5
Ridgeway Avenue	C3-C4

Royal Crescent	B7
Royal Parade	B6-B5
St James Street	B5
St Joseph's Road	C7
St Paul's Road	C2-C1
St Peter's Avenue	B8-B7
Salisbury Terrace	B5
Severn Avenue	C1-C2
Severn Road	B2-C2
Shrubbery Avenue	A8-B8
Shrubbery Road	A7-B7-B8
Shrubbery Terrace	A8
Shrubbery Walk	A7-B7
South Parade	B6
South Road	A8-B8
Southside	C6
South Terrace	B7-B6
Station Road	C4
Sunnyside Road	C2
Sunnyside Road North	C3-C2
Tichbourne Road	C7
Tower Walk	B8
Upper Church Road	A7-B7
Victoria Park	B7
Victoria Square	B5
Victoria Quadrant	C6
Walliscote Road	B1-B2-B3-B4-C4-C5
Waterloo Street	B6-C6
West Street	B6

Whitecross Road	B2-C2-C3
Wilton Gardens	B4
York Street	B5

Burnham-on-Sea

Abingdon Street	B2
Adam Street	B2-B3
Berrow Road	B4
Briar Close	C2
Broadhurst Gardens	C1
Charlestone Road	B4
College Street	B3
Cross Street	B3
Dunstan Road	B3
Esplanade	A2-B2-B3-B4
Gloucester Road	C4
Highbridge Road	C1
High Street	B2-B3
Jaycroft Road	B2-B3-C3
Kilarny Avenue	C1-C2
Kingsway Road	B3
Love Lane	B3-C3
Lynton Road	B2
Manor Road	B4-B3
Maple Drive	B1
Margaret Crescent	A1-B1
Marine Drive	B2-B1-C1
Oxford Street	B3-B2-C2-C1

Pier Street	B2
Princess Street	B3
Quantock Close	C3
Rosewood Avenue	C2-C3
Rosewood Close	C3
Rosewood Drive	C2
St Andrew's Road	B3-B4
St John's Road	B4-C4
St Marks Road	C4
St Mary's Road	C3-C4
St Michael's Road	C4-C3
St Paul's Road	B4-C4
St Peter's Road	C3-C4
Sea View Road	B4
South Esplanade	A1-A2
South Street	B2
Steart Avenue	B2-B1
Steart Drive	A2-B2
Technical Street	B2
Victoria Street	B4-B3
Westfield Road	B4-C4
Winchester Road	C4-C3
Worston Lane	C1

WESTON-SUPER-MARE

The piers and good beaches of Weston-Super-Mare attract over three million visitors a year, and town spectaculars such as the aircraft displays of Great Weston Air Day and the summer carnival are another powerful draw.

Central Dorchester

Central Weymouth

Central Bridport

Key to Town Plan and Area Plan

Town Plan
AA Recommended roads
Restricted roads
Other roads
Buildings of interest
Churches †
Car Parks P
Parks and open spaces
One Way Streets →

Area Plan
A roads
B roads
Locations   Piddletown ○
Urban area

Street Index with Grid Reference

Weymouth
Abbotsbury Road	A3
Alexandra Road	A6
Avenue Road	B5-B6
Barrack Road	B2-C2
Bath Street	A4
Bond Street	B3
Brownlow Street	A5-B5
Brunswick Terrace	B5-B6-C6
Carlton Road North	A6
Carlton Road South	A6-B6
Cassiobury Road	A5-A6-B6
Charles Street	A5
Chelmsford Street	A5-B5
Commercial Road	A4-A3-A2
Crescent Street	B4-B5

Weymouth

King George III favoured the ancient port of Weymouth and as a result the town aquired a certain fashionable status as a resort in the late 18th century. Still popular with holidaymakers, it offers good bathing, fishing and golf, and it is also a busy Channel Islands ferry port. Georgian houses – many of which have been turned into guest houses – overlook the broad esplanade, but near the harbour older buildings line narrow, picturesque streets and alleyways. One of the 17th-century houses in Trinity Street has been restored and refurnished in contemporary style, and another place of interest is the museum in Westham Road.

Dorchester is essentially still the busy market town Thomas Hardy featured in many of his novels. He was born at nearby Higher Bockhampton and several of his personal possessions are displayed in the Dorset County Museum in Dorchester. A series of fires in the 17th and 18th centuries left the town rather short of historic buildings, although St Peter's Church, which dates back to the 1400s, survived, as did the Old Shire Hall – scene of the trial of the Tolpuddle Martyrs in 1834.

Bridport's wide pavements used to be called 'ropewalks' because new ropes were laid out on them for twisting and drying. The 750-year-old industry continues to this day, and relics of the old trade are kept in the museum in South Street.

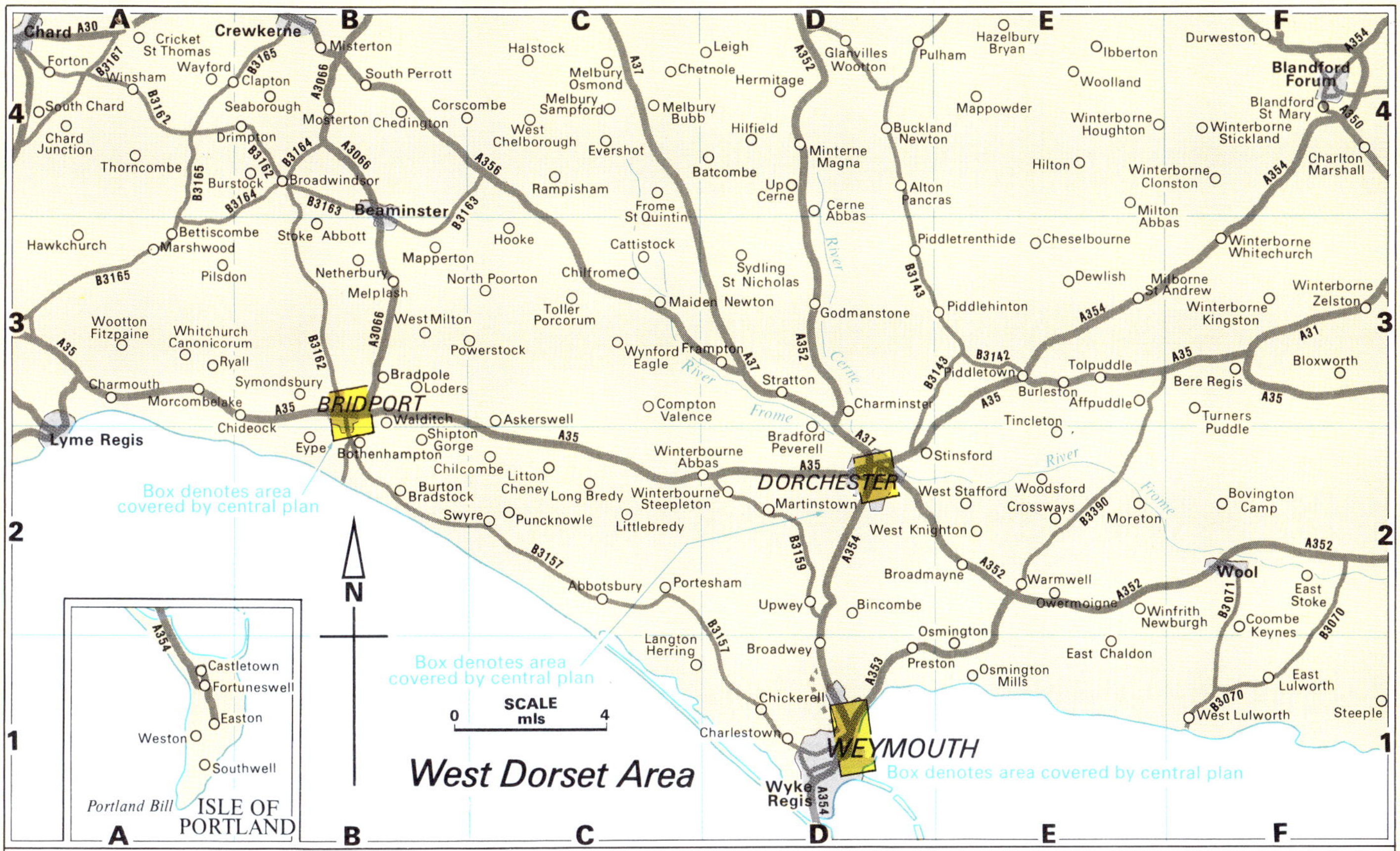

West Dorset Area

SCALE 0 mls 4

N

Box denotes area covered by central plan

ISLE OF PORTLAND

Custom House Quay	B2	Ranelagh Avenue	A5-B5	
Derby Street	A5-B5	Rodwell Avenue	A1-B1	
Dorchester Road	A6-B6	Rodwell Road	A1-A2	
East Street	B2-B3	Royal Terrace	B3-B4	
Embankment Bridge	A3	St Alban Street	B2	
Esplanade	B5-B4-B3-B2-C2-C3	St Leonard's Road	A1-B1	
Franchise Street	A1-B1-B2	St Mary Street	B2-B3	
Glendinning Road	A6	St Thomas Street	A2-B2-B3	
Gloucester Mews	B4	Spring Avenue	B1	
Grange Road	B5-B6	Spring Gardens	A1	
Great George Street	A3-B3-B4	Spring Road	B1	
Greenhill Road	B6-C6	Stavordale Road	A3	
Hanover Road	A6	Town Bridge	A2-B2	
Hardwick Street	A5-B5	Trinity Road	B2	
High Street	A2	Trinity Terrace	A2-B2	
Hope Street	B1-B2	Victoria Street	B5	
Horsford Street	B1-B2	Walpole Street	A5-B5	
Kempston Road	A1-B1	Waterloo Place	B5-B6	
King Street	A4-B4	Wesley Street	A4	
Kirkleton Avenue	A6-B6	Westerhall Road	B6	
Lennox Street	A5-B5	Westham Road	A3-B3	
Love Lane	A1-A2	Westway Road	A2-A3	
Lower Bond Street	A3-B3	William Street	B5-B6	
Lower St Alban Street	A2-B2	Wyke Road	A1	
Maiden Street	B2-B3			
Market Street	B2			
Maycroft	A1	**Bridport**		
Melcombe Road	B6	Alexandra Road	A1-A2	
Newberry	B1	Barrack Street	B2-B3-C3	
Newberry Road	B1	Beaumont Avenue	C4	
Newtons Road	B1	Broadmead Avenue	A4	
Nicholas Street	A2-A3-B3	Chardsmead Road	B3	
North Parade	B2-C2	Church Street	B2	
North Quay	A2	Claremont Road	C4	
Nothe Walk	C2	Coneygar Lane	C4	
Oakley Place	B1	Coneygar Road	B4-C4	
Orion Road	A1	Crock Lane	C1-C2	
Park Drive	A3-A4	Delapre Gardens	C3	
Park Street	A3-A4-B4	Downes Street	B2-B3	
Penny Street	A5	East Road	C2	
Portway Close	A1	East Street	B2-C2	
Queen Street	B4-B5	Elizabeth Avenue	A1	
Radipole Park Drive	A4-A5-A6	Folly Mill Lane	B2	

Fulbrooks Close	A4	Colliton Street	B4	
Fulbrooks Lane	A4	Cornwall Road	A2-A3-A4	
Gundry Lane	A2-B2	Cromwell Road	B1	
Hardy Road	C3-C4	Culliford Road	C1-C2	
Kenwyn Road	C3	Damers Road	A2-A3	
King Street	B2	Durngate Street	B3-C3	
Nordons	C1	Edward Road	A1-A2	
North Allington	A3-A4	Fairfield Road	A2-B2	
North Street	B3	Friary Hill	C4	
North Mills Road	B4	Friary Lane	C4	
Osbourne Road	B4	Frome Terrace	C4	
Parsonage Road	A4	Glyde Path Road	B4	
Pasture Way	C1	Great Western Road	A2-B2	
Princess Road	A1-A2	High Street	C4-C3	
Priory Lane	A2	High East Street	B4-C4	
Rax Lane	B2-B3	High West Street	A4-B4	
Rope Walks	A2	Icen Way	C2-C3-C4	
St Andrews Road	C3	Lancaster Road	C2	
St Michael's Lane	A2-A3	Linden Avenue	C3	
St Swithin's Avenue	A4	London Road	C4	
St Swithin's Road	A3-A4-B4	Maumbury Road	A1-A2	
Sea Road	B1-C1-C2	Monmouth Road	A1-B1-C1	
Sea Road North	C2-C3	North Square	B4	
Slades Grove	C1	Orchard Street	C4	
South Street	B1-B2	Poundbury Road	A4	
Sparacre Gardens	B3-C3	Princes Street	A3-B3-B4	
Tannery Road	A2-A3	Prince of Wales Road	B2-C2-C1	
Victoria Grove	A3-B3-B4	Queens Avenue	A1	
West Allington	A3	Rothesay Road	B1	
West Street	A3-A2-B3-B2	St Helens Road	A3	
		South Street	B2-B3-B4	
		South Court Avenue	B1-C1	
Dorchester		South Walks Road	B2-C2-C3	
Acland Road	C3-C4	The Grove	A4	
Albert Road	A3-A4	Trinity Street	B2-B3-B4	
Alexandra Road	A2	Victoria Road	A2-A3	
Alfred Road	B1	West Walks	A3	
All Saints Road	C3	West Mills Road	A4	
Ashley Road	B1	Weymouth Avenue	A1-A2-B2	
Bridport Road	A4	Weymouth Road	A1	
Charles Street	B2-B3-C3	Wollaston Road	C3	
Coburg Road	A1	York Road	C2	

WEYMOUTH
Little has changed along the town's seafront since George III first came to the resort in the late 18th century to try out a new-fangled contraption called a bathing machine. A statue of the King stands on the esplanade.

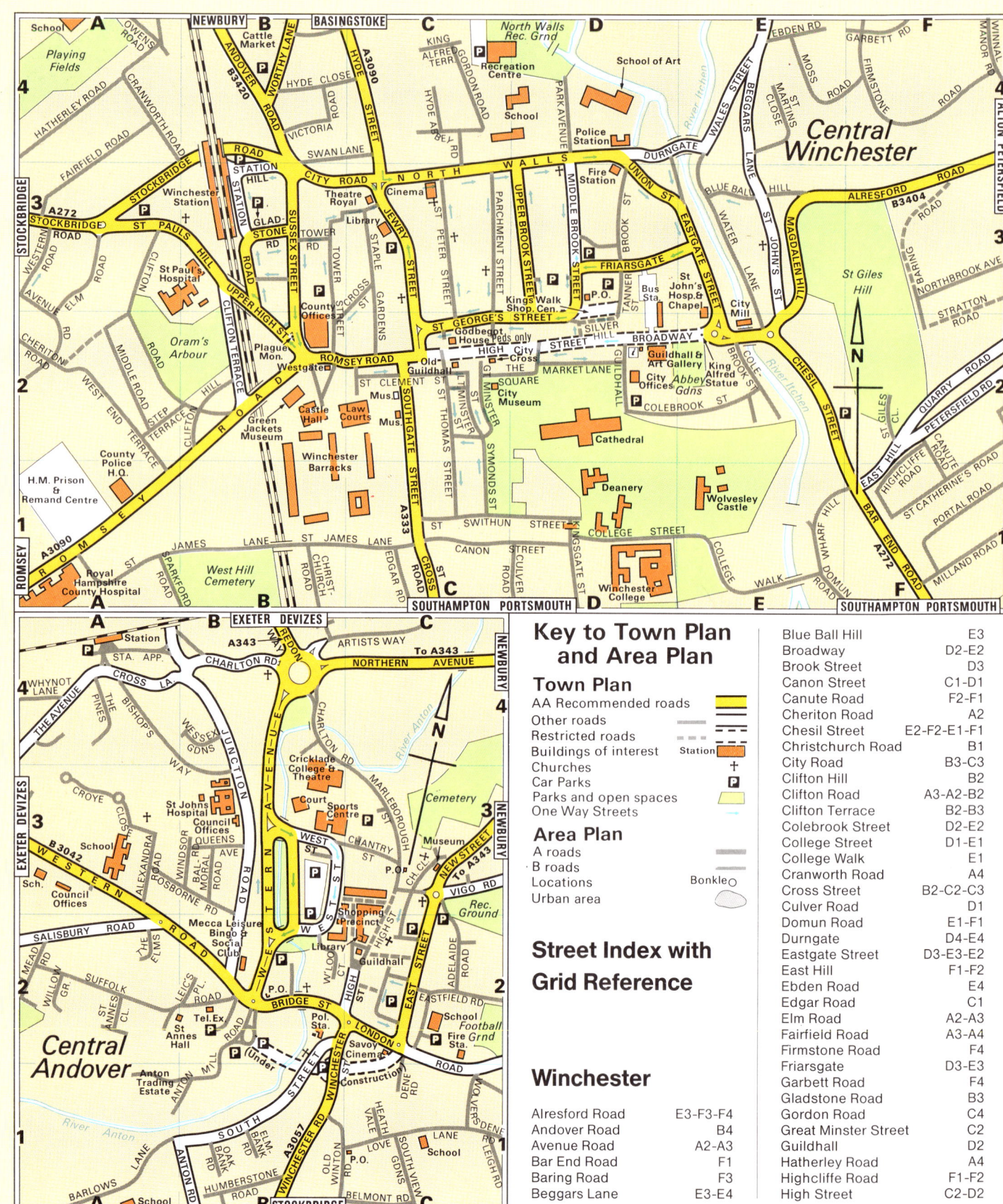

Key to Town Plan and Area Plan

Town Plan
AA Recommended roads
Other roads
Restricted roads
Buildings of interest   Station
Churches
Car Parks
Parks and open spaces
One Way Streets

Area Plan
A roads
B roads
Locations   Bonkle ○
Urban area

Street Index with Grid Reference

Winchester

Alresford Road	E3-F3-F4
Andover Road	B4
Avenue Road	A2-A3
Bar End Road	F1
Baring Road	F3
Beggars Lane	E3-E4

Blue Ball Hill	E3
Broadway	D2-E2
Brook Street	D3
Canon Street	C1-D1
Canute Road	F2-F1
Cheriton Road	A2
Chesil Street	E2-F2-E1-F1
Christchurch Road	B1
City Road	B3-C3
Clifton Hill	B2
Clifton Road	A3-A2-B2
Clifton Terrace	B2-B3
Colebrook Street	D2-E2
College Street	D1-E1
College Walk	E1
Cranworth Road	A4
Cross Street	B2-C2-C3
Culver Road	D1
Domun Road	E1-F1
Durngate	D4-E4
Eastgate Street	D3-E3-E2
East Hill	F1-F2
Ebden Road	E4
Edgar Road	C1
Elm Road	A2-A3
Fairfield Road	A3-A4
Firmstone Road	F4
Friarsgate	D3-E3
Garbett Road	F4
Gladstone Road	B3
Gordon Road	C4
Great Minster Street	C2
Guildhall	D2
Hatherley Road	A4
Highcliffe Road	F1-F2
High Street	C2-D2

Winchester

King Alfred designated Winchester capital of England, a status it retained until after the Norman Conquest. Although gradually eclipsed by London, the city maintained close links with the Crown until the reign of Charles II.

Tucked away unobtrusively in the heart of Winchester is the impressive cathedral which encompasses Norman, and all the later Gothic styles of architecture. William of Wykeham was a bishop here in the 14th century and it was he who founded Winchester College, one of the oldest and most famous public schools in England. The buildings lie just outside the peaceful, shady Close where Pilgrims' Hall can be visited. Nearby are the Bishop's Palace and remains of Wolvesley Castle, one of Winchester's two Norman castles. Of the other, only the Great Hall, just outside the Westgate, survives. Here hangs the massive circle of oak claimed to be King Arthur's Round Table.

The streets of the city, which cover a remarkably small area, are lined with many charming old buildings of different periods. A walk along the pedestrianised High Street takes you past the former Guildhall – now a bank – and the old Butter Cross, into the Broadway where a statue of King Alfred stands near the River Itchen. A delightful path follows the river alongside the remnants of the old city walls.

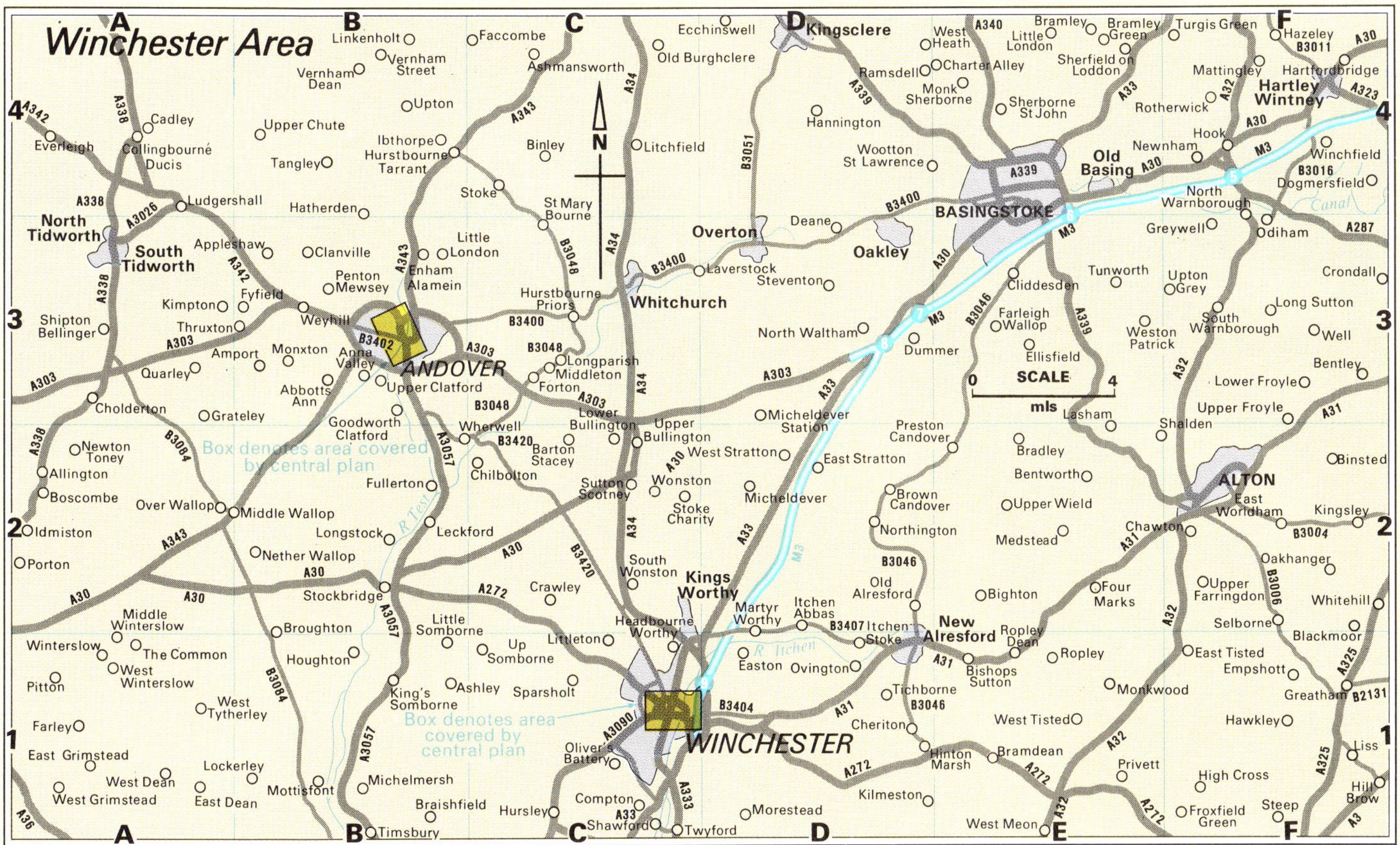

Winchester Area

WINCHESTER
Standing on the site of the old Hall of Court in the Broadway is the city's Guildhall. Built in 1873, its style was influenced by Northampton Town Hall. It is now a centre for culture and the arts.

75

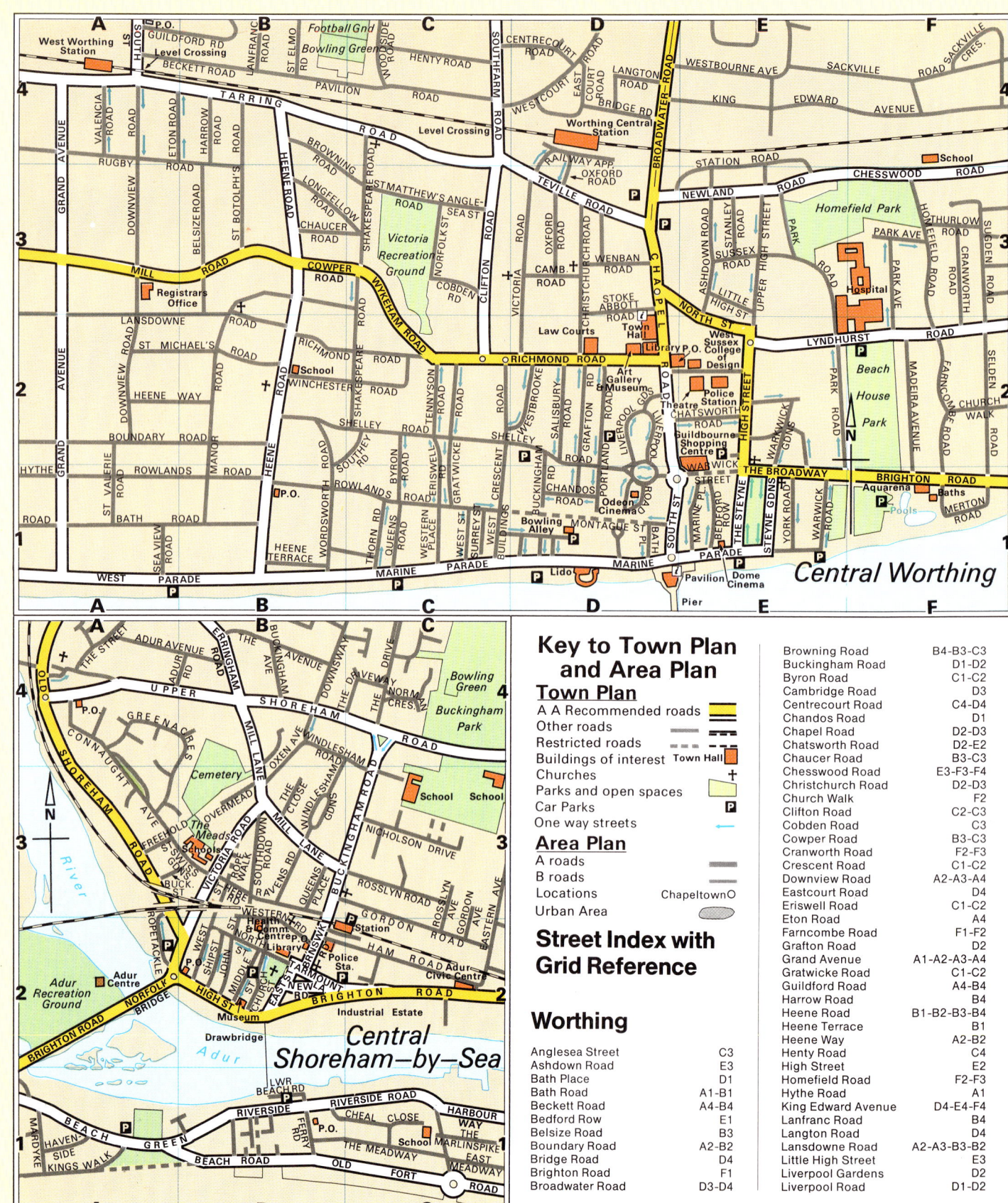

Key to Town Plan and Area Plan

Town Plan
A A Recommended roads
Other roads
Restricted roads
Buildings of interest — Town Hall
Churches
Parks and open spaces
Car Parks
One way streets

Area Plan
A roads
B roads
Locations — Chapeltown○
Urban Area

Street Index with Grid Reference

Worthing

Anglesea Street	C3
Ashdown Road	E3
Bath Place	D1
Bath Road	A1-B1
Beckett Road	A4-B4
Bedford Row	E1
Belsize Road	B3
Boundary Road	A2-B2
Bridge Road	D4
Brighton Road	F1
Broadwater Road	D3-D4

Browning Road	B4-B3-C3
Buckingham Road	D1-D2
Byron Road	C1-C2
Cambridge Road	D3
Centrecourt Road	C4-D4
Chandos Road	D1
Chapel Road	D2-D3
Chatsworth Road	D2-E2
Chaucer Road	B3-C3
Chesswood Road	E3-F3-F4
Christchurch Road	D2-D3
Church Walk	F2
Clifton Road	C2-C3
Cobden Road	C3
Cowper Road	B3-C3
Cranworth Road	F2-F3
Crescent Road	C1-C2
Downview Road	A2-A3-A4
Eastcourt Road	D4
Eriswell Road	C1-C2
Eton Road	A4
Farncombe Road	F1-F2
Grafton Road	D2
Grand Avenue	A1-A2-A3-A4
Gratwicke Road	C1-C2
Guildford Road	A4-B4
Harrow Road	B4
Heene Road	B1-B2-B3-B4
Heene Terrace	B1
Heene Way	A2-B2
Henty Road	C4
High Street	E2
Homefield Road	F2-F3
Hythe Road	A1
King Edward Avenue	D4-E4-F4
Lanfranc Road	B4
Langton Road	D4
Lansdowne Road	A2-A3-B3-B2
Little High Street	E3
Liverpool Gardens	D2
Liverpool Road	D1-D2

Worthing

A mecca for bowls devotees, Worthing hosts both national and international competitions on the excellent greens at Beach House Park. Golf and sailing are popular pastimes, and more than adequate facilities exist for other sports.

Worthing became a fashionable resort in the 18th century and today it offers the visitor a pleasant mixture of Victorian buildings and areas

of modern development: this is one of the major shopping centres of West Sussex, and several pleasant precincts and covered centres have been built. Brooklands Pleasure Park and a good range of shows in the summer season are another draw for visitors. Worthing Museum and Art Gallery has collections of costumes and toys as well as items of local interest, and exhibitions of arts and crafts are held here regularly. At Tarring, one mile from the town centre, a group of 15th-century

cottages has been restored and now houses the Sussex Folklore Museum.

Shoreham has been the site of a port since Roman times, and by the early 14th century it had become a major shipbuilding town. Lying at the mouth of the River Adur, it still keeps up a thriving maritime life in the shape of a busy harbour and several yachting and sailing clubs. The Marlipins Museum, which explores the history of the area, concentrates on Shoreham's nautical connections.

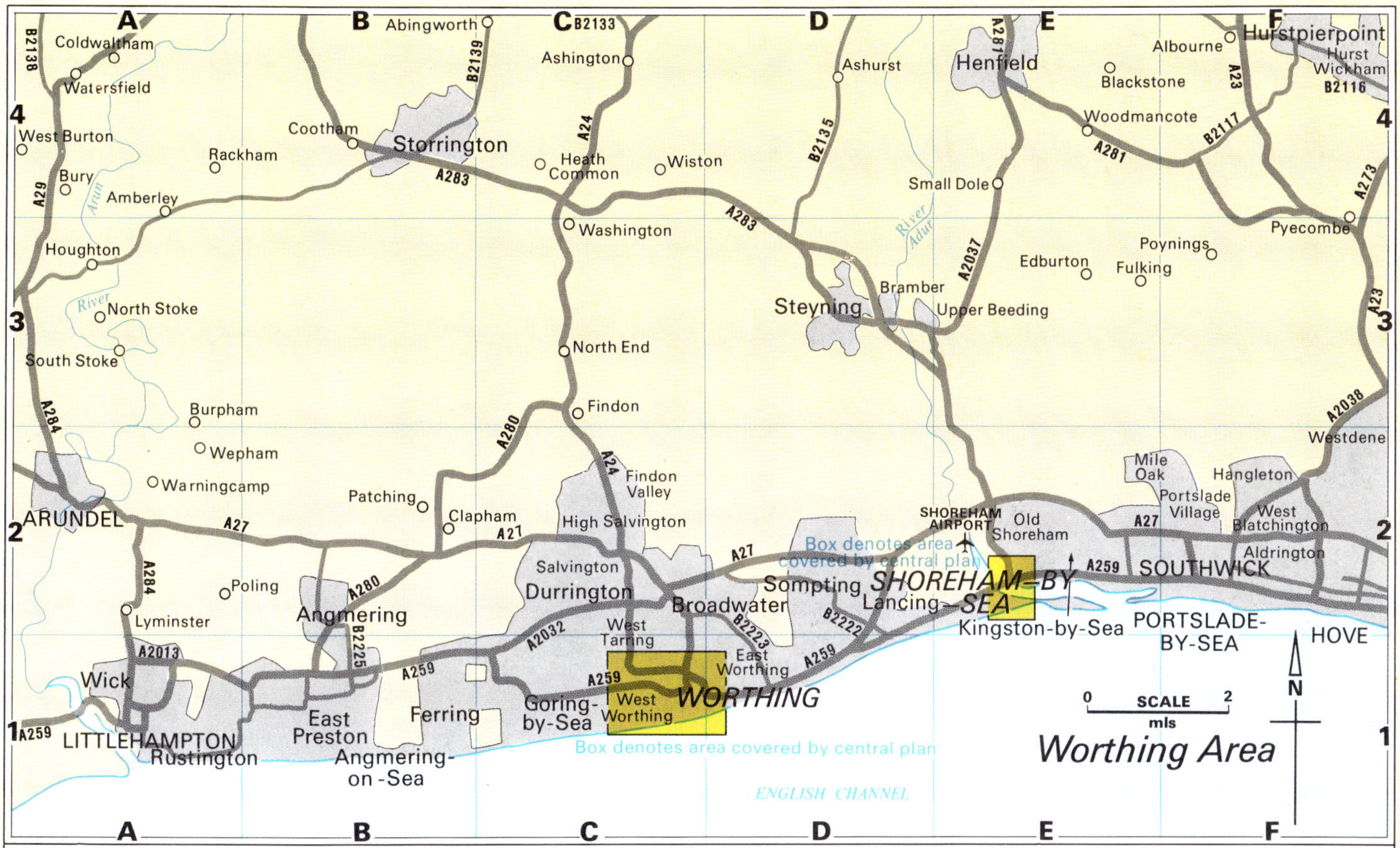

Worthing Area

Map labels (north to south, west to east):

B2138 · Coldwaltham · Watersfield · West Burton · Bury · Amberley · Houghton · North Stoke · South Stoke · A284 · A29 · River Arun · ARUNDEL · A27 · A284 · Poling · Lyminster · A2013 · Wick · LITTLEHAMPTON · A259 · Rustington · East Preston · Angmering-on-Sea · Ferring · Angmering · A2225 · A280 · A259 · Goring-by-Sea · West Worthing · WORTHING

Rackham · Cootham · Storrington · A283 · Heath Common · Washington · A24 · North End · Findon · Burpham · Wepham · Warningcamp · Patching · Clapham · A27 · A24 · High Salvington · Findon Valley · Salvington · Durrington · A2032 · West Tarring · Broadwater · B2223 · A259 · A27

Abingworth · Ashington · B2133 · B2139 · Wiston · A283

Ashurst · Henfield · A281 · Small Dole · Steyning · Bramber · Upper Beeding · A2037 · Edburton · Fulking · River Adur · B2135 · Sompting · Lancing · B2222 · A27 · A259 · Kingston-by-Sea · SHOREHAM AIRPORT · SHOREHAM-BY-SEA · Old Shoreham

Albourne · Hurstpierpoint · Hurst Wickham · B2116 · Blackstone · Woodmancote · A281 · B2117 · Poynings · Pyecombe · A23 · A273 · A2038 · Westdene · Mile Oak · Hangleton · Portslade Village · West Blatchington · A27 · SOUTHWICK · Aldrington · PORTSLADE-BY-SEA · HOVE

Box denotes area covered by central plan

SCALE 0 2 mls N

ENGLISH CHANNEL

Street	Grid
Longfellow Road	B3-C3
Lyndhurst Road	E2-F2
Madeira Avenue	F1-F2
Manor Road	B1-B2
Marine Parade	B1-C1-D1-E1
Marine Place	E1
Merton Road	F1
Mill Road	A3-B3
Montague Street	C1-D1
Newland Road	D3-E3
Norfolk Street	C3
North Street	D3-E3-E2
Oxford Road	D3-D4
Park Avenue	F2-F3
Park Road	E1-E2-E3
Pavilion Road	B4-C4
Portland Road	D1-D2
Queens Road	C1
Railway Approach	D3-D4
Richmond Road	B2-C2-D2
Rowlands Road	A1-B1-C1
Rugby Road	A4-B4-B3
St Boltolph's Road	B3-B4
St Elmo Road	B4
St Mathew's Road	C3
St Michael's Road	A2-B2
St Valerie Road	A1-A2
Sackville Crescent	F4
Sackville Road	E4-F4
Salisbury Road	D2
Sea View Road	A1
Seldon Road	F1-F2
Shakespeare Road	C2-C3-C4
Shelley Road	B2-C2-D2-D1
South Street	A4
South Street	D1-E1
Southey Road	B2-C2
Southfarm Road	C4
Stanley Road	E3
Station Road	D3-E3-E4-E3
Steyne Gardens	E1

Street	Grid
Stoke Abbott Road	D3
Sugden Road	F2-F3
Surrey Street	C1
Sussex Road	E3
Tarring Road	A4-B4-C4-C3
Tennyson Road	C2
Teville Road	C4-D4-D3
The Broadway	E1
The Steyne	E1
Thorn Road	C1
Thurlow Road	F3
Upper High Street	E2-E3
Valencia Road	A4
Victoria Road	D2-D3
Warwick Gardens	E2
Warwick Road	E1
Warwick Street	E1
Wenban Road	D3
West Buildings	C1
West Parade	A1-B1
West Street	C1
Westbourne Avenue	D4-E4
Westbrooke	C2-D2
Westcourt Road	C4-D4
Western Place	C1
Winchester Road	B2-C2
Woodside Road	C4
Wordsworth Road	B1-B2
Wykeham Road	C2-C3
York Road	E1

Shoreham

Street	Grid
Adur Avenue	A4-B4
Adur Road	A4-B4
Beach Green	A1-B1

Street	Grid
Beach Road	A1-B1
Brighton Road	A1-A2, B2-C2
Brunswick Road	B2
Buckingham Avenue	B4
Buckingham Road	B3-C3-C4
Buckingham Street	A3-B3
Cheal Close	B1-C1
Church Street	B2
Connaught Avenue	A3-A4
Downsway	B4-C4
East Meadway	C1
East Street	B2
Eastern Avenue	C2-C3
Erringham Road	B4
Ferry Road	B1
Freehold Street	A3
Gordon Avenue	B3-C3-C2
Gordon Road	B3-C3-C2
Greenacres	A4-B4-A4-A3
Ham Road	B2-C2
Harbour Way	C1
Havenside	A1
Hebe Road	B3
High Street	B2
John Street	B2
Kings Walk	A1
Lower Beach Road	B1
Mardyke	A1
Middle Street	B2
Mill Lane	B3-B4
New Road	B2
Nicholas Drive	C3
Norfolk Bridge	A2
Norman Crescent	C4
North Street	B2
Old Fort Road	B1-C1
Old Shoreham Road	A4-A3-A2-B2
Overmead	B3
Oxen Avenue	B3-B4
Queens Place	B3
Ravens Road	B3

Street	Grid
Riverside	B1
Riverside Road	B1-C1
Ropetackle	A2-A3
Rope Walk	B3
Rosslyn Avenue	C2-C3
Rosslyn Road	C3
Ship Street	B2
Southdown Road	B3
Swiss Gardens	A3-B3
Tarmount Lane	B2
The Avenue	B4
The Close	B3
The Drive	C4
The Driveway	C4
The Marlinspike	C1
The Meadway	B1-C1
The Street	A4
Upper Shoreham Road	A4-B4-C4
Victoria Road	A2-B2-B3
West Street	B2-B3
Western Road	B2-B3
Windlesham Gardens	B3-B4
Windlesham Road	B4-C4-C3

WORTHING
The Marine Parade and West Pier — now the largest town in West Sussex, Worthing was a small fishing village until Princess Amelia, youngest daughter of George III, set a new trend by holidaying here in 1798.

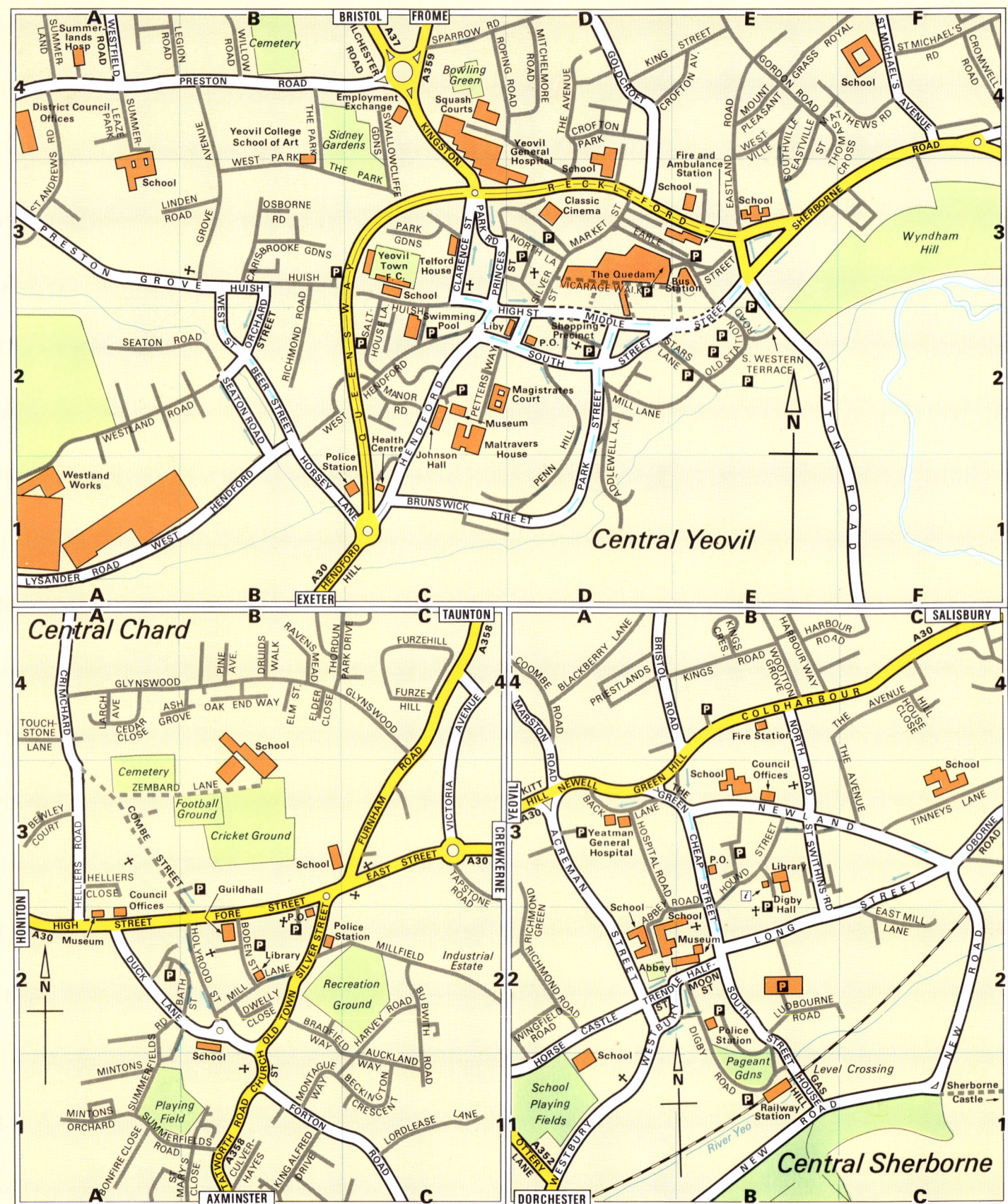

Yeovil

Home of the Westland helicopter and aircraft factory — as a result of which it suffered bomb damage in the Second World War — and six miles south of the Fleet Air Museum at Yeovilton, the market town of Yeovil is also known for its more homely glovemaking. There is a fine 14th-century church, and a collection of firearms and local interest items at Hendford Manor.

Sherborne Full of medieval buildings built in the golden Ham Hill stone, Sherborne has a magnificent, mainly 15th-century, abbey church. Of the town's two public schools, the 1550 boys' school occupies some of the abbey buildings, and the abbey gatehouse has a museum.

East of the town are two castles: a Norman structure which was partly destroyed after the Civil War, and the 'new' castle, a fine Elizabethan house built and occupied by Sir Walter Raleigh, and full of treasures.

Chard was the scene of one of Judge Jeffreys' Bloody Assizes, held in the courthouse (built 1590) here after the Monmouth Rebellion of 1685. The town's grammar school was founded in 1671, the Choughs Hotel is Elizabethan and the porticoed Town Hall dates back to 1834. All stand in the main street, from which streams flow north to the Bristol Channel and south to the English Channel — at 400ft (122m), this is the county's highest town.

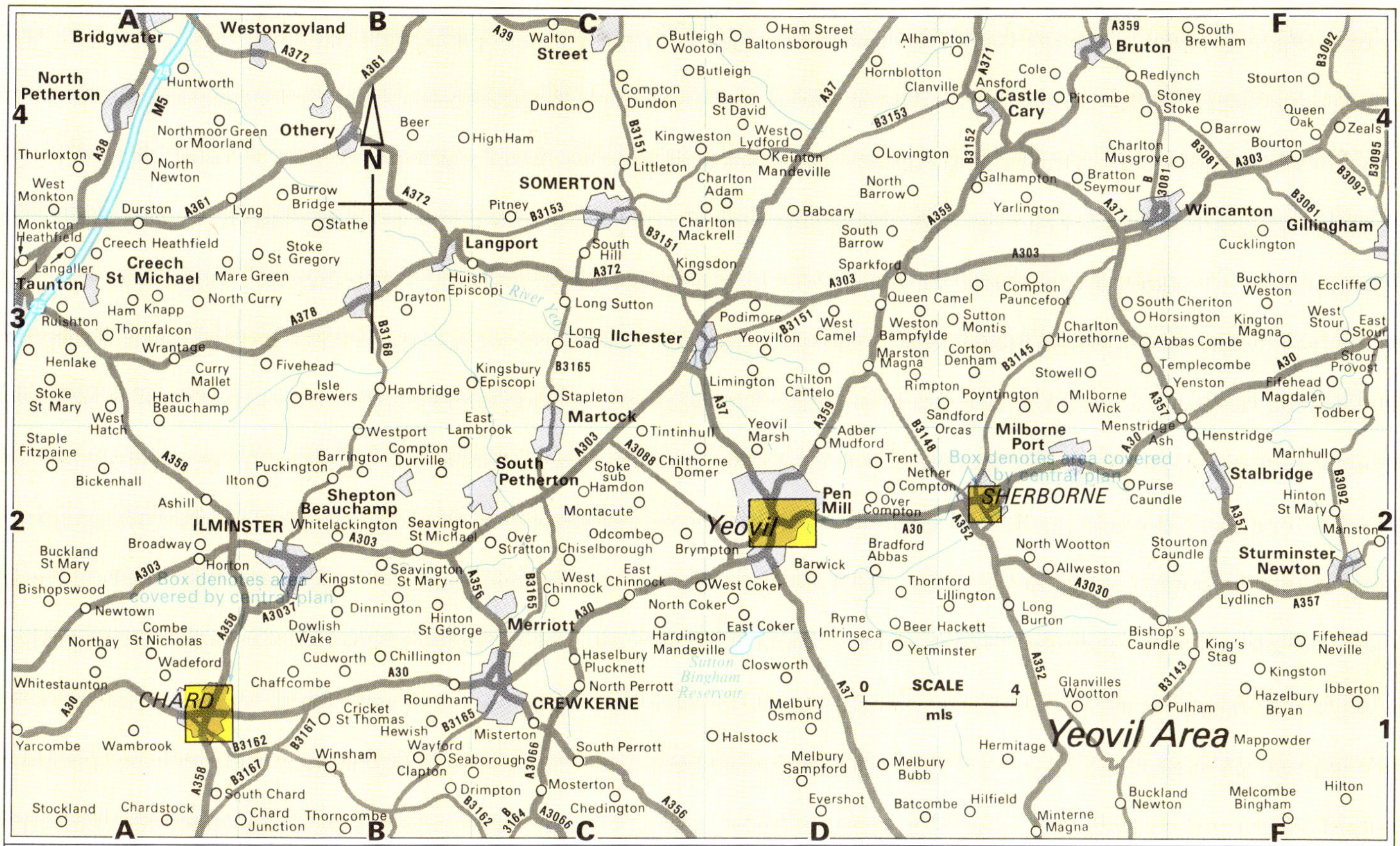

Map of Yeovil Area showing towns including Bridgwater, Taunton, Somerton, Langport, Ilchester, Ilminster, Chard, Crewkerne, Yeovil, Sherborne, Wincanton, Gillingham, Bruton, Castle Cary, and surrounding villages.

Key to Town Plan and Area Plan

Town Plan
AA Recommended roads	
Restricted roads	
Other roads	
Buildings of interest	Library
Car Parks	P
Parks and open spaces	
Churches	+

Area Plan
A roads	
B roads	
Locations	Terry's Green ○
Urban area	

Street Index

Yeovil
Addlewell Lane	D1-D2
Beer Street	B2
Brunswick Street	C1-D1
Carisbrooke Gardens	B3
Clarence Street	C3
Crofton Avenue	D4-E4
Crofton Park	D4
Cromwell Road	F4
Earle Street	D3-E3
Eastland Road	E3-E4
Eastville	E3-E4
Goldcroft	D3-D4
Gordon Road	E4
Grass Royal	E4-F4
Grove Avenue	B3-B4
Hendford	C1-C2
Hendford Hill	B1-C1
High Street	C2-D2
Horsey Lane	B2-B1-C1
Huish	B3-C3
Ilchester Road	C4
King Street	D4-E4
Kingston	C3-C4
Legion Road	A4
Linden Road	A3-B3
Lysander Road	A1
Manor Road	C2
Market Street	D3
Matthews Road	E4-F4
Middle Street	D2-E2-E3
Mill Lane	D2
Mitchelmore Road	D4
Mount Pleasant	E4
Newton Road	E3-E2-F2-F1
North Lane	C3-D3
Old Station Road	E2
Orchard Street	B2-B3
Osborne Road	B3
Queens Way	C1-C2-C3
Park Gardens	C3
Park Road	C3
Park Street	D1-D2
Penn Hill	D1-D2
Petters Way	C2
Preston Grove	A3-B3
Preston Road	A4-B4-C4
Princes Street	C3
Reckleford	C3-D3-E3
Richmond Road	B2-B3
Roping Road	C4-D4
St Andrews Road	A3-A4
St Michael's Avenue	F4
St Michael's Road	F4
St Thomas Cross	E4
Salthouse Lane	C2-C3
Seaton Road	A2-B2-B1
Sherborne Road	E3-F3-F4
South Street	C2-D2
Southville	E3-E4
South Western Terrace	E2
Sparrow Road	C4-D4
Stars Lane	D2-E2
Summerlands	A4
Summerleaze Park	A4
Swallowcliffe Gardens	C3-C4
The Avenue	D3-D4
The Park	B4-B3-C3
Vicarage Walk	D3
West Hendford	A1-B1-B2-C2
West Park	B3
West Street	B2-B3
Westfield Road	A4
Westland Road	A1-A2-B2
Westville	E4
Willow Road	B4

Chard
Ash Grove	A4-B4
Auckland Way	C1
Bath Street	A2-B2
Beckington Crescent	B1-C1
Bewley Court	A3
Boden Street	B2
Bonfire Close	A1
Bradfield Way	B2-C2-C1
Bubwith Road	C1-C2
Cedar Close	A4
Church Street	B1-B2
Combe Street	A3-B3-B2
Crimchard	A3-A4
Culverhayes	B1
Druids Walk	B4
Duck Lane	A2-B2
Dwelly Close	B2
East Street	C3
Elder Close	B4
Elm Street	B4
Fore Street	B2-B3
Forton Road	B1-C1
Furnham Road	C3-C4
Furzehill	C4
Glynswood	A4-B4-C4
Harvey Road	C1-C2
High Street	A2-B2
Helliers Close	A3
Helliers Road	A2-A3
Holyrood Street	B2
King Alfred Drive	B1
Larch Avenue	A4
Lordlease Lane	C1
Mill Lane	B2
Millfield	B2-C2
Mintons	A1
Mintons Orchard	A1
Montague Way	B1
Oak End Way	B4
Old Town	B2
Pine Avenue	B4
Ravensmead	B4
St Mary's Close	B1
Silver Street	B2-B3
Summerfields Road	A2-A1-B1

Sherborne
Tapstone Road	C3
Tatworth Road	B1
Thordun Park Drive	B4-C4
Touchstone Lane	A4
Victoria Avenue	C3-C4
Zembard Lane	A3-B3
Abbey Road	A2-B2-B3
Acreman Street	A2-A3
Back Lane	A3
Blackberry Lane	A4
Bristol Road	A4-B4
Cheap Street	B2-B3
Coldharbour	B4-C4
Coombe Road	A4
Digby Road	B1-B2
East Mill Lane	C2
Gas House Hill	B1
Green Hill	A3-B3-B4
Halfmoon Street	B2
Harbour Road	B4-C4
Harbour Way	B4
Hill House Close	C4
Horse Castle	A1-A2
Hospital Road	A3
Hound Street	B3
Kings Crescent	B4
Kings Road	A4-B4
Kitt Hill	A3
Long Street	B2-C2-C3
Ludbourne Road	B2-C2
Marston Road	A3-A4
New Road	B1-C1-C2-C3
Newell	A4
Newland	B3-C3
North Road	B3-B4
Oborne Road	C3
Ottery Lane	A1
Priestlands	A4
Richmond Green	A2-A3
Richmond Road	A2
St Swithins Road	B2-B3
South Street	B1-B2
The Avenue	C3-C4-B4-C4
The Green	A3-B3
Tinneys Lane	C3
Trendle Street	A2-B2
Westbury	A1-A2-B2
Wingfield Road	A1-A2
Wootton Grove	B4

SHERBORNE
The 'new' castle was built by Sir Walter Raleigh in 1594, and is said to be the place where a servant, horrified at the sight of smoke rising from his newfangled tobacco pipe, promptly doused him with ale to 'put out the fire'.

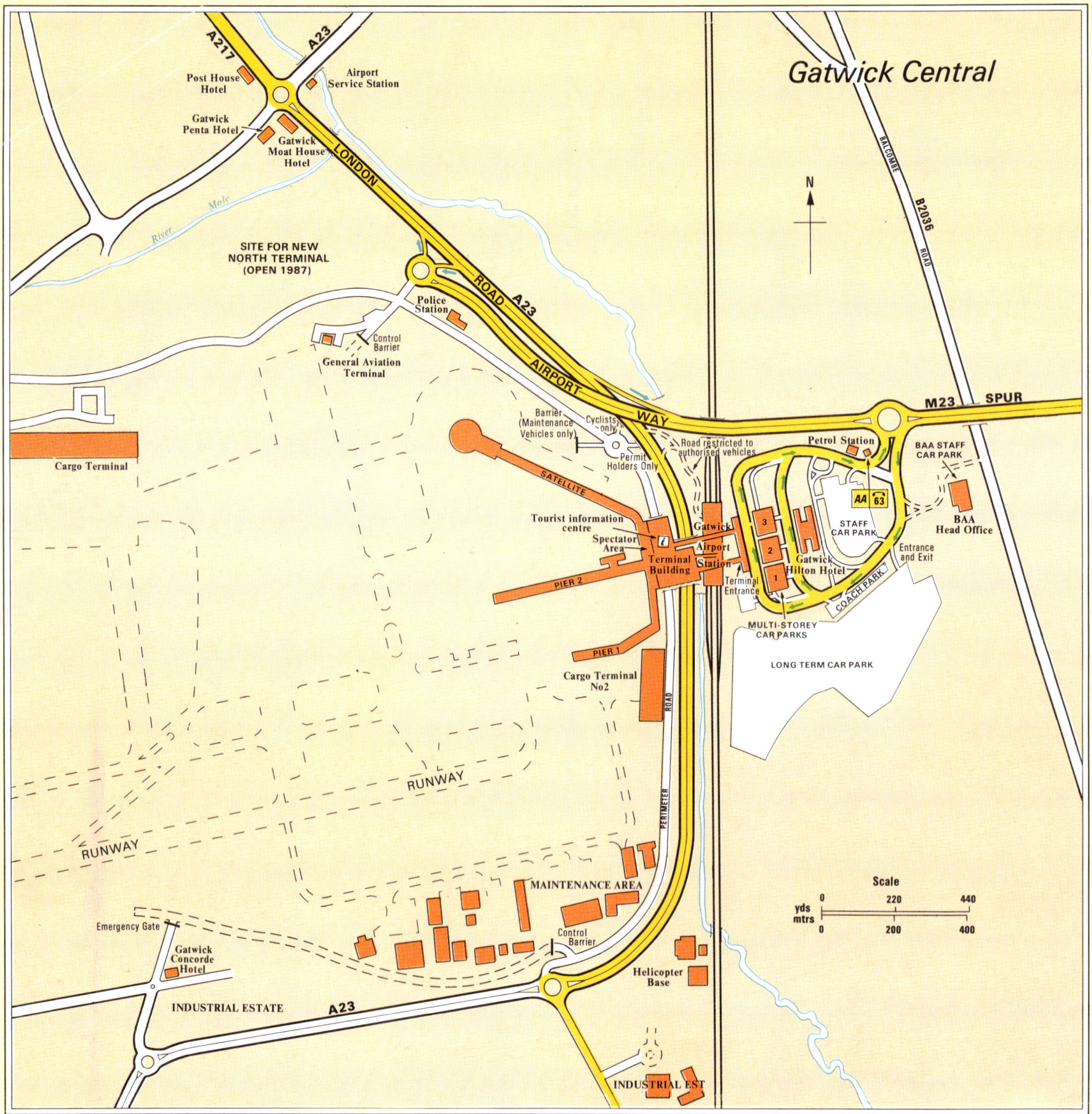

Map labels:

A217
A23
Post House Hotel
Airport Service Station
Gatwick Penta Hotel
Gatwick Moat House Hotel
LONDON
River Mole
ROAD
A23
AIRPORT
WAY
M23 SPUR
BALCOMBE ROAD
B2036
N
SITE FOR NEW NORTH TERMINAL (OPEN 1987)
Police Station
Control Barrier
General Aviation Terminal
Barrier (Maintenance Vehicles only)
Cyclists only
Permit Holders Only
Road restricted to authorised vehicles
Petrol Station
BAA STAFF CAR PARK
Cargo Terminal
SATELLITE
Tourist information centre
Spectator Area
Gatwick Airport Station
Terminal Building
PIER 2
3
2
1
STAFF CAR PARK
Gatwick Hilton Hotel
AA 63
Entrance and Exit
BAA Head Office
Terminal Entrance
MULTI-STOREY CAR PARKS
COACH PARK
PIER 1
Cargo Terminal No2
LONG TERM CAR PARK
RUNWAY
RUNWAY
PERIMETER ROAD
Scale
yds 0 220 440
mtrs 0 200 400
MAINTENANCE AREA
Control Barrier
Emergency Gate
Gatwick Concorde Hotel
INDUSTRIAL ESTATE
A23
Helicopter Base
INDUSTRIAL EST

Inset map:

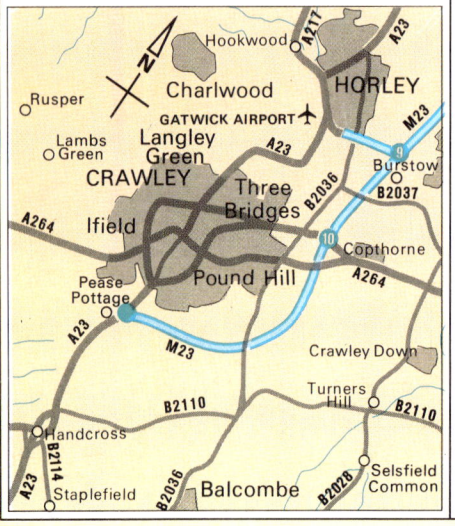

N
Hookwood
A217
A23
Charlwood
HORLEY
Rusper
GATWICK AIRPORT
M23
9
Lambs Green
Langley Green
Burstow
CRAWLEY
B2036
B2037
Three Bridges
Copthorne
A264
Ifield
10
A264
Pease Pottage
Pound Hill
M23
Crawley Down
B2110
Turners Hill
B2110
Handcross
B2114
Staplefield
A23
B2036
Balcombe
B2028
Selsfield Common

Gatwick Airport

Gatwick is London's second busiest airport, coming second only to Heathrow. Well situated near the new town of Crawley, West Sussex, for easy access via the A23 and M23 London to Brighton motorway, it also has its own adjoining British Rail mainline railway station. Fast 15-minute frequency trains make a link 24 hours a day between Victoria Station and Gatwick, and a link is also provided to the capital by a Green Line Coach service. Coach connections to Heathrow and Luton, are available.

Lying on the edge of the North Downs, this has been the site of an airport since 1936. It was taken over by the Air Ministry, which established a training school for RAF pilots on the site in 1937. Wartime saw Gatwick's expansion into an RAF station of major importance, so much so that it had to be extended to take in the nearby racecourse. After the war, it went over to commercial use, but was only opened as an international airport in 1958, after extensive modernisation. At that time, it was hailed as the most advanced airport in Europe, with its linking of road, rail and air facilities.

Today this busy air traffic centre is used by most major airlines and by charter services of other airline companies, as well as being open in case of need to aircraft diverted from Heathrow. Passengers travelling between the two airports of Gatwick and Heathrow can also enjoy the service of rapid helicopter flights from one to the other. This helicopter airlink is run daily and takes only about quarter of an hour.

A spectators' viewing area, signposted through the International Arrivals section, allows visitors to watch the ever-changing panorama of an important international airport in action. A small fee is charged for this. The viewing area is open daily until dusk, and includes car parking facilities. Three linked multi-storey car parks and an open air car park are also provided for travellers and other visitors to the airport.

Several bars and eating places catering for different tastes have been established within the airport, and can be found on the 'catering level' above the international arrivals hall.